Taming Lust

EARLY AMERICAN STUDIES

Series editors:
Daniel K. Richter, Kathleen M. Brown,
Max Cavitch, and David Waldstreicher

Exploring neglected aspects of our colonial,
revolutionary, and early national history and culture,
Early American Studies reinterprets familiar themes
and events in fresh ways. Interdisciplinary in character,
and with a special emphasis on the period from about
1600 to 1850, the series is published in partnership with
the McNeil Center for Early American Studies.

A complete list of books in the series
is available from the publisher.

TAMING LUST

Crimes Against Nature in the Early Republic

DORON S. BEN-ATAR AND RICHARD D. BROWN

PENN

UNIVERSITY OF PENNSYLVANIA PRESS

PHILADELPHIA

Published by
University of Pennsylvania Press
Philadelphia, Pennsylvania 19104-4112
www.upenn.edu/pennpress

Printed in the United States of America
on acid-free paper

1 3 5 7 9 10 8 6 4 2

Library of Congress Cataloging-in-Publication Data
Ben-Atar, Doron S.
Taming lust : crimes against nature in the early Republic /
Doron S. Ben-Atar and Richard D. Brown.—1st ed.
p. cm.— (Early American studies)
Includes bibliographical references and index.
ISBN 978-0-8122-4581-3 (hardcover : alk. paper)
1. Bestiality—United States—Case studies. 2. Bestiality—
United States—History—18th century. 3. Criminal justice,
Administration of—United States—History—18th century.
4. United States—Civilization—18th century. I. Brown, Richard D.
II. Title. III. Series: Early American studies.
HQ71.5.B47B46 2014
306.0973—dc23   2013033187

CONTENTS

∿

Crimes Against Nature

This book treats a most unusual offense—one that evokes laughter for some and disgust in others.[1] Our account of John Farrell and Gideon Washburn, two elderly New England men tried separately for bestiality in the 1790s, runs counter to the instinctual sense of what it means to be human, while also reminding us of the animalistic demons we hold in check. Researching and writing about bestiality, even reading this book, is an act of transgression—an affront, perhaps, to the good taste that seeks to keep the unseemly part of human existence hidden.

Prepare to be startled. Some of the analysis places cherished elements of Western culture in uneasy proximity to a despised practice. We point to elements in high art and religion where bestiality is part of both context and subtext. And our historical analysis necessitates consideration of bestiality as a subcategory of sodomy—a highly offensive association that might fuel homophobic prejudice—but one that is grounded in the statutory record. As far as the law in the early modern period was concerned, bestiality was a subcategory of sodomy. Even the enlightened philosopher Montesquieu spoke of bestiality and sodomy as one and the same—"crimes against nature." Currently we associate sodomy with human anal penetration and male homosexuality. However, before the middle of the nineteenth century sodomy was a rather broad category—a catchall word that represented all nonreproductive sex as well as general moral degeneracy. A sodomite was a man who committed sexual acts prohibited in the Bible. Sodomy stood for the broader threat of sexual degeneracy. Finally, sodomy was the opposite of manliness—and all the gendered social and cultural associations that went with it.[2]

Bestiality occupies an anomalous place in the range of sexual violations. It features elements similar to the two most abhorrent sexual crimes, rape and pedophilia—the power imbalance, the abuse of the weaker and dependents, and the unnerving intimate blurring of the lines between aggression and desire.[3] Yet discussion of bestiality often triggers amusement or disgust at bestial humans rather than sympathy for its animal victims. Significantly, humorists have been joking about bestiality for centuries, in caricatures, fiction, theater, and film. Indeed, since we stumbled onto the Farrell and Washburn episodes we have become professorial magnets for bestiality references, stories, and jokes. When we have described our research, a listener may respond with a long-forgotten bestiality story.[4] Whereas historian Robert Darnton in his essay "The Great Cat Massacre" famously asked why eighteenth-century Parisian apprentices laughed at the sadistic killing of cats, the question for us is why do men, especially, laugh at bestiality? In his analysis of jokes Sigmund Freud noted that his patients often found the "uncovering of unconscious material . . . comic." Whether this laughter originates in some primeval unconscious longing to violate the sexual taboo against bestiality or not, mockery relegates the phenomenon to the world of marginal curiosities. This renunciation, however, "does not abolish the instinct," as philosopher Judith Butler astutely observed. On the contrary, "it deploys the instinct for its own purposes." Renunciation through laughter, then, highlights the distance between present-day attitudes and those of the early modern period we are considering, a period when sodomy, and its subcategory bestiality, could be regarded not as humorous, but as among the most heinous of capital crimes.[5]

Bestiality has existed in every known human society.[6] Psychologists, sexologists, and psychoanalysts have long recognized this behavior as part of the range of male sexual activity. Havelock Ellis, the founding father of modern sexology, saw bestiality as "the sexual perversion of dull, insensitive and unfastidious persons. . . . It flourishes," he claimed, "among primitive peoples and among peasants. It is the vice of the clodhopper, unattractive to women or inapt to court them." Freud explained in *Three Essays on the Theory of Sexuality* (1905) that excessive libido led some men to "sexual intercourse with animals, which is by no means rare." Soviet studies of rural sexual practices in the 1920s found that 8 percent of the peasants had intercourse with animals in their youth and that in farming communities this was considered a natural stage in the sexual development of men. In the United States, Alfred Kinsey's analysis of male sexual behavior in the 1940s similarly reported that 8 percent of his subjects had sexual contact with animals, and in farm country the percentage shot up, with nearly 50 percent of all men admitting to some bestial experimentation. In the American countryside of the first half of the twentieth century, so it seemed to Kinsey, animals were more accessible as sexual outlets than girls or women. And a longitudinal study of the decades from 1880 to 1950 in Sweden found that most offenders were adolescent males who reported that they turned to sex with animals because they did not have access to women. Yet the absence of available women does not adequately explain bestiality, since most rural adolescent males choose masturbation over bestiality. According to psychologists, sex between rural adolescents and farm animals is rooted in psychosexual disorders, not—as Kinsey surmised—the fact of easy access to animals instead of women. Indeed, the Soviet statistics and Kinsey's figures seem inflated because, while it is impossible to determine actual rates of bestiality, most researchers believe only a tiny fraction of human sexual activity engages animals. Still, bestiality has been and remains a fact of life in every society, particularly in rural regions.[7]

Modern psychiatry has classified the phenomenon as zoophilia, a subcategory of paraphilia—sexual desires or acts toward nonconsenting nonhuman subjects that involve suffering by one or both participants.[8] Historically, the overwhelming majority of identified bestial actors were always rural young men. Freud long ago noted the powerful connections between male sexual and aggressive drives, writing that the "sexuality of most male human beings contains an element of *aggressiveness*—a desire to subjugate." Apart from rape, bestiality, more than other sexual practices, attests to this connection.[9] A few daring writers have explored the fantasy of sex between animals and women, but bestiality—in desire, mythology, and practice—belongs almost exclusively to the fantasy worlds of men. Social science reinforces this observation. In a study of the sexual preferences of 1,300 American juvenile delinquents, 70 percent of whom were girls, only boys displayed bestial desires. And in the 1880–1950 Swedish study, over 99 percent of those charged with bestial acts (2,319) were men, and just 14 women were accused, and none of these women were charged with actual intercourse with an animal. Bestiality is a male phenomenon, and the idea of female participation is either a pornographic fantasy or a libel aimed at discrediting powerful women.[10]

Bestiality comprehends a multitude of phenomena whose foundation in the physical world may never be quite clear. Its origin lies in the prohibition of sexual contact between man and beast, even though the boundaries between the lovingly humane and the sexually "perverse" are subjective and socially constructed. It is a transnational, transhistorical phenomenon extending around the globe and across the millennia. And while the offense seems more or less constant, societies' responses have varied markedly. Nearly every known human society—ancient and modern—has criminalized bestiality; yet inconsistent enforcement, irregular legal proceedings, and the doubtful evidentiary basis for nearly every specific case has made the prosecution of bestiality a complicated, historically specific bundle of social and cultural phenomena, some demonstrably real, some imagined, and all individual and personal. Since a certain percentage of the sexual activity in society at any given moment, particularly in rural areas, crosses the boundary between humans and other species, our task as historians is to explain why officials in the New England interior chose to prosecute John Farrell and Gideon Washburn for the hanging crime of bestiality in the late 1790s.[11]

All through the autumn of 1796, eighty-five-year-old John Farrell, recently convicted by the Massachusetts Supreme Judicial Court of engaging in "a venereal affair with a certain female Brute Animal called a Bitch," wondered what his fate would be as he waited in the dank county jail at Northampton, Massachusetts. After Christmas, Farrell learned the worst. Governor Samuel Adams and the Governor's Council had not only denied his latest petition for clemency but on December 26, 1796, the governor signed Farrell's death warrant. The governor had given the order to the Hampshire County sheriff that in just a matter of weeks, on February 23, 1797, "between the hours of Twelve and Three in the Afternoon," as punishment for "the crime of Sodomy" Farrell must be "taken to the usual place of Execution," there "to suffer the pains and penalties of Death." Prayer, it seemed, was Farrell's only recourse. He could pray that the governor would, miraculously, change his mind; or, more realistically, he could pray that God would save his soul.[12]

Almost exactly three years later, in the autumn of 1799, eighty-three-year-old Gideon Washburn, convicted of the same crime, was languishing in the Litchfield County, Connecticut, jail—some seventy miles southwest of where Farrell had been incarcerated. In a case that was wholly separate from Farrell's, a Superior Court jury had decided on September 2, 1799, that the old man "hath lain with beasts or brute Creatures by carnal copulation." In front of a crowded courtroom that probably included his wife and son, Judge Jesse Root declared he himself was "smitten with horror and amazement at the atrocity" of Washburn's "vile drudgery of sin and Satan" and ordered that he must hang "by the neck between the heavens & the Earth until he shall be dead." So like Farrell before him, Washburn now awaited his ride to the gallows, scheduled for Friday, November 15, 1799. His fate, too, lay with God.[13]

John Farrell and Gideon Washburn were not sentenced to hang for bestiality in the seventeenth century, when Puritans prosecuted and executed witches, religious dissenters, and sexual offenders, but more than a century later—after the American and French Revolutions—in the era known as the age of reason. By that time neither Massachusetts nor Connecticut had executed anyone for bestiality for at least 120 years. Yet suddenly, without warning, in the late 1790s and in villages in the same region, high courts determined that two old men would hang for the crime. Though the statutes were clear, there was no apparent social logic to these prosecutions. For even if the two elderly men did commit sexual acts with animals, bestiality did not seem to be a grave concern to people at the time. Indeed, despite Judge Root's expression of horror and amazement, few men who dwelled in late eighteenth-century New England could have reached middle age wholly ignorant of the reality that, forbidden or not, some boys and men did actually violate that barrier. Such knowledge might have come to them in barnyard and tavern gossip and jocular stories; or they might have known such misbehavior at first or second hand. But as Root's words convey, the fact that they were conscious of this particular human failing does not mean they accepted it or did not find such stories scandalous. We doubt that any householder would have questioned the language of Farrell's and Washburn's criminal indictments, which spoke of violations "of the order of Nature"; nor would they disagree with the judge who condemned the bestial act as a "dishonor done to human nature."[14] On the other hand, boys shared secrets and neighbors gossiped about what took place in barns and pastures; but only on rare occasions did authorities bring charges against offenders. Prosecuting ancient men for this offense was unknown.

More astonishing than the crime was the punishment. Bestiality was a sin, a violation of the order mandated by creation—a strange and perhaps disgusting act. But was it a crime that required hanging? Even in the 1790s executing elderly white men for nonviolent, victimless crimes ran contrary to the penal practices of many states. To be sure, the old English penal code prescribed hanging for those convicted of sodomy or bestiality. In 1757 New

Jersey hanged a man for bestiality and as recently as 1785 Pennsylvania had executed a man for "buggery"; and though that state and several others had recently deleted sodomy from their slate of capital crimes, every New England state retained the death penalty for sodomy, which encompassed bestiality. Moreover Massachusetts and Connecticut were known to operate the gallows with some frequency, having executed some thirty-two people during the 1780s. And though there were no old men who swung from their gallows, the two states had hanged three women and a twelve-year-old girl. In the 1790s these states executed fewer people than in the prior decade, but their penal scorecards remained deadly.[15]

In the wake of American independence political leaders eagerly and confidently reduced the list of capital offenses and adopted penal practices infused with an Enlightenment rationality they believed to be both practical and humane. Moreover the citizens of Massachusetts and Connecticut were not especially eager to hang convicts. Like people in other states, these New Englanders were rethinking questions of crime and punishment within the larger framework of Enlightenment social and political reform as well as the context of Christian revival. Though both states had passed up the opportunity to revise their criminal codes in recent years, it was not out of ignorance. Their political and legal elites had been familiar with the reformist writings of Count Cesare di Beccaria, whose 1764 *Essay on Crimes and Punishments* quickly became the dominant Enlightenment authority on the subject. Beccaria criticized the cruel and arbitrary European penal statutes and called for replacing them with a rational system of punishments that suited particular crimes. As early as 1770 John Adams had quoted Beccaria when he defended the Boston Massacre soldiers; and in 1786 the *New-Haven Gazette and Connecticut Magazine* reprinted Beccaria's *Essay on Crimes and Punishments*, including his chapter on "Crimes of Difficult Proof," which dealt specifically with sodomy.[16] Cosmopolitan New Englanders recognized that states such as New York, New Jersey, Pennsylvania, and Maryland, which before the Revolution had relied on British penal codes resting on capital punishment, had recently reformed their laws so as to incorporate the humane dictates of Enlightenment ideals. All had cut back on the death penalty. At the grassroots level, some Massachusetts voters were so reluctant to sit in judgment on the lives of others that by the mid-1790s they chose to pay the fine for nonservice rather than serve on a jury that might condemn a man to death.[17] Juries did, of course, convict, and the authorities hanged the guilty; but only after a step-by-step legal process—never by acts of vigilante justice.

Yet in 1796 Massachusetts, a state that had led in the Revolution and that possessed an advanced republican constitution drafted by John Adams, was, under Governor Samuel Adams (a Harvard graduate like his cousin), prepared to execute an eighty-five-year-old physician because a jury ruled he had committed sodomy with a dog. And three years later Connecticut, the home of Yale College and a key state for the creation of the United States Constitution, was ready to send an eighty-three-year-old farmer to the gallows for much the same offense. Why were these men prosecuted? Why did prosecutors, juries, judges, and political leaders insist on the death penalty? And what do these bizarre and deadly proceedings teach us about the culture and society of the early republic? Stripped of historical context, these two New England prosecutions of the 1790s may seem like bolts from the blue, utterly incomprehensible expressions of "witch-hunting" justice in the new American republic. But we are convinced there is more to the story.

We began investigating the Farrell and Washburn cases independently and were alerted to each other's research by our colleague John Murrin, the eminent historian and author of a landmark essay on bestiality prosecutions in colonial America.[18] We shared our findings, took part in panels at professional meetings, and realized that the two prosecutions must be studied together. It could be argued that the episodes are *sui generis*, that each stands on its own, and that the proximities and similarities are merely accidental. And certainly historical episodes are always and everywhere intrinsically unique. Each one happens at a particular time and place and in a context that has not been exactly duplicated anywhere else. This is true of the cases we examine in the chapters that follow. To a statistician the cases we are examining could be simply a random cluster. We considered this explanation carefully, but finally ruled it out. Nothing of the kind had happened before or since in the entire span of early American history and in the many jurisdictions of the new republic. Yet the Farrell and Washburn episodes occurred almost simultaneously and almost in the same place. This in a society where the median age was eighteen years and only a vanishingly small fraction of men lived into their ninth decade. Yet Massachusetts and Connecticut chose to prosecute these two octogenarians even unto death for criminal behavior typically associated with young men. And these obvious similarities, as the chapters that follow demonstrate, merely scratch the surface. The more deeply we examined the cases in their broader cultural-historical context, the more we realized that the Farrell and Washburn cases offer unusual insights into the mysterious, only partly understood storm of worries that engulfed New England in the late 1790s.[19]

A decade of historical detective work, combing through local and regional archives for traces of these marginal outcasts, enabled us to put together their stories.[20] But the tale, with all its twists and turns, is embedded within a range of questions about the proceedings themselves and the broader cultural contexts they engaged. With the death penalty looming, why did neighbors report on these harmless old men? Why did communities in the New England interior where violations of the taboo were usually overlooked choose this historical moment for strict enforcement of the prohibition with capital prosecutions? It cannot have been chance that led them to pick on two old men rather than youthful offenders. Did these particular men possess some specific characteristic, some "mark of Cain" that not only called down the wrath of Hampshire and Litchfield Counties but also the full punitive apparatus of their respective states? We seek to understand what forces in *fin de siècle* New England propelled these cases toward their deadly destinations.[21]

The Farrell and Washburn episodes take us to the margins of historical understanding of the late eighteenth century, to the liminal space in the New England interior where the ideas of the Enlightenment, the new modes of communications and culture, and the political upheaval of the American Revolution and its aftermath generated excitement and anxiety in villages and farms. At times, New Englanders embraced the new age and at other times they fought to preserve the world of their fathers and grandfathers. In an era when old, deeply felt ideals were under siege, and when hitherto rock-solid assumptions about masculinity, age, deference, and order were being challenged publicly, acts that provincial leaders had long understood to be merely deviant became frighteningly subversive. And as the century drew to a close, a zealous Puritan flashback gained the upper hand. Conspiracy theories multiplied, in which secret sects plotted to destroy the Christian society they had known and cherished. Christian and Federalist Jeremiahs warned against the encroachment of French political ideas and sexual debauchery. Popular epistolary novels featured sorry tales of young women who succumbed to temptation, sin, and death. And in some locales courts vigorously pursued sexual offenders.

The stories of Farrell and Washburn are less about the two men accused of sexual relations with domestic animals than about the local elites that enabled these otherwise bizarre prosecutions to proceed from accusation to indictment, to trial, and to death warrants. Local elites, while riding the rough waves of modernity, revived the prohibitions of their forefathers. As the anthropologist Mary Douglas astutely noted, "taboo-maintained rules will be as repressive as the leading members of society want them to be."[22] By reflecting on the circumstances of a divided elite, one whose mutual suspicions and bitter invective shaped public policy, we can begin to understand why the usually disciplined and rational ruling class did not contain the consequences of sodomy accusations. New England's religious and political conflicts not only destroyed cohesion among respectable "gentlemen," they also divided common folk who identified themselves with different religious sects and parties as well as their own neighborhood and kinship clans. At a moment when long-standing assumptions about God's creation and the stability of the social order were wavering, the law appeared to be the one sanctuary to which an anxious elite could repair. Though the wisdom and justice of the penal code might be doubtful, the law must be enforced. Otherwise the agents of misrule would engulf their villages, their countryside, their cities, and their nation. In a time of religious awakening, Satan did not slumber.

CHAPTER 1

~

The Sisyphean Battle Against Bestiality

Interspecies intercourse is part of the foundational mythologies of Western civilization. Cave paintings depicted men mounting animals. Cultures of the ancient Mediterranean world frequently depicted half-human–half-animal creatures, and in Greek and Roman mythologies animals and humans frequently have interspecies sex yielding heroic offspring. Shows at the Roman coliseum included sex between animals, domesticated and wild, and human partners. Centuries later, Rashi, the most important medieval Jewish interpreter of the Bible, commented that the Genesis creation story implied that before God created a woman, "Adam attempted to find [a mate] amongst all the animals and beasts and he was not satisfied with them until he discovered Eve." Some Christian commentaries on "the Fall" suggested that Eve had sex with the serpent, and an explicit version of this interpretation is prominently displayed in the sculpture of Adam and Eve at the Notre Dame Cathedral in Paris. A passage in Luke suggests the kind of interspecies contact practiced by the Greek deities when the angel Gabriel announces to Mary that the Holy Spirit will "come upon" or "overshadow" her, leading to the birth of the Son of God. Although the claim that human beings are made in the image of God mitigates the transgression, as a metaphor Christian religious paintings of the Annunciation routinely depict the Holy Spirit as a dove and angels as hybrid humans with birdlike wings. Winged cherubs, according to Ezekiel in the Hebrew Bible, possess four faces—a lion, an ox, an eagle, and a man. Moreover the prophet describes them as having the hands of a man, the feet of a calf, and four wings. In the New Testament the same creatures appear in Revelation.[1]

Cultural, literal, and artistic fantasies of such mythologies are common. All over the world rituals of animal masquerades symbolically enact

Figure 1. *The Annunciation*, attributed to Francesco Mazzola (Parmigianino) (1520?). Mary and the angel who descends upon her are facing each other. Both look down toward her genital area as her right hand points the way. Represented as a winged human, the angel blurs the boundary between human and animal. Courtesy of the Metropolitan Museum of Art / Art Resource, NY.

interspecies relationships, which have led some psychoanalytically inclined critics to speculate on the relationship between the ritualized fantasy of phallic domination and the construction of the psychic fear of castration. Greek mythology had Zeus in the shape of a swan, bull, and stallion having intercourse with women. We have even been telling our children tales with animal-human motifs, such as "Beauty and the Beast," and "Little Red Riding Hood." Early modern tales told of fairies or bad men who replaced human babies with wild ones in their cradles, and the mothers themselves could not tell the difference. These themes appear in some of the most cherished images of European civilization, from the ruins of Pompeii, which featured the satyr Pan having sex with a she-goat, to countless paintings through the ages of Zeus in the form of a swan entwined with the princess Leda.[2] Beautiful Helen of Troy was born out of this fateful seduction, and in 1924 poet W. B. Yeats narrated in vivid detail that moment of bestial lust, when the swan seduces the "staggering girl," until "a shudder in the loins engenders" the calamity of the Trojan War after which the god's "indifferent beak could let her drop."[3]

But though bestiality was long recognized and embedded in mythologies, it was also regarded as a dangerous temptation and uniformly condemned. Ancient Hittite law decreed death for men who had sex with a dog or a pig; while for men who had "intercourse with a horse or mule, there is no punishment," though such a man "shall not approach the king, and shall not become a priest." While classical Greece celebrated human sexuality, and some have argued ancient Greeks even privileged sodomy between males over heterosexual intercourse, the Greeks vigorously condemned bestiality. Plato's *Republic*'s philosopher warned that in "the wild and animal part" of man's mind "there is nothing it will not dare," even going so far as "to attempt sexual intercourse with a mother or anyone else—man, god, or beast." Twenty-five hundred years later the anthropologist Clifford Geertz reported a similar attitude in Bali. He noted that the "Balinese revulsion against any behavior as animal-like can hardly be overstressed. Babies are not allowed to crawl for that reason. Incest, though hardly approved, is a much less horrifying crime than bestiality. (The appropriate punishment for the second is death by drowning, for the first being forced to live like an animal.)" Human rejection of sex with animals, it appears, is an all but universal norm.[4]

Europeans believed interspecies intercourse was common among the "barbarian" nations of Asia, Africa, and the Americas. And past and present

Figure 2. Pan copulating with a female goat, a marble sculpture from the ancient Roman city of Herculaneum. Buried by the eruption of Vesuvius in C.E. 79, the sculpture was excavated in 1752. Courtesy of the National Archeological Museum, Naples / Art Resource, NY.

cultural critics have used bestial imagery to represent the lowest possible human moral degradation. John Marston's *The Scourge of Villanie* (1599), which criticized the women in the Elizabethan court, portrayed its heroine as a nymphomaniac who takes a donkey as a lover. In England of the 1680s, a polemical drama on the supposed libertine culture of the court of Charles II invoked bestiality to represent the debauched state of the monarch's court. A century later critics of Marie Antoinette hinted that she engaged in unspeakable sexual acts with animals, while the Marquis de Sade's iconoclastic attack on the culture of eighteenth-century France asserted that bestiality was "a simple passion . . . altogether natural," and discussed the sensual benefits of penetrating goats. Rivals of the Russian empress Catherine the Great spread the malicious tale that she died when the horse with whom she was having intercourse fell on her, crushing her to death. And

Figure 3. This 1530 copy of Michelangelo's *Leda and the Swan* by one of his followers recalls the myth in an explicitly sexual manner. The intertwined bodies and the peck on the lips is an example of anthropomorphic depictions of bestial intercourse. Courtesy of the National Gallery, London.

in twenty-first-century America some prominent opponents of gay unions claim that allowing gay people to marry would open the door to marriage between humans and animals.[5]

The Bible called on the children of Abraham to be fruitful and multiply, and it condemned nonprocreative sex. Scripture-based sexual regulations penalized victimless acts—such as men engaged in consensual same-sex relations. Homosexuality, masturbation, and bestiality have been seen as undermining the procreative foundations of society. The Torah prohibits bestiality four separate times and in four different contexts. In Exodus it is written that "whoever lies with a beast shall be put to death." The preceding verse commands that a sorceress not be allowed to live. Both directives are anomalies in a chapter dedicated to property law and charitable treatment of strangers, the poor, widows, and orphans. The prohibition also appears twice in Leviticus. Among the laws against sodomy is this one: "Do not lie with a male as one lies with a woman; it is abhorrence. Do not have carnal relations with any beast and defile yourself thereby; and let no woman lend herself to a beast to mate with it; it is perversion." It is significant that these rules appear in a chapter that asserts Israel's moral superiority over the Canaanites, who are said to defile themselves with such abominations. Two chapters later, Leviticus, as part of the sexual code of laws, spells out the punishment, death to both human perpetrators and their animal partners. Finally, in Deuteronomy, Moses commands the Levites, after they conquer the land of Israel, to publicly call out, "cursed be he who lies with any beast," to which the people are commanded to respond with "amen [let it be so]."[6]

The New Testament did not explicitly address sex between men and animals, though Paul's declaration that "effeminate, and abusers of themselves with mankind" will not "inherit the kingdom of God" probably applies to bestiality. The moral code of the Torah, with the exception of the changes specifically revised by Christianity like doing away with the kosher dietary laws and male circumcision, remained in effect. Whereas Judaism embraced heterosexual sexuality, Christian scripture disparaged sexual pleasure, even within marriage. Paul, for example, believed it was "good for a man not to touch a woman," and even recommended that married men avoid the pleasures of the flesh. Three centuries later Saint Augustine condemned sex altogether. His most important theological work, *City of God*, centered on the Fall of man, where he argued that God inflicted uncontrolled erections on men to remind us of the original sin, asserting that before the Fall, in the Garden of Eden, Adam could control his erections. And whereas sex for pleasure among married couples was a forgivable offense, vices against nature were not. In his *Confessions* Augustine declared: "offenses against nature are everywhere and at all times to be held in detestation and should be punished. Such offenses, for example, were those of the Sodomites; and, even if all nations should commit them, they would all be judged guilty of the same crime by the divine law, which has not made men so that they should ever abuse one another in that way. For the fellowship that should be between God and us is violated whenever that nature of which he is the author is polluted by perverted lust." Augustine made no specific mention of bestiality. But the biblical grouping of it with sodomy suggests that he understood the church's position on both subjects as similar.[7]

But Augustine's anathemas against sodomy and its subcategory bestiality did not carry the day. Not immediately, at least. The vast penitential literature of late Roman and early medieval Europe equated bestiality with the venial sin of masturbation, not sodomy. Punishment was rare and often mild, the major exception being the sin of copulating with a Jew, which was considered a form of bestiality and sometimes sanctioned with the death penalty. Commonly, early Christian theologians believed that animals were radically different from humans and that brutes were naturally lustful and could not be faulted for wanting sex with humans. Consequently men in some compromised states could be forgiven for succumbing to the temptation. Near the end of the first millennium, however, the Augustinian anti-desire ideology swept over Christendom. As the historian John Boswell noted, the age's "main innovation was to privilege and make real widespread voluntary celibacy, implicitly or explicitly suggesting that heterosexual matrimony was a mere compromise with the awful powers of sexual desire."[8]

Sex for the purpose of procreation was tolerated, but God expected humans to resist lust. Bestial intercourse merely gratified lust; it had no reproductive potential. When man and beast mated, both must be held accountable for the offense. Indeed in late medieval and early modern Europe a tradition of charging animals with seducing men emerged. While animals implicated in bestiality were usually convicted and burned at the stake, some were accorded the orderly procedures of a trial and acquitted. As late as 1750 a female donkey in France was exonerated; but the man who had relations with her was convicted and hanged after a local aristocrat testified that the animal was raped. In four years' acquaintance, the seigneur claimed, he knew the animal was not wanton, but well behaved.[9]

Following the biblical command from Deuteronomy referring to the wages of male homosexual prostitutes as "the pay of a dog"—because they practiced their trade in the stance of a dog—early modern theologians prescribed face-to-face intercourse between men and women as the proper way humans have sex, preferably in the missionary position. In contrast, the dorsal position, where the male mounts from behind, invoked proximity to the anus, which was associated with evil and the devil. Eleventh-century theologian Burchard of Worms prescribed a punishment of ten days on bread and water to husbands who made love to their wives in this forbidden way. His ruling proved mild in comparison to later Christians. In the thirteenth century, severe sanctions against bestiality were practiced in continental Europe. The era's leading theologian, Thomas Aquinas, declared "the unnatural intercourse of man and beast" more base than the other three sexual sins: masturbation, homosexuality, and sex in a dorsal position. Going beyond Burchard of Worms, Aquinas, whose writings defined Christian orthodoxy for centuries, asserted that "not observing the natural manner of copulation, either as to undue means, or as to other monstrous and bestial manners of copulation" generated excessive desire.[10]

In contrast to the church, which sometimes devised ways to atone for the sin of bestiality, the European monarchs who seized jurisdictional authority in the late medieval and early modern eras revived the biblical death penalty for sodomy—a term used interchangeably to describe both homosexual and bestial intercourse. In late medieval Spain convicted sodomites were hung upside down with their severed genitals placed around their necks—a punishment replaced in 1497 with burning at the stake. Fourteenth-century Florence prescribed castration and whipping, and later the death penalty for multiple offenses. Venice decided in 1464 to behead offenders and then to burn their corpses. And in the first decade of the sixteenth century, throughout its domains, the Holy Roman Empire prescribed burning for bestiality.[11]

Enforcement of such harsh punishments, however, remained sporadic. Whereas Sweden executed hundreds of men for bestiality in the seventeenth and eighteenth centuries, in neighboring Norway there is no evidence of a similar bloodbath. In the Iberian Peninsula the Inquisition policed such transgressions: over half of the men executed for sodomy in Spain between 1570 and 1630 were actually convicted of having sexual intercourse with animals. Neighboring Portugal, on the other hand, saw only thirty executions for both offenses in the more than two centuries from 1587 to 1794. Generally, punishment in Christendom was exacted most often for religious heretics and Jews. Early modern church exteriors in Germany featured images carved in stone of hideous Jews engaged in a variety of sexual acts with pigs. In sixteenth-century Paris a French Catholic was burned at the stake together with a Jewish lover because, the jurist argued, "coitus with a Jewess is exactly the same as if a man were to copulate with a dog." And some seventeenth-century Englishmen spread stories of sexual intercourse between Quakers and horses.[12]

A century earlier when the English monarchy under Henry VIII broke with the Catholic Church, the Crown took sexual regulations out of the hands of the clergy. In 1533 Parliament and the king prescribed death for "the detestable and abominable vice of Buggery committed with mankind or beast." Thirty years later, Elizabeth's Parliament revived the law against those committing the "most horrible and detestible [*sic*] vice of Buggerie," mandating not only death but the loss of all property as well. And regulations against bestiality hardened in the seventeenth century as post-Reformation theologians became obsessed with separating man from beast. They admonished Britons to cover their bodies and cut their hair because nudity and long hair belonged to the seductive lust of the animal world. They forbade swimming because, they argued, only fish swim, whereas men walk the earth. Sir Edward Coke, chief justice of the Court of Common Pleas from 1607, and after 1613 chief justice of the King's Bench, condemned nighttime burglary as worse than daytime robbery because men rest at night whereas beasts run wild. In this context, bestiality was more than just a repellant, sinful practice; it erased the boundary between man and beast, confusing categories and violating injunctions against the sanctity of God's distinction between man and animal. In some respects it was worse than murder or treason. Declaring that buggery, meaning both bestiality and sodomy, was "a detestable and abominable sin amongst Christians not to be named," Coke proclaimed it a felony, a crime "committed by carnal knowledge against the ordinance of the Creator, and order of nature, by mankind with mankind, or with brute beast, or by womankind with brute beast."[13]

Proscribing bestiality was easy, and so was making scandalous charges; but proving guilt according to law in a criminal court was difficult. To protect subjects from nasty gossip, early modern English law required sworn testimony to actual penetration as the criterion for consummation of the bestial act. Convictions relied on testimony about a presumably secret act from eyewitnesses who were rarely close enough to determine the fact of actual penetration with certainty. In 1677, for example, London's Central Criminal Court acquitted a man accused of having sex with a mare, and the court reporter explained that the witness was "near Threescore yards distant, [so] they [the jury] could not make that direct and positive Proof which the Law exacts." At other times convictions could depend on the behavior of the suspected animals. The same court that doubted distant eyewitness testimony sought confirmation of eyewitness accounts of sexual relations in that rarest of cases, one concerning a woman and a dog, by enlisting the animal's testimony. The prosecutor brought the dog to court and, "being set on the Bar before the Prisoner, owned her by wagging his tail, and making motions as it were to kiss her, which 'twas sworn she did do when she made that horrid use of him." The jury found the woman guilty and, following the statute, the judge ordered her to hang.[14]

Yet as outrageous as such a case now seems, in comparison to Spain and Sweden, bestiality prosecutions were infrequent in early modern England. Although the rising age of marriage from the sixteenth to the eighteenth centuries meant that most rural and lower-class young males had no legitimate outlets for their sexual impulses, and while some surely engaged in sex with farm animals, few were prosecuted. In fact, only eleven bestiality trials took place at London's Old Bailey court from 1674 to 1834. Sometimes even the most conspicuous, proven incidents were not prosecuted to the full extent of the law. So in 1734 eleven-year-old Jeffery Skuse was caught with his penis "fasten'd" to a dog, but "on account of his Youth the court tho't fit to shown him Compassion, and order'd him discharge'd." A generation later, in 1758, the king granted a full pardon to a royal marine who had been convicted for "buggery upon the body of a she-goat." Though the goat was summarily executed, because the marine "was the most illiterate, ignorant, stupid young fellow . . . being deprived of all natural capacity and next to an idiot," he was deemed to deserve mercy.[15] Such episodes, coupled with the relative paucity of bestiality trials, suggest a measure of practical acceptance of behavior that was so severely proscribed in principle. And while religious moralists denounced the evils of bestiality, English prosecutors did not distinguish between homosexual and bestial penetration. Indeed for English political culture in the second half of the eighteenth century, whose celebrated masculinity was epitomized by John Wilkes's attack on the court of George III and its supposed buggery and effeminacy, homosexual relations were the chief threat. For English authorities the sodomy of man on man was the great danger, not the sodomy of man on beast.[16]

Nearly every known human society—ancient and modern—criminalized bestiality; yet inconsistent enforcement, irregular legal proceedings, and the doubtful evidentiary basis for nearly every specific case has made the prosecution of bestiality a complicated bundle of social and cultural phenomena, some demonstrably real, some imagined, and all individual and personal. In the long history of bestial sexuality few "offenders" have ever "come out" as zoophiles voluntarily, though some early modern defendants confessed, and a few convicted offenders actually identified their own partners in the forbidden act so that man and beast could be killed and buried together. The admissions, however, are not necessarily credible. Sometimes they were prompted by torture or by hopes of reduced punishment, and sometimes by theological considerations of heaven and hell;

moreover Christendom, as Michel Foucault put it, has made man a "confessing animal." While historians can speculate as to why some men chose to confess to sexual relations with animals, our task is to understand why society wrung confessions, false or true, from certain men at certain times. We must determine why societies that have usually lived with violations of a taboo choose specific historical moments to enforce the taboo strictly by prosecuting transgressors to deadly ends.[17]

The seventeenth-century Britons who settled the New World shared their countrymen's concern for human backsliding into a bestial condition. Indeed when Puritans made homes for themselves surrounded by wild beasts, they felt a particular anxiety about regression in North America's "howling wilderness." In an age when many believed it possible that monks could lactate and women could grow penises, the birth of badly disfigured babies was often attributed to intercourse between women and beasts. And why not? Travel literature of the New World reported the discovery of hybrid species—trees with oysters, or snakes with multiple heads, even unicorns and mermaids. Writers who had never visited America depicted its native inhabitants as half-man–half-beast. To eradicate bestiality among the natives was among the first priorities of both Catholic and Protestant missionaries. In the European imagination of the seventeenth century, North America stood for a place where the distinct categories of species were regularly violated, where lust could readily tempt men to quit civilization so as to pursue the pleasures of the body. This perception was so important that English pamphleteers promoting Virginia immigration felt compelled to refute rumors that Chesapeake natives were degenerates who engaged in bestiality.[18]

Several colonies in North America held bestiality trials—including Bermuda and Virginia in addition to Connecticut, Massachusetts, New Haven, and Plymouth. We doubt that the people who settled in New England were more inclined to bestiality than others. But because they settled in small communities that pursued the mission of erecting an ideal Christian society, one that would serve as the model for English and Continental Protestants, they were more eager to prosecute. Anxious over the tenuous hold of God, humanity, and civilization on the sinful world, and engaged in a radical utopian experiment, Puritans believed that men always stood at the edge of turning into beasts. Plymouth looked with horror at Thomas Morton's tiny Merry Mount settlement, where Englishmen abandoned civilization and embraced living with Indians. The Pilgrims, wrote their leader, William Bradford, could not tolerate unchecked lust and "beastly practices" in such close proximity. They attacked and destroyed Merry Mount, establishing, as Nathaniel Hawthorne put it two centuries later, the authority of the "grizzly saints . . . over the gay sinners."[19]

Whereas campaigns to purge society of its sins were episodic and incomplete in the mother country, and subversive sexual practices—marital infidelity, homosexuality, and bestiality—were occasionally punished violently in every colony, eradicating subversive lust became an essential element of the Puritan utopian project. Seventeenth-century concern with bestiality originated in the Puritans' uneasy relationship with the surrounding forests. On the one hand they celebrated the authenticity of the wilderness that allowed them to connect with their God without ungodly artificial structures. In this way the wild New World assisted the larger Puritan project of creating a church of saints with direct links to God, independent of mediation by ecclesiastical hierarchies. On the other hand, the wilderness could tempt men and women to exchange the rules of civilization for spontaneous responsiveness to bodily impulses. Allowing such corporeal seduction would have subverted the Puritan journey to North America. Protestants at home and in Europe could never consider a society that fell short in "civilization" as worthy of emulation. And there was no more dramatic symbol of the incomplete dominion of God and civilization over humankind than sexual contact with animals. As the Reverend Samuel Danforth admonished, such connections embodied a "monstrous and horrible Confusion: it turneth a man into a bruit Beast. He that joyneth himself to a Beast, is one flesh with a Beast."[20]

The eradication of sexual contact between people and animals was a religious duty. Barely six years after the founding of the Massachusetts Bay Colony, the Reverend John Cotton, its leading minister, composed a model legal code, "Moses His Judicials," which he drew from the book of Leviticus, including the death penalty for "unnatural filthiness . . . whether sodomy, which is carnal fellowship of man with man, or woman with woman, or buggery, which is carnal fellowship of man or woman with beasts or fowls." Puritans aimed to endow their English penal code with scriptural authority. Several years later the colony of New Haven based its laws on Cotton's draft. And while the "Body of Liberties" the Massachusetts Bay Colony enacted in 1641 departed from Cotton's code, when it came to bestiality it toed the Leviticus line, mandating, "If any man or woman shall lie with any beast or bruit creature by Carnal Copulation, They shall surely be put to death. And the beast shall be slain, and buried and not eaten." The laws in the other New England colonies echoed similar sentiments, and also mandated executions.[21]

Soon after they drafted their codes, Puritan concern with bestiality erupted in the early 1640s, following the expulsion of Roger Williams and Ann Hutchinson from Massachusetts and just as the outbreak of civil war in England began to attract Puritans back to the European front. As the historian Virginia DeJohn Anderson writes, between 1640 and 1647 a "bestiality panic" seized New England. In an Anglo population of around 13,000 men, women, and children, authorities brought eight men to trial and executed four of them. Seemingly, John Winthrop's fear that "as people increased, so sin abounded, and especially the sin of uncleanness," was being realized. In May 1642 a Salem woman looking out her window saw William Hackett, a young servant, "in buggery with a cow, upon the Lord's day." Hackett admitted only "the attempt and some entrance," yet the court found him guilty of the whole crime and sentenced him to death "lest sinful men in love of their lust" think that confession and repentance can excuse such vile sins. On the day of execution, officials ceremoniously killed the polluted cow before Hackett's eyes and then hanged him. Three decades later, Massachusetts's authorities executed seventeen-year-old Benjamin Goad and his mare. The Reverend Danforth, who presided over the execution, justified killing both man and beast: "The Church cannot be cleansed, until this wicked person be put away from among us. . . . If we will not pronounce such a Villain Accursed, we must be content to bear the Curse our selves. The land cannot be cleansed, until it hath spued out this Unclean Beast. The execution of Justice upon such a notorious Malefactor, is the onely way to turn away the wrath of God from us, and to consecrate our selves to the Lord, and obtain his Blessing upon us."[22] The survival of the colony demanded strict, exemplary punishment.

New England's other Puritan colonies also acted to eradicate bestiality from their midst. In prosecuting teenager Thomas Granger for buggery with "a mare, a cow, two goats, five sheep, two calves and a turkey," Plymouth followed the Mosaic code. The offender had to identify his sexual partners to the authorities: the herd of sheep "were brought before him" so he could identify those he had defiled. As Governor William Bradford reported, on September 8, 1642, Plymouth executed Granger and the beasts he had penetrated: "first the mare and then the cow and the rest of the lesser cattle were killed before his face, according to the law, Leviticus xx. 15 and then he himself was executed. The cattle were all cast into a great and large pit that was digged of purpose for them, and no use made of any part of them."[23]

Whereas Massachusetts and Plymouth relied on conventional legal proceedings—eyewitness testimony and confessions—Connecticut and New Haven were more proactive. The colony of Connecticut executed John Nubery after he voluntarily came forward to confess that he attempted buggery with a few animals and that with one there was some "penetration, but not to the effusion of seed." And the New Haven Colony harkened back to medieval proceedings. Charges against George Spencer originated with the birth of a pig "without hair and some human resemblances," and with "one eye blemished," visual reminders of Spencer's own disfigurement. Authorities presumed that Spencer must have been the father of the misbegotten piglet. Spencer confessed and then recanted, but magistrates refused to accept his recantation. Because the common law conditioned conviction upon confirmation from a second witness, officials took the exceptional step of treating the piglet's appearance as a second testimony; so in 1642 they executed Spencer and the piglet. Proceedings five years later stretched ordinary legal procedures even further when a settler named, ironically, Hogg denied fatherhood of yet another deformed piglet. As no eyewitness could testify to Hogg's misbehavior, the town's elders brought the sow to him in prison and made him fondle it to see whether this intimacy would rekindle ardor between Hogg and the sow. The judges observed that the swine's lust was aroused, but since the prisoner refused to confess, and there was no witness to the act, Hogg's life was spared. Before uniting with Connecticut toward the end of the century, the small New Haven Colony executed two more offenders: fifteen-year-old Walter Robinson in 1655 and sixty-year-old William Potter in 1662. The fact that Robinson was merely a youth and Potter an old man did not reduce the harshness of punishment. In all of New England, New Haven was the most severely Puritan society. The same colony also executed two men for sodomy, one of whom had also committed the additional sin of teaching youths to masturbate.[24]

Seventeenth-century New Englanders vigorously prosecuted real and imagined violators of the boundaries between man and beast. Convictions and executions followed the testimonies of witnesses against mostly young offenders. Whereas New Englanders did not ascribe legal accountability to animals, in some cases charges rested on their "testimony."[25] Because eye-witness testimony of penetration could easily be challenged, the seven men executed for bestiality actually aided their prosecutors by confessing to the act when denial could have spared their lives. In seventeenth-century New France when a French soldier was sentenced to death, the colony council conditioned the execution on a confession, and when the soldier, withstood torture and refused to confess, he was released. But Puritans so emphasized the importance of confession for the expiation of sins that they could often persuade offenders that their public admission of guilt would improve their chances in the next world.[26]

In the New World in the seventeenth century, accusations, trials, and even harsh measures of interrogation were not unique to New England. Men were prosecuted and even convicted in other parts of English America, as well as in the Spanish and French North American possessions.[27] But only the religious colonies of Connecticut and Massachusetts executed men and beasts. Acting on doubtful evidence, suspect confessions, and public alarm, the Puritan prosecutions recall the witch hunts that swept medieval and early modern Europe and North America.[28] The book of Exodus had grouped the two offenses together and in antiwitchcraft mania bestial imag-ery often took center stage. European writers imagined Satan and his agents appearing as animal "familiars" who seduced women to become agents of the devil. The fifteenth-century guide to witchcraft *Malleus Maleficarum* warned against sexually predatory werewolves who used sexual intercourse to turn women into witches. When Henry VIII's wife Anne Boleyn gave birth to a deformed fetus, the king, as was appropriate for the age's connec-tion of fetal deformity to sex with the devil and his bestial agents, withdrew from Boleyn and promptly began the proceedings that would lead to her execution. Later, in 1621, an English drama, *The Witch of Edmonton*, which was believed to chronicle actual events, told of an English woman who sold her soul to the devil by having sex with a black dog named Tom. And spectral accounts of sexual relations between witches and the devil appear-ing in the form of an animal led to convictions and executions in Salem in 1692.[29]

The comparison of witchcraft and bestiality prosecutions is not only plausible; some spasms of bestiality and witchcraft prosecutions actually coincided. From 1642 to 1662, for example, New England colonies executed six men for bestiality and thirteen women and two men for witchcraft. Bestiality accusations could serve as the sword of social control to police male transgressors, just as witchcraft accusations threatened women who challenged authority. A 1659 satirical broadside about a Quaker who "attempted to Bugger a Mare," wondered if "a Quaker turns *Italian*" because the logic of Quakerism leads to the conclusion "That a *Mare's* as good as a *Madam.*" The violent campaign against the Quaker challenge in Massachusetts, culminating in the 1660 execution of Mary Dyer, coincided with associations of Quakers with witchcraft and bestiality in England. And Dyer herself seemed to combine the identities of a heretic and a bestialist. In 1637 she gave birth to a deformed stillborn child whose appearance shocked John Winthrop, who remarked that the feet of the fetus resembled a "young foul [*sic*]."[30]

But the prosecutions of witchcraft and bestiality in colonial New England were markedly different from each other in key ways. Whereas it is undeniable that sexual contact between humans and animals sometimes happened, the same assertion cannot be made for supernatural connections. Witchcraft is always a fantasy; but bestiality can be real. Moreover, unlike witchcraft, bestiality was a wholly gendered crime. Whereas some men were accused, tried, and executed for witchcraft, only two women were ever prosecuted for bestiality and none executed in seventeenth- and eighteenth-century America. A further difference is that in New England a confession of guilt typically spared a convicted witch from the gallows so she (or he) could rejoin the community. Bestiality prosecutions, however, used confessions of sex with animals to confirm the verdict and justify the sentence.

In early America bestiality was prosecuted as both sexual and religious deviance, whereas witchcraft was a religious violation. And though witchcraft provided a viable explanation for inexplicable phenomena in the sixteenth and seventeenth centuries, during the Enlightenment of the following century such supernatural explanations collapsed. While Salem marked both the high-water mark and final chapter of deadly prosecutions of witchcraft in America, deadly prosecutions of men for bestial acts persisted in the English colonies. Contemporaneous with the accusations against Farrell and Washburn, a judge in Portland, Maine (then part of Massachusetts) ridiculed two men who brought an accusation of witchcraft against the widow Elizabeth Smith. Rather than taking their claims seriously, he "endeavored to convince them of their error, and [that] the difficulties and dissentions, in the neighborhood, arose rather from ignorance in themselves, than from witchcraft in the poor old woman."[31] We have found no record of a magistrate in a bestiality case ever telling an accuser that the alleged crime was imaginary.

For more than a century no one was sentenced to death for witchcraft in New England after 1692 or for bestiality after the 1674 trial of Benjamin Goad. No one, that is, until the convictions of John Farrell in 1796 and Gideon Washburn in 1799. Though a handful of men were accused and tried, courts were able to shelve the death penalty by acquitting the accused or by convicting offenders of the lesser crime of attempting to commit the unspeakable act. The only known eighteenth-century convictions that led to death sentences in Anglo-America came not from "Puritan" New England but from the mid-Atlantic region, from New Jersey and Pennsylvania.[32]

Throughout Britain and British North America the penalty remained essentially constant in law across the long eighteenth century. William Blackstone, the foremost legal authority of the era considered "the infamous crime against nature, committed either with man or beast," to be a repulsive offense worthy of forceful disciplining by the "avenging sword" of the state, even to the point of withholding from the condemned a visit from the clergy before hanging. Following Blackstone, in the first treatise on American law in 1795 Zephaniah Swift reported the current Connecticut "statute inflicts the punishment of death on the offender, and to inspire the deepest detestation of the deed, directs that the very beast shall be slain and buried." Swift affirmed that the early modern criterion for conviction was unchanged: "to constitute this crime, there must be an actual penetration."[33]

Bestiality remained a capital crime in most colonies, and later states, for much of the eighteenth century. Some colonies, like Georgia and Maryland, did not address the offense specifically, probably because of the belief that it was not necessary to duplicate the English statute. Initially, Pennsylvania, the Quaker colony, had enacted a nonlethal form of disciplining offenders. In the 1680s the punishment was set at whipping, loss of one-third of one's property, and six months' imprisonment for a first offense, with life imprisonment the price of a second conviction. In 1700, the colony revised the punishment to one-year imprisonment for a first offense, and life and whipping every three months of the first year for a second offense. Convicted married men also faced "Castration, and his Wife may have a Bill of

Divorce." The Privy Council in London, however, disallowed the punishment of castration before it was ever enforced. In 1714 Pennsylvania mandated life imprisonment and hard labor for buggery, and finally, in 1718, the colony adopted the British code: death for offenders.[34]

But the tone of antisodomy laws moderated in the eighteenth century. Initially, statutes in both Massachusetts and New Hampshire employed biblical rhetoric in describing the offense as a "detestable and abominable Sin." And Connecticut cited Leviticus, chapter 20, as the authority for its laws against "carnal Copulation." By midcentury, however, when Connecticut reaffirmed the death penalty for offenders, it did not cite the authority of the Bible. In the courts, caution replaced urgent prosecutions and hasty convictions. Blackstone warned that "it is an offence of so dark a nature, so easily charged, and the negative so difficult to be proved, that the accusation should be clearly made out: for, if false, it deserves a punishment inferior only to that of the crime itself." And Swift reported the acquittal of a man whom he believed guilty on the technical grounds that only one eyewitness came forward to testify to penetration whereas, he wrote, common law required the testimony of two for such capital convictions.[35]

Trials persisted and some defendants were punished harshly, but concern for legal procedures and reluctance to employ the death penalty for nonviolent and "victimless" crimes made convictions so unusual that executions seemingly ended in New England. In 1701 a Rhode Island court tried Nathaniel Bowdish, Jr., for having sex with a dog, but he was convicted only "of an Attempt of Buggery with a doge." Jurors spared the man's life; the judge fined him thirty pounds and ruled that Bowdish's right hand thumb be branded with the letter R (probably for rape). In addition Bowdish was to be publicly humiliated by being "tyed to a carts taile" and moved to three locations in Newport where at each stop he would "Recive ten stripes on his Naked back well Layd." Finally, Bowdish had to stand for three days "upon a stock neare ye Collony hous" with a sign reading, "heare I stand ffor Commiting the Most Horrid & Beastly Sin of Bugery or Sodomy with A dog." Three years later in Salem, Massachusetts, in another dog-related case, Edward Twist and Benjamin Doroty were charged with assaulting Abigail Moulton, in which they "in a most filthy and obscene manner did handle & move the Genitalls of the sd dog close to the Body of sd. Abigail Moulton and in a most wicked & inhumane manner allowed the sd Abigail that the Dog was very Capable of Copulating." In this 1704 case the court acquitted Doroty, but it convicted Twist of threatening Abigail Moulton with the dog's genitals and ordered him to "be whipt ten stripes on the naked back or Pay a fine of Three Pounds." In Connecticut charges were brought against Andrew Davis of Groton in 1718 after numerous neighbors suspected he had sex with his mare. Eyewitnesses reported seeing him standing behind her "with one of his hands on the taile of—maire or in the—of it, and his other hand on hr back towards her mane." Davis denied the charges and was acquitted.[36]

As in the seventeenth century, accusations tended to come in clusters. Bowdish's 1701 trial was preceded four years earlier by a 1697 scandal in Fairfield, Connecticut, and was followed in 1704 by the accusation against Doroty and Twist. Nine years later the New London county court convicted two residents of Colchester, Connecticut, Joseph Chapman and John Brown in 1713. And in 1718 Davis faced similar charges at the same court. These men, however, were not convicted of capital crimes and so were whipped and subjected to mock hanging—that is, to sit on the gallows for an hour with a rope around the neck.

Almost two generations passed before Hannah Corkin of Monmouth County, New Jersey, was convicted in 1757 of attempted buggery and sentenced to twenty lashes, to be administered in four sets in four different towns. Corkin, the only woman in colonial America punished for a bestiality-related offense, fell victim to the brief spasm of prosecutions in the mid-Atlantic region. These trials may have been encouraged by a frequently reprinted 1755 English newspaper report describing how George Chambers was convicted of bestiality and sentenced to death. The onset of the French and Indian War, which threatened Pennsylvania and New York especially, fed public anxieties. In addition, enthusiasm for biblical rhetoric, inspired by the midcentury evangelical revivals, may also account in part for the deadly turn of prosecutions. In 1756 the *New York Mercury* published a jeremiad-style letter declaring that God had sent recent catastrophes to "reform vicious people," just as he sent Joshua to destroy the Canaanite nations as punishment for their sins, which included sodomy and bestiality. In the same year that Corkin faced her accusers, the court at Salem, some forty miles south of Philadelphia at the southwest corner of New Jersey, convicted "Charles Conoway, for the detestable and unnatural Sin of Bestiality, with a Mare" and executed him on May 9, 1757. Prosecution of all sexual crimes peaked in Pennsylvania in the 1760s, and while most targeted fornication, in 1761 a court in Lancaster, Pennsylvania, sentenced Nehemiah Armstrong to death for committing bestiality. Farther south, North Carolina tried John Everitt for having sex with a mare in 1764 and Robert Johnson the following year for penetrating a cow. And while the language of the indictments echoed charges filed in New England—the offenses were described as "a venereal affair" and "the detestable and abominable Crime of buggery (not to be named among Christians)"—neither man was executed.[37]

Accusations and trials for bestiality persisted fitfully in the eighteenth century, but the keen sense of urgency inspired by fear of divine punishment that had once surrounded them faded. The religious zeal and supernatural beliefs of the previous century made way for a new spirit of religious moderation and enlightened scientific and philosophic inquiry. Although the new mood mitigated the urge to exterminate the sinners and sin in a violent manner, the logic of the biblical prohibition was now joined by a scientific effort to understand the world by creating clearly defined categories. This Enlightenment effort to make sense of the natural world led intellectuals to examine the strange, the exotic, and the deformed. Now such phenomena must be explained in natural, not supernatural terms. The age, after all, tried to banish Satan, not God. Consequently the appearance of "freakish" creatures could no longer be explained as the work of the devil; freaks challenged notions of divine order.

In a world where Satan became dormant and God a distant watchmaker, sexual intercourse between humans and animals seemed a logical explanation for the birth of "deformed monstrosities," an idea, after all, that had led to the execution of a New Haven man in the previous century. Now many educated men, even some trained in medicine, could believe a 1726 account of an illiterate English woman, Mary Toft, who claimed to have given birth to seventeen rabbits. A fair in the Netherlands featured Siamese twins whose abnormality was explained by their sinful mother's watching dogs mating during her pregnancy. And different editions of *Aristotle's Master-Piece*, the pseudoscientific pornographic treatise on sex and procreation, which went through more editions in eighteenth-century America than all the other books on the subject combined, explained that monstrous births are "also begotten by women's bestial and unnatural coition."[38]

Prominent New Englanders were no less susceptible to believing that human-animal intercourse could lead to monstrous offspring. Isaac Backus, New England's leading Baptist minister, recorded the finding of a dead sheep at a Massachusetts farm. The farmer, he noted, "cut her open when to his great surprise there came out a thing which had some features of a lamb, but much more of a negro female child . . . its back and thighs shaped like a child and smooth all over except a wooly hair upon its head." Backus went on to report that "great numbers of people flockt to see it and dr. Isaac Otis dissected it and found that inwardly as well as outwardly it had more resemblance of a child than a beast, and tis suspect to be the effect of the beastiality of a Negro in the neighbourhood."[39] The science of autopsy could be used to confirm the fertility of interspecies sexual contact—a natural rather than a supernatural explanation for a freakish curiosity. And while the conclusion that the features resembled "a Negro in the neighborhood" confirmed eighteenth-century racialist fantasies about the "biological" proximity of Africans and animals, unlike the deadly 1642 New Haven case, the similarities to the local black man did not lead to a trial.

This cultural fascination with the odd and deformed was accompanied by a scientific effort to document and explain the natural world. Eighteenth-century naturalists extended species differentiations to humanity, dividing people into geographical subgroups with distinct physical and mental characteristics. Carolus Linnaeus's *Systema Naturae* (1735) became the zoological textbook for the next century. Linnaeus was intrigued by the phenomena of *Homo Ferus*, wild children supposedly raised by wolves. He classified them as hybrids of humans and beasts. One theory of early childhood education warned that babies might revert into animalistic existence. Crawling was considered an animal-like form of locomotion suitable for beasts but below the dignity of humans. Parents thus discouraged toddlers from crawling to make sure they encouraged human, not animal, characteristics. Though the founders of Rome, Romulus and Remus, had been suckled by wolves, this was no model for eighteenth-century Americans.[40]

The age of reason was also the era of creating boundaries and confirming hierarchies within the emerging category of national identity. By reinforcing the idea of a distinct biological identity for the hegemonic group natural philosophers also confirmed the legitimacy of the social order. Even the most influential voices of the Enlightenment believed that ancient interspecies sex yielded humanoid offspring. Denis Diderot's scientific dialogue *Le Rêve de D'Alembert* (1769) invoked the specter of the creation of goat men. And Voltaire, though famed as a skeptic, interpreted the biblical prohibition on bestiality as evidence that the practice must have been widespread among the ancient Hebrews.[41] Other naturalists subscribed to the Enlightenment's "Great Chain of Being" belief system that organized the natural world in a hierarchical order where each species occupied a distinct place in the ladder of creation. Yet this ladder assumed the possibility of reproduction as a result of sexual contacts between adjoining species. At the top humans, "partly divine, partly animal," might—as in the case of Mary and the Holy Spirit—reproduce.[42]

Scientific reflections on species boundaries and sexuality carried powerful political implications. Some European commentators believed that Native Americans occupied a transitional place in the biological chain and thus engaged in trans-species sexual unions. One commented in 1660 that Pueblo "men and women have sexual intercourse in bestial fashion." The term *mulatto* originated in the Spanish word for young mule, *mulato*, suggesting that the sexual contacts between people of African and European descent were similar to cross-species intercourse between horses and donkeys. Educated Westerners commonly believed Africans had sexual intercourse with apes. English medical literature of the eighteenth century, for example, blamed the spread of venereal diseases on Africans who contracted them from bestial intercourse. Upon observing interracial sex in South Africa, one Swedish observer noted: "An Englishman will occasionally take *a dear black sweetheart,* and an urbane Frenchman does not miss the chance of throwing himself *aux pieds de sa belle brune.* My own innocent countrymen, however, generally consider this to be bestiality."[43]

Racial definitions of Africans as different species rendered sex between master and female slave a bestial act. Thomas Jefferson speculated in *Notes on the State of Virginia* that the sexual desire of blacks for whites was just "as widespread as the preference of the orangutan for the black women over his own species." Ironically, in the eyes of a racialist thinker like Jefferson, his own relations with Sally Hemings must have possessed a bestial undercurrent, made explicit by an 1804 political cartoon that mocked the Jefferson-Hemings relationship with animal imagery to portray the couple.

Jefferson's thoughts on the relationship between Africans and apes suggest his own carnal desire for the "inferior species." In fact, the fantasy world of sadism and bestial imagination helps explain European-Americans' preoccupation with the sexuality of African Americans—and their routinely violated taboo against interracial sex, interracial attraction, and its suppression when it concerned black men and white women. In sex, as Freud pointed out, the greater the violations of prescribed sexual norms, the more people are engrossed in both fantasizing about the forbidden and ridding themselves of their own sexual guilt by violent reaction to any manifestations of such activities. The desire to violate taboos, Freud wrote, "persists in the unconscious; those who obey the taboo have an ambivalent

Figure 4. This caricature of Thomas Jefferson and Sally Hemings draws on bestial connotations to disparage the president and his slave paramour. *A Philosophic Cock*, Newburyport, Massachusetts (c. 1804) by James Akin. Charles Peirce Collection. Courtesy of the American Antiquarian Society.

attitude toward what the taboo prohibits. The magical power that is attributed to the taboo is based on the capacity for arousing temptation."[44] And in eighteenth-century society there was no greater sexual taboo than bestiality.

The scattered and incomplete nature of colonial archives makes it impossible to assert positive quantitative claims about the number of bestiality cases that came before eighteenth-century New England courts. We surmise that neighbors occasionally accused one another of bestiality, but public officials typically blocked further proceedings entirely, or else reduced accusations to lesser charges, such as attempted sodomy or lewd and lascivious behavior.[45] We have found seven men who faced bestiality charges in eighteenth-century Connecticut; two were convicted, though neither was executed: one escaped from jail, and the other was whipped. In 1767 the grand jury of New London County charged that sixteen-year-old Amos Green "wickedly devilishly feloniously and Against the Order of Nature" committed "that Detestable sin called Buggery" with a cow. The indictment retained the old Puritan language, declaring that Green was "moved and seduced by the Instigation of the devil." But whereas such rhetoric backed by questionable testimonies had led to execution in the seventeenth century, the New London jury discounted the testimony of eyewitnesses, took the defendant's youth into consideration, and acquitted Green.[46]

Three years later in 1770, three of twelve jurors in Hartford refused to convict for several days, leading to the acquittal of Thomas Alderman, who had been accused of the "foul and unnatural Crime of Bestiality." A year later John Sennet of Wenham, New Hampshire, was arrested for committing the "unnatural crime, Bestiality," in broad daylight "in the sight of several people" on the Boston common. The court reporter noted that Sennet, a married man with children, "was in Liquor at the time he committed the detestable Act," and that the owner of the mare "had her immediately put to Death." With several eyewitnesses to testify, it is likely that a century earlier Sennet would have been convicted and executed. But the Boston court convicted him only of attempted buggery and in 1772 sentenced him to be whipped, humiliated by an hour of mock execution on the gallows, and "pelted by the populace," a punishment depicted in a broadside the following year. The same reluctance to convict for the capital crime was evident six years later when the laborer John McKney was indicted in Middlesex County for committing "Buggery . . . upon a certain Beast & Brute Creature called a Cow," but acquitted. Here, unlike in the Alderman case, the prosecuting attorney, Robert Treat Paine (a signer of the Declaration of Independence), persisted. He tried McKney a second time six months later for "assault with an intent to commit . . . Buggery," and this time after McKney pleaded guilty, like Sennet he was sentenced to thirty-nine stripes on his "naked back" and an hour seated on the gallows "with a Rope about his Neck"—in addition to paying the costs of his prosecution. It was a severe punishment, especially because he was probably indentured for a year or more so as to pay court costs. But it was not hanging.[47]

Remnants of the old order remained. Inflammatory rhetoric appeared in two separate slander cases filed in 1770 in New London County Court by men alleging that their good names were sullied by rumors that they committed bestiality. In stating their case for monetary compensation, the plaintiffs' complaint described the offense as a "heinous & detestable" crime that would bring the plaintiffs "Discredit and Contempt" because bestiality was "abhor[ed] and hated of all Mankind." And when charges were filed by the state of Connecticut against sixteen-year-old Henry Burden in 1782 for "having carnal knowledge of or copulation with said Mare," authorities ordered the constable of the town of Norwich to "arrest s[ai]d mare" to make sure of her appearance at the trial. Burden's trial proceeded, eyewitnesses testified, the mare was viewed by the jury (probably outside the courtroom), but Burden won acquittal.[48]

The tide was turning. Sennet and Alderman were accused of violating nature, not of committing a capital sin against God, and juries spared their lives. As far back as 1760 John Adams had reported his seventy-year-old father telling a bestiality joke one evening as the family sat around the keeping-room hearth: "Old Horn . . . a little crooked old Lawyer in my fathers youth," overtook a "Market Girl" on her way to Boston "and asked to let him jigg her." The girl replied "by asking what is that? What good will that do? He replied it will make you fat! Pray be so good then says the Girl as to Gigg my Mare. She's miserably lean."[49] In the previous century we doubt a Harvard graduate would record a story that carried such irreverent, subversive implications. But now his father, born in 1690, evidently felt no embarrassment in amusing his family with this off-color anecdote. One doubts Adams, Senior, would have told this story to his parson, but during the eighteenth century the severity of Puritan sentiments faded among

many Yankees. And although the old rhetoric reappeared in Henry Burden's 1782 indictment, eyewitness testimony did not lead to conviction. By
the time the state of Connecticut acquitted this sixteen-year-old, bestiality
executions in New England had come to seem outdated relics of the Puritan
past.

Montesquieu's and Beccaria's assault on the death penalty in *The Spirit
of Laws* (1748) and *On Crime and Punishment* (1764), which demanded
rational and proportional punishments for crime, had echoed across the
Atlantic. Montesquieu's rosy celebration of England's political system made
The Spirit of Laws an instant hit in Britain, where it went through at least
seventeen editions in English from 1750 to 1768. The work was equally popular in the colonies, where numerous writers cited the *philosophe*. Montesquieu declared that "the crime against nature will never make any great
progress in society" and argued against executing offenders: "let it, like
every other violation of morals, be severely proscribed by the civil magistrate; and nature will soon defend or resume her rights." Beccaria's *On
Crime and Punishment* was even more popular in America. It was reprinted
serially in *The New-Haven Gazette and Connecticut Magazine* from March
through May 1786, and its readers knew that in the enlightened Atlantic
world it was no longer proper to execute people due to violations of biblical
sexual prohibitions. Discussion of the horror of bestiality moved from
homilies against violating scripture, to a secular response to a repulsive act
against nature. Zephaniah Swift openly acknowledged his intellectual debt
to Montesquieu and Beccaria and defined the transgression as "the unnatural connection between the human being and a brute," not as detestable
sin. Bestiality remained a detestable crime, but the mood in North America
had swung decidedly in favor of sparing the lives of those convicted of the
offense.[50]

Executions for such crimes seemed to be a thing of the past. In 1777
Thomas Jefferson proposed that the newly independent state of Virginia
punish offenders by castration instead of hanging, a proposal the legislature
rejected. In Pennsylvania, which had sentenced Jeremiah Sturgeon, "a
young man under 18," to hang in 1783 for committing "buggery" with a
mare and executed Joseph Ross for bestiality in 1785, the legislature reacted
by replacing the capital penalty in 1786 with forfeiture of property and a
prison term of up to ten years. Maryland ended the death penalty for sodomy in 1793, substituting a term of convict labor, and New York and New
Jersey followed suit three years later. Rhode Island turned in 1798 to a mock

execution for the first offense, though a second conviction remained a capital crime. Most heterosexual offenses—excepting rape, prostitution, and adultery—were widely overlooked, and now, after the American Revolution, the statutory penalties for "unnatural" sexual transgressions, including sodomy and bestiality, moderated and prosecutions came to a halt almost entirely.[51]

But astonishingly, in the late 1790s, as we have seen, courts in the New England interior reversed direction, convicting and sentencing to death two men in their mid-eighties for the crime of sexual intercourse with animals. Over a century earlier, when Puritans were striving to fulfill Mosaic law, such proceedings would have been more understandable. But after the Revolution and the Enlightenment had swept through the region, these prosecutions were as rare as they were unexpected. At the end of the eighteenth century, presumably, the incidence of sodomy was more frequent in populous maritime towns like Salem, Boston, Providence, or even New Haven than inland towns like Leverett and Litchfield. And acts of sodomy with animals—bestiality—must have been a somewhat familiar offense throughout southern New England, where farmers regularly put cattle and sheep to pasture, and horses and oxen provided everyday transportation as well as plowing. In a land where young men vastly outnumbered the old, it was teenagers and young men, not the elderly, who most likely engaged in bestial acts.[52] Indeed punishing young men for this crime had been the history of bestiality prosecutions for over 150 years. But in the late 1790s accusers and public officials in two inland counties did not target youths and young men. Instead they pursued two men who were regarded as ancient.

At the beginning of the eighteenth century the Puritan cleric Increase Mather testified that those "who have attained to three score . . . are everywhere accounted as old men"; and indeed before the Revolution barely 5 percent of the population lived beyond the age of sixty years. According to scholars, "seventy [years] was considered the maximum lifespan for men and women in the early national period"; so men in their eighties were extremely rare—just one-eighth of 1 percent among white males in Hartford, Connecticut, in 1830. If a man achieved such a great age, he was supposed to be a wise patriarch, one who could rule "over society and dispense the wisdom of past generations." Puritans had prescribed the highest social rank for such elders, regarding their longevity as a mark of God's favor and, because they were said to be "sober, temperate, grave, and patient"— beyond the reach of passion.[53]

In fact, of course, only a few men actually fulfilled such exalted roles. As far back as 1721 the eminent eighty-two-year-old divine Increase Mather grumbled that "he was shown little respect or veneration." Three generations later in 1805 the seventy-four-year-old Reverend Joseph Lathrop, speaking of his own aged cohort, bemoaned the fact that "once we were of some importance in society; now we are sunk into insignificance." The wisdom of elders was prized more in rhetoric than in fact: "once our advice was sought and regarded; now we are passed by with neglect," Lathrop complained.[54]

Still, even when old men were not sought out for their wisdom, there was a general expectation that they could and should be sober examples to the young. In the Old Testament the Lord had announced that "days should speak, and the multitude of years teach wisdom." In 1781 the Hingham, Massachusetts, pastor Ebenezer Gay, after citing this text, preached on his eighty-fifth birthday that "old age hath peculiar advantages. . . . It abateth the violence of sensual inclinations; and it exempteth from many temptations to sin, in which youth betrayeth men." When the signer of the Declaration of Independence Benjamin Rush, the early republic's preeminent physician, reported on his study of octogenarians in 1797, he observed that though their memories were sometimes faulty, "their intellectual, moral, and religious powers were completely unimpaired." Though the elderly—and old men in particular—did not necessarily command reverence, they normally possessed respect. Widely regarded as being more trustworthy and virtuous than younger people, old people, many believed, had attained a sort of "moral expertise."[55]

So why, we ask, were these two octogenarians accused, tried, convicted, and sentenced to hang? The charges seem preposterous. Could men in their eighties be capable of actually penetrating dogs, cows, and horses? The strangeness of the accusations is conspicuous when one considers the record of all the men incarcerated in Connecticut for sex crimes from 1794 to 1827. The list of convicts held by the state at its New Gate Prison demonstrates that sex criminals were being confined only for violent, rape-related charges. Not a single one was imprisoned for sodomy or bestiality. Moreover the average age of these sexual offenders was 28.2 years, with a median age of twenty-seven years, exactly the age one would expect for men guilty of sexual offenses. The oldest offender in this thirty-three-year period was Job Roswell, convicted in 1826 at the age of—not eighty-four or eighty-five—but fifty-six years old. English prosecutions of offenders confirm that bestiality was an offense young men committed, usually during the summer.[56]

Table 1. Sexual Offenders in New Gate Prison, 1794-1827

Name	Age	Race	Convicted In	Trial Date	Charge	Sentence
Ezekiel Ball	40	White	New Haven	Aug. 27, 1813	Rape	Life at New Gate Prison
John Baptist	30	Black	Fairfield	Aug. 10, 1812	Attempted Rape	Life at New Gate Prison
Shadrach Burr	24	Black	New Haven	Aug. 23, 1817	Rape	Life at New Gate Prison
John Ely	33	White	Hartford	Dec. 1, 1804	Attempted Rape	Life at New Gate Prison
Stephen Franklin	27	White	Fairfield	Oct. 12, 1824	Attempted Rape	2 years at New Gate Prison
Charles Freeman	29	Black	New London	Oct. 29, 1823	Attempted Rape	6 years at New Gate Prison
Elias Freeman	19			May 1, 1826	Attempted Rape	3 years at New Gate Prison
Edward Green	30	Black	New London	Jan. 26, 1815	Attempted Rape	Life at New Gate Prison
Jacob Hazard	31	Black	Windham	Jan. 28, 1823	Attempted Rape	
John Ide	37	White	Windham	Sept. 27, 1822	Attempted Rape	14 years at New Gate Prison
Moses Johnson	45	White	Fairfield	Aug. 20, 1794	Attempted Rape	Life at New Gate Prison
Deming Latimer	14	White		? 2, 1809	Attempted Rape	7 years at New Gate Prison
Reuben Larence	30	Indian		? 2, 1810	Attempted Rape	
Eli Lyon	28	White	Fairfield	June 11, 1805	Rape	Life at New Gate Prison
Joseph Mawwee	22	Black	Litchfield	Aug. 25, 1820	Attempted Rape	Life at New Gate Prison
Job Roswell	56			Aug. 26, 1826	Incest	4 years at New Gate Prison

Name	Age	Race	Convicted In	Trial Date	Charge	Sentence
John Sahm	27	White		? 9, 1806	Attempted Rape	Life at New Gate Prison
Jacob Smith	25	Black	Fairfield	Oct. 6, 1823	Attempted Rape	7 years at New Gate Prison
Willaim Thayer	16			Aug. 29, 1825	Attempted Rape	5 years at New Gate Prison
Philip Vincent	26	White	Hartford	Sept. 10, 1817	Attempted Rape	Life at New Gate Prison
David Wells	20	White	Litchfield	March 1, 1824	Attempted Rape	5 years at New Gate Prison
Henry Wilson	25	Black	Fairfield	May 4, 1822	Rape	Life at New Gate Prison
George Wright	15	White		May 27, 1827	Attempted Rape	15 years at New Gate Prison

Average Age: 28.2: Median Age 27.0

18 Attempted Rape, 4 Rapes, 1 Incest

11 Whites, 8 Blacks, 1 Indian, 3 No race given

Two Black Men Executed for Rape, 1798–1817

Name	Age	Race	Convicted In	Trial Date	Charge	Sentence
Amos Adams	28	Black	Fairfield (Danbury)	1817	Rape	Executed
(Negro) Anthony	?	Black	Fairfield (Danbury)	1798	Rape	Executed

From data compiled by Karin E. Peterson, Museum Director, Old Newgate Prison, Connecticut State Historic Preservation Office, Department of Economic and Community Development.

Historically, and in the present day, hormone-driven young males have been the subjects of the overwhelming majority of psychological literature on bestiality. Such men have been described as suffering from a wide range of personality disorders that lead them to engage in a variety of other forms of antisocial behavior, such as violent sexual and nonsexual attacks, child abuse, and animal torture. Aged offenders, and there are very few such cases, are believed to suffer from repetition-compulsion disorders starting from youthful exploration or violent sexual abuse in early adolescence. But the two old men we are studying, Farrell and Washburn, do not, so far as our research can tell, fit this profile. And until the execution of Ephraim Wheeler in 1806 for committing rape on his daughter, the only men who were executed for sexual crimes in post-Revolutionary New England were black. So it was not merely unexpected to send two old white men to the gallows for any reason, it was extraordinary to consign two old white men to hang for nonviolent, victimless crimes.[57]

Why, then, in the early American republic—a nation founded on Enlightenment ideas—would neighbors accuse, officials prosecute, and juries condemn old men for a young man's offense?[58] Why didn't Farrell and Washburn sue their accusers for slander as some men did in New London County in the 1770s? Surely, if local elites were deeply concerned with bestiality, they would have targeted young offenders in Hampshire and Litchfield Counties, not Farrell and Washburn. Since bestiality is a reality in every society, the scandal it generates is less about specific transgressions than it is an expression of the conflicts and anxieties of an age. We turn, then, to a close examination of the Farrell and Washburn cases in the context of both the sexual revolution that transformed the Anglo-American world in the eighteenth century and the way leaders in the New England interior fought against what they perceived as the unleashing of the destructive power of passion.[59]

~

CHAPTER 2

The Unlikely Prosecutions of John Farrell
and Gideon Washburn

The story of John Farrell begins in the hardscrabble farming town of Lever-ett, located about 105 miles west of Boston in the eastern hills of Hampshire County, the countryside that had so recently supplied foot soldiers for Dan-iel Shays's army of insurgents. First settled around 1750 and incorporated in 1774, the town of Leverett erected a meetinghouse by 1776. But the parish, which could never provide a handsome livelihood, did not secure a regular pastor for almost a decade, until 1784, when the Reverend Henry Williams settled there. Williams was ordained, but he was not a college graduate. Over the course of his twenty-seven-year career he published just a single evangelical sermon, one he preached in neighboring Shutesbury in 1809, two years before his death. Among Leverett's hallmarks of advancing culti-vation, the town set a bounty on wolves' heads in 1783, constructed a pound to hold domestic animals in 1788, and—seven years before John Farrell's arrival—erected stocks to display wrongdoers in 1789.[1]

Evidence on the particular character and history of the Leverett com-munity is scarce. During the town's early decades the clerks' records—there were five clerks between 1774 when the town was set off from the southern part of Sunderland and 1796—display only the barest literacy skills. They illustrate the characteristic sketchiness of record keeping in recently settled towns where farming, grazing, and harvesting timber occupied most fami-lies; and where merchants, traders, and lawyers were scarce. Through the 1780s and 1790s Leverett was among the minority of towns that possessed no resident justice of the peace: indeed there is no evidence that anyone possessing a college degree resided in the town during its first two generations.

Leverett's localism and the frugality of its householders are reflected by the fact that, though the town was entitled to send a delegate to the Massachusetts General Court annually, only once during the entire decade from 1787 to 1797 did Leverett elect a representative, militia captain Stephen Ashley. That was in 1787 during the tumultuous aftermath of the Shays uprising, when the number of towns choosing to send delegates jumped suddenly by forty percent from the preceding year. And early in 1788, when Massachusetts held a convention to ratify or reject the proposed U.S. Constitution, Leverett sent John Hubbard to represent his neighbors. Suspicious of central authority, Hubbard, together with sixty-three percent of Hampshire County delegates, voted against ratification of the Constitution. Hubbard was a backbencher, part of the majority who neither spoke on the floor of the Convention nor served on any of its committees. Like most delegates who came from small farming communities, he was more comfortable with the provincial insularity of Leverett and its neighboring towns than the worldly cosmopolitanism of Boston and the learned gentlemen whose rhetoric dominated the convention.[2]

When Ashley and Hubbard returned to Leverett they resumed their local stations in a town consisting of roughly twenty-six square miles of uneven land, watered by several streams and where, as of 1790, there were eighty-six houses—mostly scattered farmsteads—in which dwelled 155 white males over the age of sixteen years, and 524 people overall. Only a single household was headed by a man of color, Adam Freeman, whose wife was white. By the time John Farrell was accused six years later, the community had grown to perhaps 640 people living in one hundred or so families, with a village center beginning to form in the southern quarter of the town, by road at least ten miles east of the Connecticut River and separate from the principal east-west and north-south travel routes. At that time Farrell, an eighty-five-year-old Irish-born physician, was a newcomer to Leverett. According to the advertisement Farrell placed in the *Greenfield Gazette*, he had opened for business close to the emerging village center in the house of Dr. Silas Ball on May 2, 1796. According to Farrell, he "had great success in curing many of the long standing" cancers.[3]

Whether Farrell's medical claims were accurate or inflated, some of his former patients testified to his success. Cancer doctors during this period practiced in the hazy borderland between trained allopathic physicians and self-taught quacks. Using surgery to cut out cancerous growths and also applying chemical salves and plasters, physicians like Farrell could

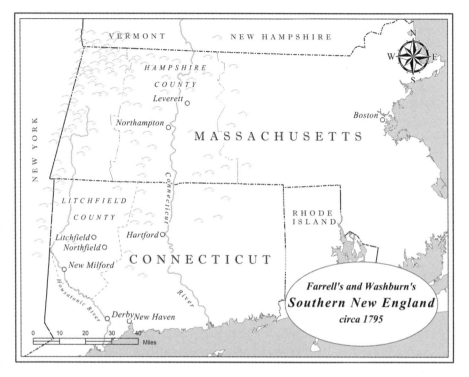

Figure 5. Farrell's and Washburn's Southern New England: Created by Brian Perchal, Cartographer, University of Connecticut Libraries, Map and Geographic Information Center (MAGIC).

sometimes succeed, although among residents of urban centers like Philadelphia, New York, or Boston they were seldom employed unless more respectable physicians had given up. As a "cancer doctor," Farrell was unlikely to have been university trained or entirely respectable; however, in rural communities where patients enjoyed few options, a doctor who could sometimes provide remedies found support.[4]

Why this old medical man should have landed in out-of-the-way Leverett is a mystery, though he had recently treated patients in Pelham and Shutesbury, similarly remote farming towns in Hampshire County less than a day's travel from Leverett. Judging from Farrell's record, the Irish immigrant was a transient who in the previous dozen years had dwelled in at least half a dozen rural communities. The earliest record we have found is an advertisement dated August 1785, and it includes a testimonial from six residents of Beekman, New York, who announced that Farrell "has in sundry instances proved himself infallible in curing the worst of CANCERS, contrary to almost every persons [sic] expectations." So successful was Farrell that the Beekman men declared they had "never heard of his failing in any one instance, among the many patients he has undertaken." Six years later four Connecticut gentlemen—including a justice of the peace, a Yale-trained Congregational pastor, and two physicians—one with an M.D. degree—testified that "several cancers and kings'-evils have been compleatly [sic] cured . . . by John Ferrill [sic]." The following year three patients who had long suffered with cancer—two men and a woman—certified that "within about two years have obtained a complete cure, through the blessing of God on the means used by Doctor JOHN FARRELL."[5]

But notwithstanding such testimonials, after less than two months in Leverett, it is clear that whether or not he had made friends or admirers in his new community, he possessed at least two acquaintances that were ready to accuse him of having sex with a dog. The charge first came to the ears of Justice of the Peace Simeon Strong of Amherst, Massachusetts, in June 1796 when men from neighboring Leverett brought their potentially deadly complaint before him. As the law directed, Strong held a justice's court to hear the accusation and Farrell's response to it before ordering the old man's arrest. Though the identities of his accusers are not known, court records show that nine men, seven from Leverett, one from Pelham, and the county sheriff, Elisha Parker of Hadley, were paid for their time and travel as witnesses—Farrell's accusers among them. The Leverett witnesses included five farmers: Burden Cole, Webster Cole, Jonathan Field, Lewis Shumway, and Joseph Willard—all listed as yeomen—as well as the tavern keeper William Hubbard and Farrell's landlord, Dr. Silas Ball, a fifty-two-year-old local fixture who had held the office of town clerk in 1782–83. In addition, John Conkey of Pelham served as a witness. So far as can be determined, all the witnesses were adult men, nearly all husbands, fathers, and household heads. When they testified as to what they had seen and heard, their words would not be the mere gossip of Hubbard's tavern, but sworn statements in a capital trial before the Supreme Judicial Court.[6]

Farrell's claim that "the Resentment of his Persecutors" inspired their testimony and that they "were prompted to give evidence against him from interested motives" is credible, even probable, although no proof to support Farrell's claim survives. To speculate that Dr. Silas Ball, who had so recently welcomed him as a lodger, should now have found cause to turn against his fellow medical practitioner is plausible; but it is also reasonable to suppose that Ball was called to testify only because he was familiar with Farrell's comings and goings and perhaps the presence or absence of the dog in question. Without any record of the testimony—which would have required a witness to swear he saw Farrell actually penetrate the dog—one can only speculate as to what might have led some of the farmers, the doctor, or the tavern keeper to make the accusation. Yet Farrell's claim that he was being attacked due to hostile intent is persuasive: an examination of other sodomy and bestiality cases in early America, and especially the eighteenth century, reveals official passivity, even reluctance—not zeal—to press charges against the crime. Charges moved forward only when accusers pressed them.[7]

Supposing that one or two of Farrell's new acquaintances or neighbors had witnessed a forbidden act, they were not compelled to bring the grotesque formal accusation of bestiality. Elsewhere, in the exceedingly rare cases where neighbors did make complaints of bestiality, the accusations were ordinarily quashed before trial or, if tried, reduced to lesser noncapital charges. Occasionally such behavior could be a matter of common, jocular gossip of the sort that John Adams recorded in 1760 concerning Braintree's Deacon Savil, who, though "an old Man 77 Years of Age, [was] discovered to have been the most salacious, rampant, Stallion, in the Universe—rambling all the Town over, lodging with this and that Boy and Attempting at least the Crime of Buggery." Though Adams was himself a lawyer and "Deacon Savils Affair has become public," it never led to any legal proceedings.[8] And in the case of Gideon Washburn in Litchfield, Connecticut, neighbors kept their accusations out of court for years, only complaining to the authorities when vengeance was the likely catalyst. So whatever the witnesses against John Farrell believed they had seen, their decision to bring their stories to Justice of the Peace Simeon Strong, and to swear complaints against Farrell should be construed as hostile.

The centuries-old language of the state's indictment against Farrell was not merely hostile but threatening. Composed by Simeon Strong, the justice of the peace who was also serving as the state's prosecuting attorney, the time-honored words rang out in the Supreme Judicial Court when it met at Northampton in September 1796: John Farrell, late of Leverett in Hampshire County, was charged with "feloniously, wickedly, diabolically, and against the order of Nature," engaging in "a venereal affair with a certain female Brute Animal called a Bitch." On June 23, 1796, in Leverett, Farrell, "not having the fear of God before his Eyes nor regarding the order of Nature but being moved and seduced by the instigation of the Devil, did commit & perpetrate that detestable and abominable Crime of Sodomy (not to be named among Christians) to the great displeasure of Almighty God, to the great scandal of all human kind, [and] against the . . . Statute." Now, after hearing the testimony of the witnesses and the arguments of the attorneys, it would be up to the jury to determine Farrell's life or death.[9]

Because no detailed account of the trial was ever made, the testimony of the witnesses, the arguments of the prosecution and defense, and the judge's charge to the jury cannot be known. However, a newspaper reported that when the Supreme Judicial Court met at Northampton the previous spring, Chief Justice Francis Dana had delivered a partisan charge to the grand jury warning of the dire threat to "the American nation" posed by the "restless spirit of the factious few." Later, when Farrell came to trial in September, the heated presidential contest between John Adams and Thomas Jefferson was approaching a climax, so the judges—all eastern Massachusetts Federalists—most likely conveyed their own sense of anxiety in the courtroom. For jurors in this most Federalist of Massachusetts counties, their apprehension resonated. Back in April the Federalist press had reported that Judge Dana's speech "on the present alarming aspect of our public affairs" had been "so well received, that the Grand Jurors agreed unanimously to request a copy for the press."[10] The courtroom was deep-dyed with Federalist sentiment.

The prosecuting attorney, Simeon Strong, was himself a Federalist and the same official who ordered Farrell's arrest in June. Strong, who had graduated from Yale forty years earlier, was a sixty-year-old Northampton native who had practiced law all his adult life. Because he had gained his legal training with the prominent Loyalist John Worthington of Springfield, Massachusetts, Strong's own loyalties were suspected during the Revolution. As of 1790, however, he was prospering—heading a household of eleven people, including one servant of color. By the 1790s he had gained public trust and, five years after he prosecuted Farrell, his second cousin Governor Caleb Strong would appoint him to the state's highest tribunal, the Supreme Judicial Court. When Simeon Strong issued Farrell's arrest warrant and wrote out the old physician's indictment, there is no evidence that he was especially eager to prosecute Farrell; but in his own life he was a model of staunch orthodox Christianity and orthodox sexual life. After fathering eight children during his twenty-one-year marriage to his first wife, he had remarried after her death, to a widow with whom he would pass his remaining seventeen years of life. Strong may not have wished to see Farrell executed, but he doubtless believed that sodomy with man or beast was sinful and must be punished according to law.

Certainly Farrell's own lawyers, the future governor Caleb Strong and John Hooker, also Federalists, held similar beliefs. But as court-appointed attorneys for the defendant in a capital case, their first responsibility according to both law and professional ethics was the defense of their client. And they were powerful defenders. Hooker, the junior member, a 1782 Yale graduate and the son and namesake of Jonathan Edwards's successor in the Northampton pulpit, was already a leading attorney in nearby Springfield. His sister had married his senior colleague Caleb Strong—the most notable member of the Hampshire County bar. Strong, a nearly blind fifty-one-year-old Harvard graduate, had taken leading roles in Massachusetts politics from the beginning of the Revolution onward. He had been elected to the Massachusetts General Court from 1776 to 1788, where he served both in the House and the Senate, and his colleagues had chosen him to represent Massachusetts at the Constitutional Convention at Philadelphia in 1787. When Strong returned home, in contrast to the majority of Hampshire delegates, including Leverett's John Hubbard, Strong vigorously supported the U.S. Constitution as a Northampton delegate to the ratifying convention in Boston in 1788. The very next year the legislature sent him back to Philadelphia as one of Massachusetts's U.S. senators. Two years before Farrell's trial, Strong had been living there as a U.S. senator when the Pennsylvania legislature ended the death penalty for rape and sodomy—indeed, for every crime except murder. Now, just back from Philadelphia and his U.S. Senate service, he joined Hooker in defending Farrell. With these gentlemen as his advocates, the old man stood a fair chance of winning acquittal, no matter what stories might have been told about him and the dog.

The town of Northampton, which had only recently won selection in 1794 as the county seat for Hampshire, Massachusetts's largest county, was about three times the size of Leverett, with a population in 1796 of about two thousand people.[11] At the beginning of Farrell's trial in Northampton's new courthouse, the press reported nothing unusual; so evidently the only pretrial publicity his case provoked was limited to word of mouth among the people of Leverett and their neighbors. Printed trial reports, commercial ventures that would provide near-verbatim accounts of courtroom proceedings, had not yet come to Massachusetts or Connecticut, so we can only speculate as to the arguments presented to the jury.[12]

Based on the conduct of capital trials just a few years later, we may presume that the prosecution began by emphasizing the reliability of its witnesses and the heinous nature of the crime. In response, the defense attorneys sought to cast doubt on the motives of the witnesses and the truth of their claims. If they could demonstrate that Farrell's accusers acted from malicious or interested motives, then they could reduce the weight of witness testimony. But because Farrell was new to Leverett, as he later described, "a Stranger and friendless in that part of the Country when his Trial took place," his attorneys could not call on witnesses in the usual way so as to testify to Farrell's good character and that they had known the virtue and moral fiber of the old physician for years. And since Massachusetts law forbade defendants from testifying on their own behalf—in case they might be tempted to perjure themselves and so be doomed to hell—Strong and Hooker had to stress the implausibility of an eighty-five-year-old committing the crime. They would then rely on their rhetorical skills to exonerate their client. That they did not choose to raise the issue of dementia suggests that, based on Farrell's observable behavior, the argument that he was *non compos mentis* would have seemed spurious and thus tantamount to admitting that Farrell had actually committed the bestial act. So Hooker and Strong questioned the soundness and motives of the testimony against him and argued that Farrell was not guilty of the specific charge in the indictment. Yet despite their best efforts the two prominent attorneys could persuade the jury neither to acquit nor reduce the charge to the noncapital offenses of either "attempted sodomy" or the more common "lewd and lascivious" behavior.[13]

As in other trials, the proceedings ended with a charge to the jury from one of the justices. Since they were all—Francis Dana, Robert Treat Paine, Increase Sumner, Nathan Cushing, and Thomas Dawes—eastern Massachusetts Federalists who were troubled by the rising tide of pro-French Jeffersonian politics, we can be confident that the charge to the jury emphasized enforcement of the law. At the same time, however, the judge who spoke to the jury would have admonished jurors to weigh the evidence carefully and to render their judgment dispassionately. Judges invariably counseled juries to seek a fair conclusion that could withstand the test of

Figure 6. *Northampton in 1786*, as depicted in 1936 by Maitland de Gogorza. Courtesy of Forbes Library, Northampton, Massachusetts.

reasonable doubt. The goal of the trial, after all, was not punishment but justice.

A day after the jury brought in its verdict the court pronounced Farrell's sentence. As the local paper laconically reported, "*John Farrel*, a native of Ireland, for the crime of Sodomy—was found guilty by the jury, and on the day following received sentence of DEATH." A newspaper twenty miles down the Connecticut River at West Springfield reported the two notable judgments of the September 1796 session of the Supreme Judicial Court sitting at Northampton: Noah Barns was found guilty of "counterfeiting, &c. and was sentenced to stand in the pillory one hour, to be cropped [to have his ears cut off], and to make a visit to Castle Island [the state prison] for the term of seven years"; and "John Farrol, a Frenchman, aged 85 years (as he says) was convicted of Sodomy & received sentence of death." The latter report was reprinted in no fewer than seven newspapers in New England and New York with the additional editorial comment that this was "the first conviction of the kind we ever recollect."[14] Though brief—no mention was made of the convict's occupation or prior residence—this newspaper report was momentous. If, as expected, the state enforced this sentence of its highest tribunal, Massachusetts would, for the first time since 1674—the first time in the eighteenth century—hang a man for sodomy. Notwithstanding Enlightenment doubts about the death penalty for crimes like sodomy—as well as arson, burglary, rape, and robbery—the North-ampton jury, composed of voters drawn from a dozen of Hampshire's sixty-two towns, delivered a guilty verdict and the justices assigned the stat-utory punishment by sentencing Farrell to hang.

One would suppose that the accusation, trial, and sentencing of John Farrell were unique—after all a half-dozen printers had never heard of such a case; yet just three years later in Litchfield, a Connecticut town about seventy miles southwest of Northampton, there was another trial of an old man for the very same capital crime. And remarkably, the outcome repeated the Massachusetts result. Moreover, as in Massachusetts, it had been over a century—137 years to be exact—since the authorities had exe-cuted anyone for such a crime.[15] Now the defendant, Gideon Washburn, was not a peripatetic immigrant, but a married man, a Yankee, with deep roots in Connecticut.

If the state actually followed the path prescribed for the convict by stat-ute, Washburn would suffer the most disgraceful end Connecticut could visit on one of its sons, a man descended from an old and respectable yeoman family. Gideon's own grandfather, Hope Washburn of Bengeworth, in Worcestershire, had come to Connecticut sometime before 1660, the year that he married Mary Stiles of Hartford. Thereafter the Washburns moved to Milford and Stratford on the Connecticut shore, before settling in Derby, the first English settlement on the Naugatuck River, about a dozen miles west of New Haven. After the original immigrant Hope Washburn's death in 1696 his estate was divided between his sons William (Gideon's father) and Samuel. As the eldest son, William inherited the family house and first choice of half his father's land.

A few months before Hope Washburn's death, Gideon's father William had married Hannah Wooster, also of Derby, in August 1696. Together the couple had five boys and three girls. Gideon, born on November 15, 1715, was their seventh child and last boy in a prosperous family. William Washburn's name appears prominently in Derby records as one of the town's proprietors, a land surveyor, and a fence viewer. In 1708 he was among the first townsmen to take the freeman's oath; and as a leading citizen he pledged to pay both a minister and a physician to settle in Derby. Town tax records estimated William Washburn's property in 1719 at £90; and though he was not wealthy, he did rank among the top fifteen percent of the town taxpayers. When his father died in 1741 Gideon was twenty-six years old, and his status as the son of a proprietor supplied benefits. For when the town divided the remaining common land, the descendants of eighty-three original residents shared in it equally. Though the value of the acreage was modest, all of William Washburn's children, Gideon included, gained land from this distribution.[16]

As of 1741 there was no evidence that Gideon's life was remarkable; and certainly it did not foretell his later disgrace. His family had provided him land and reputation. Indeed, on his grandmother's side he was related to the clergymen Isaac Stiles and his son, Ezra, a younger contemporary of Gideon who, after graduating from Yale and serving a Congregational parish in Newport, Rhode Island, went on to the Yale College presidency. On October 6, 1743, at the age of twenty-eight, Gideon married twenty-three-year-old Esther Alling of New Haven. Together the couple had eight children; the first birth, a daughter named Philene, was recorded as coming on July 6, 1744, exactly nine months after the wedding.[17]

After their wedding the young couple settled on thirty acres Gideon purchased from the widow of an uncle. Thereupon he set out to establish himself as a Derby yeoman farmer. During the years 1741 to 1748 he bought over 155 acres, paying over £700. Washburn's trading suggests he was trying to consolidate his holdings. But by the end of the 1740s he evidently began a downward slide so that by 1763, when he finally sold his last Derby real estate, he gave up the family homestead and barn located on an eighteen-acre lot as well as three other parcels of land. Indeed, between 1744 and 1763 he had sold approximately 365 acres for over £2,716. Overall, from 1741 to 1763 he had bought or sold land twenty-six times; but when he left Derby, Gideon Washburn had sold more than twice as much land as he bought.[18]

In local records Gideon is titled "yeoman," but unlike his father he never took a prominent role in town affairs. Instead he earned a name for himself in a way that suggests he was unwilling or unable to follow his father's path. In an era when the countryside was changing from forest to farming, Gideon Washburn became known as one of the town's best hunters, and he developed connections with nearby Indians. Local lore had Washburn naming his residence "Chuse," after the Indian sachem Joseph Mauwehu Chuse, who lived near Washburn with a few Indians and who claimed the land was an ancient burying ground. Closeness between Gideon Washburn and Joseph Chuse is suggested by the fact that both belonged to the tiny St. James Anglican Church in Derby. Washburn's membership in St. James Church and his association with the Indians suggests that, notwithstanding his Puritan heritage, he did not readily find a comfortable place among his Yankee neighbors.[19]

The respectability of his origins and early years did not assure future success. Gideon's oldest brother, John, a surveyor, retained their father's standing in the community. Other members of the family, however, did not fare equally well. Some left Derby and those who remained settled in outlying sections where the future towns of Oxford and Seymour would emerge in 1798 and 1850. Gideon's brother Ephraim Washburn was an original settler of the Oxford Parish and the town built its first meetinghouse on Ephraim's land.[20] In 1741, the year of William Washburn's death and concurrent with the organization of the first parish in Oxford, Ephraim purchased a one-story house, enlarged it, and opened it as a tavern with his son Josiah running its daily affairs. This structure still stands in present-day Oxford.[21]

Gideon's own history is checkered. In June 1746, three months after the birth of his second child, Asahel, like many young men in search of adventure and a soldier's pay, he enlisted for a planned invasion of Canada.

Figure 7. Ephraim and Josiah Washburn's tavern from 1714, Oxford, Connecticut, as it appeared in 2012. Photograph by Doron Ben-Atar.

Gideon signed with a New London-based unit, whose commander recognized his age and competence by naming him as one of only four sergeants in the company. The expedition, however, never left Connecticut; so Gideon was cut loose from military service without his expected pay. Even before, however, Washburn had turned to criminal activity. In 1745 Gideon and an older brother, Edward, conspired with some Derby residents to counterfeit colonial notes. In August Gideon met blacksmith Daniel Tucker in Derby and asked him to shoe his horse. When it was time to pay, Gideon took a fresh forty shilling Massachusetts note and told Tucker that together they could have as many of them as they wanted; thereupon he hired Tucker to forge the necessary printing plates. They set up a press in Edward Washburn's house and struck off both Connecticut and Massachusetts money. But Tucker's plates and the quality of their bills proved doubtful, and in 1747 they were arrested.

Counterfeiting was a serious offense; punishable in England by death. In Connecticut anyone convicted by the Superior Court of counterfeiting or making the necessary machinery, or even for knowingly passing a counterfeit note, could face severe penalties. According to law the convict's right ear could be cut off, the letter C branded on his forehead, his entire estate forfeited, and the counterfeiter not only barred from trading in the colony but committed to a workhouse for the rest of his life. A few members of the gang received harsh sentences, but Edward Washburn escaped prosecution altogether and Gideon avoided punishment by having two of his neighbors submit affidavits guaranteeing his future good behavior. The fact that two men in Derby were willing to stand behind Washburn suggests that though Gideon had fallen, he had not reached bottom. In 1758, perhaps in an effort to earn cash, Washburn enlisted to serve in a New Haven regiment organized to fight against the French. Washburn's literacy, already suggested by his earning the rank of sergeant in 1746, is attested by the list of soldiers he signed in 1761 during this later enlistment. Joining the army, however, did not improve Gideon's standing in the community. When he submitted a deposition in a 1760 property dispute, his neighbors doubted his word. An attorney noted Washburn's "general character is not good." The judges asked about Washburn's "verasity for 10 or 12 years past," to which the attorney responded, "I take it to be not good. I have heard some talk about him, but don't know much about it." Gideon had worn out his welcome in his native town.[22]

So in 1763 Gideon and Esther Washburn left Derby and moved some thirty miles northwest up the Housatonic River to the large and hilly town of New Milford. Here Gideon purchased sixty-eight acres a few miles southwest of the village in the Steep Hill section and evidently settled into respectable life. He joined the local Anglican church, where three of his daughters, Philene, Lucretia, and Sarah, married local men. His seventh child and youngest son, William (named after Gideon's own father), lived with his parents and in 1787 married Rachel McDonald of Watertown, Connecticut. The same year, Gideon and William jointly sold their 116 acres in New Milford for £300 to William's father-in-law, Daniel McDonald (1733–92). Evidently Gideon was transferring his remaining assets to this youngest son, William, who would thenceforth provide for his aging parents—a time-honored practice among New Englanders.[23]

Gideon Washburn was already an old man in his seventies in 1788 when he and his wife, Esther, accompanied William's family to Litchfield, twenty miles northeast of New Milford. That town had been founded as a frontier settlement in the early 1720s by migrants from Hartford and Windsor.

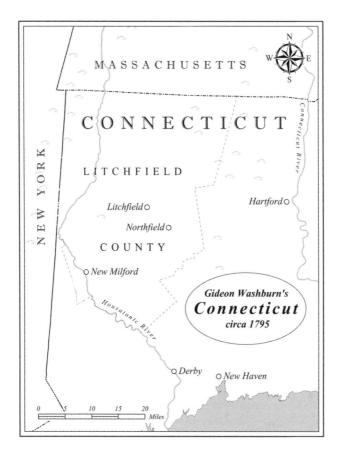

Figure 8. Gideon Washburn's Connecticut: Created by Brian Perchal, Cartographer, University of Connecticut Libraries, Map and Geographic Information Center (MAGIC).

These first European residents had struggled to earn livelihoods in the uplands of northwestern Connecticut, where the climate was colder than the Connecticut River valley, and the hilly, stony fields they cleared in the wilderness were less productive than the bottomlands they left behind. Fully a generation passed before the town began its ascent when in 1751 the legislature selected it as the seat of the newly organized Litchfield County. As the location of the county court and the center for a thriving market, Litchfield village emerged as the hub of local road networks. When the imperial crisis shook the old order in the 1760s and 1770s, most of the town's residents joined the ranks of protest and rebellion. Patriot activity in the county, from outcries against the Stamp Act in 1765 to the 1774 resolutions of solidarity with beleaguered Boston, originated in Litchfield. Although the fighting was generally distant from them, townspeople found ways to support the American cause. Litchfield's roads connected it with Massachusetts, central Connecticut, and New York. Litchfield residents stored supplies for Patriot troops, housed senior prisoners of war (including New Jersey's governor, William Franklin), and in 1776 melted a statue of King George III hauled on ox carts from New York City and molded the lead into bullets for the Continental Army.

The Revolutionary War altered the direction of the coastal trade in Connecticut away from the Long Island Sound, which was controlled by the British, to the hinterland route through Hartford and Litchfield toward the Hudson River. When the War for Independence ended, the town remained a crossroads for commercial traffic between Hartford and Albany, and between Berkshire County, Massachusetts, and New York City. Increasingly commerce and legal affairs drew merchants, tradesmen, and attorneys into the village. Most notably, in 1784 Tapping Reeve opened the first law school in the United States in his home on South Street. His tiny school became the first to teach common law, and Reeve's school and its graduates launched Litchfield into regional and national prominence. Over the course of its fifty-year existence the Litchfield Law School would graduate some eleven hundred attorneys, including two U.S. vice presidents, fourteen governors, fourteen members of the U.S. cabinet, twenty-eight U.S. senators, 100 members of the House of Representatives, three members of the U.S. Supreme Court, and a host of other public officials.[24]

Nearby, Sarah Pierce founded one of the nation's first female academies in 1792. Pierce's innovative curriculum combined academic and ornamental subjects, so that Pierce and her fellow teachers expanded the scope of women's learning for the more than three thousand students who attended the school before it, too, closed in 1833. Over its forty-one-year history, the Litchfield Female Academy attracted students from fifteen states and territories, Canada, and the West Indies. Coeducation also had a start in progressive Litchfield. In the South Farms section of town, the Revolutionary veteran Captain James Morris started an academy in 1790. In contrast to most academies, he generated controversy by welcoming girls as well as boys. Such education for girls, some complained, would be "blowing up

Figure 9. This watercolor *View of Litchfield*, a thriving county seat surrounded by fertile farmlands, was painted by Rebecca Couch Dennison, a student at Sarah Pierce's Female Academy, probably in 1805. Courtesy of the Abby Aldrich Rockefeller Folk Art Museum, Colonial Williamsburg Foundation, Williamsburg, Virginia.

their pride." The "traditionalists" versus "cosmopolitans" flavor of Litchfield's cultural conflicts was evident in a meeting held in the village's Congregational meetinghouse, where some gentlemen declared the girls at the school "would feel themselves above their mates and they would feel above labor." Morris, himself a Litchfield native and a 1775 Yale graduate, won sufficient support among the village elite to maintain his academy, but the conflict revealed a fault line in the outlook of village leaders.[25]

None of these high cultural affairs affected the Washburns directly since they did not buy land in the center of Litchfield or in Captain Morris's long-settled South Farms district. Instead William Washburn bought land in a peripheral locale called Northfield, some five miles southeast of the village. Settled first in the 1760s by a cluster of farmers from New Haven County, Northfield bordered on a part of Plymouth known as Northbury.

Thus, when residents named their settlement in the 1790s, they combined the first syllable of Northbury with the last of Litchfield to construct "Northfield." In 1788 Gideon Washburn's thirty-seven-year-old son, William, moved onto land registered under his wife's name. Two years later the U.S. census shows the younger Washburn heading a household that included three males and three females over the age of sixteen—including his father and mother. In the next few years William would make three additional purchases to enlarge his holdings.[26]

Whereas Litchfield village prospered and its cultural horizons widened, the Northfield settlement on its outskirts remained a scattered array of hardscrabble hillside farms whose soil was "stony, rough, and hard for tillage." Traveling from Northfield to Litchfield village required climbing steep hills along a winding road, a two-hour trip that was especially burdensome in the winter and the mud season that followed. Not surprisingly, resentment toward the thriving center village—Litchfield Hill—festered, and Northfield residents sought relief. In 1789 the villagers organized themselves into a winter parish and voted to hire a minister for six months each year. The next year, Northfield refused to help pay the cost of painting the Litchfield village meetinghouse. And in 1791 a group of local residents, asserting the religious liberty won by the Revolution, challenged village orthodoxy by creating their own local parish of the Episcopal Church—Gideon Washburn's denomination since long before in Derby. Three years later in 1794, Northfielders enlarged their break with village leadership when they won state recognition of their community as a separate district within Litchfield.[27]

William Washburn was a leader in Northfield's assertion of an independent course. Just a year after he moved to Northfield he was chosen in 1789 to serve on a three-member committee to choose a location for a meetinghouse and to raise subscriptions to finance its construction as well as a minister's salary. After Northfield won recognition as a district, Washburn hosted the organizational meeting of the Ecclesiastical Society of Northfield in 1795, which voted to begin construction of an independent meetinghouse. At this time his dwelling and outbuildings were sufficient to enable him to board the eight carpenters hired to build the meetinghouse, a service for which the Ecclesiastical Society paid. According to local authorities, by 1798 the value of Washburn's farm had increased by 250 percent, "owing partly to the general rise of property in the county, partly, and perhaps principally, to its local situation; lying near the center of an ecclesiastical society, lately incorporated; and also lying near two houses lately erected for public worship, and partly by the improvements made upon the farm by said Washburn."[28]

During these first half dozen years in Northfield there was nothing in the record that foretold the coming family scandal. William Washburn was respected; in fact he was selected to serve as a grand juror for Litchfield County in 1794. The following year he and several neighbors entered an agreement with the town of Litchfield whereby they provided land to assist construction of a highway. The town's tax records of 1797 identify William Washburn as the sixth most propertied man among the thirty-five heads of households listed in Northfield, owning taxable property in the value of $207.21. In his district, Gideon Washburn's son was both prominent and prosperous, though on a scale far below that of the wealthy families of Litchfield village or the South Farms district. The sloping and rock-strewn land possessed by Northfield farmers did not enable them to subsist by tillage only, so like other upland farmers in central and western New England they relied substantially on grazing cattle. By the time of his father's trial in 1799, William Washburn had assembled a yeoman's farm of seventy-three acres with a dozen livestock: four horses, two mules, and six cows.[29]

By then, however, the Washburns' situation in Northfield was troubled by William Washburn's grasping ambition to enlarge his farm—by fair means or foul. William disputed the ownership of land and buildings with his neighbor Solomon Sanford—claiming the Sanford farm actually belonged to Washburn's wife, Rachel—born Rachel McDonald. This Washburn-McDonald claim originated in a 1777 loan of one hundred pounds from Rachel's grandfather to Solomon Sanford's father. In 1781 Solomon inherited the land and responsibility to pay the debt. Three years later when Rachel McDonald inherited the debt an attorney's error inadvertently transformed Solomon Sanford's debt into a mortgage owned by Rachel McDonald, William Washburn's future wife.

For a few years all seemed well as Rachel, her father, and Solomon Sanford lived by their understanding that ownership of the land remained with Solomon Sanford, who worked his farm, improved and paid taxes on it, while also paying the annual interest on the debt he owed to Rachel McDonald. But when William Washburn married Rachel McDonald he assumed management of her properties; and he decided to take advantage of the erroneous mortgage. Armed with the documents establishing his wife

as owner of the mortgage, in 1788 Washburn demanded that Sanford pay
his debt in full. When he could not pay, Washburn had him evicted and
took possession of the property. Unable to continue in Litchfield, Sanford
moved to Rensselaer County, New York, northwest of Litchfield along the
Massachusetts border.

But the conflict between Washburn and Sanford persisted. In March
1792 Solomon Sanford sued William Washburn for debt. Washburn denied
he owed Sanford anything; however, the court ruled that Washburn owed
Sanford £2 10s 8d. Evidently Washburn paid Sanford, since no further mention of this case is entered in the court records. But the aggrieved Solomon
Sanford was not finished. Having won this small victory, he hired Litchfield's best legal minds, Tapping Reeve and his law school associate, James
Gould, to help him reclaim the family farm through the courts. In June 1795
Reeve and Gould filed Sanford's suit charging that Washburn had wrongly
deprived their client of a farm worth £500 "for a debt less than half the
value." Washburn fought back. He defended his possession of the Sanford
farm by hiring the prominent New Haven attorney and future Connecticut
chief justice, David Daggett, in addition to John Allen and Pierpont
Edwards, the two attorneys who would later defend his father.[30]

The case dragged on. In August 1797 the court appointed a three-man
committee to mediate the dispute. In October that committee held hearings
at Northfield, and in January 1798 the Litchfield Superior Court accepted
its finding in favor of Sanford's claims. Washburn, the court ruled, had
wrongly used the 1784 drafting error to cheat his neighbor, "thereby con-
verting a mistake in drawing the deed, and the confidence placed in the
faith and honor of the said Daniel McDonald, . . . [to become] the means
of injustice, fraud, and oppression." Washburn, the court decreed, must
vacate the property by November 15, 1798. But William Washburn would
not yield. Advised by Daggett, Allen, and Edwards, Washburn appealed to
the Connecticut Supreme Court of Errors and on June 13, 1799, though this
court agreed with the Litchfield judges on the facts, it agreed with Washburn's lawyers and so reversed the judgment because, it concluded, Sanford
had forfeited his claim to the property. So after a decade William Washburn
won final possession of the farm; but only on a legal technicality. The highest court had ruled that he could keep his ill-gotten gain, but the price of
this victory proved different—and higher—than he could have imagined.[31]

It took less than two months before Sheriff Lynde Lord ordered the
arrest—on August 6, 1799—of Gideon, William's father, on the charge of

bestiality. It is possible that the local enemies William Washburn had made by his aggressive pursuit of his neighbor's land were now inventing stories about his father's sexual misbehavior; but more likely they chose this moment to reveal misdeeds they had witnessed over the past several years. By accusing Gideon Washburn they would avenge their old neighbors the Sanfords and gain a kind of rough justice. But no one made a detailed record of the trial proceedings, and no witness list survives to reveal the identity of the four Northfield residents who testified against Gideon Washburn. We doubt that personal animosity toward William the son, by itself, led angry neighbors to invent such unspeakable accusations and level them at his father. Indeed at first Gideon Washburn's accusers may not have known they were charging the old man with a hanging crime; but by the time they brought their reports to a hearing before Litchfield's justice of the peace they would have learned the gravity of the charge. And they did not retract their accusations.

In August 1799 the Grand Jury of Connecticut's Superior Court issued an indictment against the eighty-three-year-old patriarch, Gideon, for committing bestiality. No fewer than six times "within five years last past," the grand jury declared, the accused "hath lain with beasts or brute Creatures by carnal copulation." They specified: "on or about the first day of April 1795 . . . with a Cow, . . . on or about the first day of May last past . . . with a mare by carnal copulation, and on or about the first day of March last past . . . with a Cow by carnal copulation, and on or about the first day of March, 1798 . . . with a Mare by carnal copulation, and at Litchfield aforesaid on or about the first day of August 1797 . . . with a heifer calf by carnal copulation."[32] If the charges were true, Washburn was a chronic offender.

The state kept the accused man in the Litchfield jail until his case came to trial before the Superior Court at the session held in the town on September 2, 1799. Outlandish as this bestiality trial may seem, like the Farrell trial it featured prominent political leaders. Washburn's prosecutors were Uriah Tracy and Daniel W. Lewis. Though Lewis, a 1788 graduate of Yale who had studied at the Litchfield Law School, was not well known, having been admitted to the bar just three years earlier, he was assisting the forty-four-year-old Tracy, a U.S. senator, who had been practicing law since 1781 and ranked among the most powerful Federalists in the nation.[33] Tracy had served in public office for over a decade, starting in the Connecticut General Assembly before moving on to the U.S. House of Representatives and the U.S. Senate, where he remained from 1796 until his death in 1807. An outspoken Federalist partisan, Tracy's political power was now at its peak. Recently he had published a scathing attack on Vice President Thomas Jefferson and the Republicans. Jefferson, he claimed, was "the soul of the Jacobins of America," and he further accused the vice president of treasonous collaboration with France, asking rhetorically "whether he has not [been] *pernicious* and is not now *dangerous* to the tranquility, security and union of this country?" Had this invective been directed at President Adams, his words would have been punishable according to the 1798 Sedition Act. Nevertheless the Federalist elite in Litchfield and the state embraced his extreme denunciation. Shortly before Washburn's trial, Litchfield honored Tracy with an invitation to deliver the town's annual Independence Day oration.[34]

But Gideon Washburn's defense was not necessarily outmanned. The two prominent lawyers who had earlier represented William Washburn in his land dispute appeared to defend Gideon in court: the Federalist John Allen and the Republican Pierpont Edwards. Like Tracy, Allen had arrived in Litchfield in the 1780s. He had come to study law with Tapping Reeve. After his admission to the bar he settled there as a lawyer. Gaining respect and popularity in Litchfield, Allen won the town's seat in the Connecticut General Assembly from 1793 to 1796, and went on to win a place in the U.S. House of Representatives, where he served from 1797 to 1799. At Washburn's trial the six-foot-tall, three-hundred-pound representative had just returned from the U.S. Congress at Philadelphia, where he had earned a reputation as one of the most vocal proponents of the 1798 Sedition Act. On the floor of the House of Representatives, Allen—not to be outdone by his Federalist colleague Uriah Tracy—had proclaimed the vicious Jeffersonian press aimed "to destroy all confidence between man and man." The Jeffersonians' idea of free speech, he proclaimed, would destroy "every ligament that unites man to his family, man to his neighbor, man to society, and to Government." This Litchfield delegate to Congress directed his rhetoric to the Almighty: "God deliver us from such liberty, the liberty of vomiting on the public floods of falsehood and hatred to everything sacred, human and divine! If any gentleman doubts the effects of such a liberty, let me direct his attention across the water; it has there [in France] made slaves of thirty millions of men." Allen believed in the necessity of "purging *all* bodies of Jacobinic characters" from the nation in order to combat "disorganization, revolution, Licentiousness, profligacy and . . . that unexampled Scourge, with which God is smiting the Earth in his wrath."[35]

Figure 10. Washburn's prosecutor, Uriah Tracy, as portrayed by Ralph Earl in 1790. Courtesy of the Litchfield Historical Society.

Ironically, though Allen toed the orthodox Federalist line enthusiastically, the Massachusetts native remained a kind of outsider in Litchfield, where neighbors circulated rumors of his drinking, particularly during his term as congressman in Philadelphia. Through his intemperance they saw the once respectable attorney squandering his wealth and reputation. Just a few days before Washburn's trial, the *Litchfield Monitor* reported Allen's decision not to seek reelection to his Congressional seat in the upcoming elections. The paper provided no explanation, but when Allen vigorously proclaimed that no question of personal conduct was involved, he indirectly recognized that local people thought otherwise.[36]

Washburn's other lawyer, Pierpont Edwards, was a political star in the Jeffersonian firmament. The eleventh and youngest son of the brilliant Great Awakening clergyman Jonathan Edwards, he had graduated from Princeton in 1768 before moving to New Haven to practice law. Drawn into public life by the Revolution, he served in the Continental Army as well as the Connecticut legislature, the Continental Congress, and the state's convention that ratified the U.S. Constitution in 1788. Later it was said that Edwards's "fame in the world as a lawyer is almost universal." President George Washington appointed him U.S. attorney for Connecticut in 1789, a position he held until Jefferson raised him to the U.S. District Court for Connecticut in 1806; he retained that post until his death twenty years later.[37] Pierpont Edwards turned his back on the clerical legacy of his father and instead, like Pierpont's own nephew Aaron Burr—and in contrast to his older brother Reverend Jonathan Edwards, Jr., and another of his nephews, Reverend Timothy Dwight—he pursued a wholly secular career. Joining the Republicans, he became, both by virtue of his brilliance and his pedigree, their most prominent state leader. His enlightened, liberal cast of mind is suggested by the fact that the Connecticut Freemasons elected him as their first grand master in 1789, and later he would also help launch Connecticut's Toleration Party, which would succeed in separating church and state in Connecticut in 1818.

Like his nephew Burr, Edwards acquired the reputation of a libertine. The Burr-Edwards correspondence in the 1780s shows that Edwards fathered an illegitimate child and that Burr served as his agent in arranging the baby's support. This affair was not fully known to the public, but many suspected that Pierpont Edwards seduced and impregnated Elizabeth Whitman, a clergyman's daughter, before abandoning her to die during childbirth, alone, in a Massachusetts tavern in 1788. As she came from a patrician

Figure 11. Washburn's defense attorney, Pierpont Edwards, as portrayed by William Jennys in 1795. Courtesy of the Yale University Art Gallery.

New England family, Whitman's death reverberated through the region and inspired Hannah Webster Foster's fictional account of her tragedy, *The Coquette; or, The History of Eliza Wharton; A Novel Founded on Fact.* Published in 1797, the novel became a best-seller, reinforcing Edwards's reputation as the scoundrel who had ruined Reverend Whitman's daughter. The character of the evil seducer, like Edwards, was an army veteran who turned his back on the religious traditions of his ancestors in order to follow a life of immoral pleasures. Most readers assumed that Elizabeth Whitman was the model for Eliza Wharton, and that Edwards was the model for her seducer. In the conservative Federalist stronghold of Litchfield, one of Gideon Washburn's defenders was a lawyer who, though a Federalist, was falling because he was a drunkard and the other was a Jeffersonian who flaunted Christian sexual morality.[38]

So notwithstanding the talents and stature of his counsel, when Washburn came before the court, Senator Tracy, the prosecutor, easily persuaded the jury of the defendant's guilt. Eyewitness testimony sustained the accusation that "this most aggravated of all possible cases, suffers by a comparison with the most beastly monsters—the conviction being substantiated on the proof of four reputable witnesses, to six various facts, from four years back to within the recent period of three Months." The crime alleged was lurid; but officials maintained the usual decorum. At the same session the court tried another capital offense—Phebe Thomson was indicted for concealing the birth of her "Bastard Child, under circumstances of violence." The court also heard a bigamy case, and the judgments displayed ambivalent attitudes toward punishment. For Phebe Thomson the jury displayed a truly Beccarian sensibility, acquitting her "after a consideration of about *ten minutes*"; but after the bigamist, Jesse Clark, pled guilty he was punished Puritan-style: "to receive ten stripes, and be branded."[39] His crime, like Washburn's, did not warrant sympathy.

Contemporaries reported that the attorneys for the prosecution and for the defense argued with a zeal and eloquence that commanded the respect of the solemn spectators who overflowed the packed courtroom.[40] And after the jury delivered its verdict, the *Litchfield Monitor* was impressed by Chief Justice Jesse Root at "the ceremony of passing sentence." The judge, who sensed public discomfort with the law's prescribed death penalty, first addressed the community. Root agreed that many would naturally feel "tenderness and pity for the unhappy man," but the issue was not Washburn, but his crimes. All should reflect "with horror and amazement at the atrocity of his guilt." The law, he said, as well as "the safety of society" required the execution of the perpetrator of such heinous crimes: "we say with one voice, it must be so." Washburn was no ordinary patriarch who properly commanded "reverence and respect from all." No, Root declared, the prisoner "has grown grey in the vile drudgery of sin and Satan." Instead

Figure 12. Litchfield Court House, designed by William Sprats, ca. 1796; the artist is unknown. Courtesy of the Litchfield Historical Society.

of sympathy, "our feelings are harrowed up and tortured with indignation and contempt" for a man whose iniquitous actions embodied "dishonor done to human nature." Turning to the convict, a man old enough to be his father, the sixty-two-year-old Root—a Princeton graduate who had once served briefly as a Hartford pastor—addressed the reprobate who stood before him:

> Washburn, God has given you to see long life and many days;—few who have been born into the world have arrived to the advanced age you are of:—This gave you an enlarged opportunity of doing much service for God, and much good for your fellow men, and has

JESSE ROOT.
Member of the Continental Congress.

Figure 13. Washburn's judge, Jesse Root, in an undated image by an unknown artist. Courtesy of the Emmet Collection, Miriam and Ira D. Wallach Division of Art, Prints and Photographs, New York Public Library, Astor, Lenox and Tilden Foundations.

greatly enhanced the score of your accountability—-and to human appearance, you have counteracted the merciful designs of your Maker, have set at naught the councils of his wisdom and his grace, and in defiance of all government and laws, divine and human, have prostituted your reason to the blind and unrestrained impulse of sensual passions; and by the furor of brutal lusts, have been hurried on to perpetrate crimes beyond the natural force of your years.

Thereupon Judge Root ordered Washburn confined in the Litchfield jail to await his doom, directing the sheriff to erect a gallows in "some Open & Convenient place for Execution" and, on November 15, 1799, to hang the prisoner "up by the neck between the heavens & the Earth until he shall be dead."[41]

There it was: almost precisely three years after Massachusetts's highest court sentenced one octogenarian to death for the crime of bestiality, Connecticut's highest court would do exactly the same thing. In the first case the convict was an unmarried, transient outsider and consequently more vulnerable than most; in the second, the convict was a married man living with his settled, property-owning family, a man who was, if not part of his town's inner circles, certainly not an outsider in Connecticut society. As we have said, the proximity of the two cases could be a matter of random probabilities, purely coincidental. But before adopting such an explanation, it is necessary to explore the alternatives.

The most obvious connection between Farrell and Washburn is the fact of their great age. In an era when most men who reached adulthood died in their sixties and only a tiny fraction survived into their eighties, convicts of any sort beyond the age of seventy years were virtually unknown. So the realization that such ancient men should be convicted and sentenced to hang is confounding. It is even more astonishing that they should be executed for committing a crime that was rarely prosecuted against anyone at all. We doubt whether random chance can supply convincing reasons why old men should be connected to this crime and this penalty at this time.

Instead, an exploration of the culture and politics of New England can, we think, assist understanding of these bizarre cases. Moreover, though New England—and the interior of southern New England in particular—may be said to have had distinctive features, the life of the region was nested within the larger culture of the early American republic and the Anglo-American world of the eighteenth century. Accordingly, to understand the people and institutions of Hampshire and Litchfield Counties in the 1790s, we need to consider the historical forces that shaped the men and cultures that prosecuted, convicted, and prepared to execute John Farrell and Gideon Washburn.

~

CHAPTER 3

Sexual Crisis in the Age of Revolution

Within the space of three years New England courts just seventy miles apart sentenced two octogenarians to hang for a rare and bizarre crime. John Farrell had, so far as we can discover, no criminal record, and although Gideon Washburn had been convicted for counterfeiting some fifty years earlier in a different county, that fact seems entirely unrelated to his sexual misbehavior. Whereas Farrell was without family, a transient who lived as a boarder, Washburn was surrounded by family, living with his wife, their son and his wife, as well as his grandchildren. Ethnicity also separated the two men. Farrell was identifiably an Irish immigrant at a time when suspicion toward immigrants, especially from Ireland, was rising, whereas Washburn was a third-generation Yankee with kinship ties reaching across the social ladder, distantly as high as the recently deceased Yale president, Ezra Stiles.[1]

Yet the similarities between these two extraordinary cases are far more important than their differences. Farrell and Washburn were outsiders—recent arrivals to Leverett and Northfield. Accusations against both men originated in small hill-country towns where personal and local disputes played a part in singling out the accused. And both trials were held in county seats, Northampton and Litchfield, villages where the era's larger cultural conflicts challenged the harmony and stability of local elites. In both of these towns and counties the turmoil of the 1770s and 1780s had come to pit customary neighborhood values against rising commercial and cosmopolitan expectations. Long-established orthodox Trinitarian Christians were facing challenges from New Light evangelicals and Baptists as well as advocates of Deist and Unitarian ideas. Moreover, though Federalists ruled both towns, Jeffersonian Republicans actively competed for power, in part by appealing to the Baptists, Episcopalians, and Deists who were disaffected from the established orthodox churches.

It is also remarkable that both of the accused men were in their mid-eighties, an age known more for sexual quiescence or impotence than unbridled lust.[2] Moreover neither Farrell nor Washburn fell victim to sudden, unreflecting vigilante justice; rather, each was independently accused, tried, convicted, and sentenced to hang for the capital crime of bestiality. Nowhere else in the United States, we believe, did such proceedings against old men take place. That the people and officials of Hampshire and Litchfield Counties chose to single out such very old men for the most severe punishment their states could inflict demands explanation.

How can one explain the prosecutions of John Farrell in 1796 and Gideon Washburn in 1799? First, one must wonder about the facts. Could men in their eighties—absent the help of modern drugs—actually penetrate dogs, cows, and horses?[3] Though witnesses testified they had seen penetration, we have doubts. In the psychological literature on bestiality the subjects of the overwhelming majority of cases are hormonally driven young men—not octogenarians. It is also unlikely that this behavior, if it actually existed, would commence at such an advanced age. Farrell's history before the age of seventy years is unknown, but in the fifteen years where his career is extant, there is no evidence of impropriety; and Washburn's earlier life, his military appointment, and his midcentury counterfeiting conviction do not suggest subversive sexuality.[4]

Were they guilty of the crime of bestiality? The historical record provides no certain answer; and in our judgment the question of their innocence or guilt is far less important than the fact that trials actually took place and that men in their eighties were sentenced to hang. For even in the case of Washburn, where four witnesses recalled six different occasions of bestiality, the testimonies do not explain elite officials' readiness to prosecute or the jury's refusal to convict the defendant of the lesser noncapital crime of attempted sodomy. The indictment charged that Washburn engaged in bestiality over a period of years, starting in 1796. But, we wonder, if the crime was actually so heinous and shocking, how are we to understand the years-long silences of witnesses who swore they remembered the old farmer mounting cows and horses? Conceivably the cumulative effect of repeated incidents mattered, but the sociologist Wayne Brekhus has observed, "we make no moral distinctions between a man who has a monogamous relationship with a goat and the one who has sex with

40 goats. The transgression of interspecies sex is such a challenge to existing social boundaries that additional violations beyond the first one have little additive effect."[5] In short, we think it unlikely that the second or third incident was qualitatively more shocking than the first. Consequently we need to explain the dramatic change in witnesses' and officials' response in Litchfield between 1796 and 1799, the alleged dates of Washburn's first and last offenses.

Guilt or innocence aside, since the factual foundations of both cases are not definitive, we are confounded by the readiness of prosecutors to indict, juries to convict, and judges to execute these ancient and marginal men. Considering seventeenth-century New England, when Puritans strove to fulfill Mosaic law, such proceedings are more understandable. After all, in that era authorities in Connecticut and Massachusetts repeatedly executed sexual offenders, religious dissenters, and witches. But in the new American Republic authorities scorned witchcraft accusations and seldom prosecuted sexual transgressions unless they involved violence and coercion against fellow humans. Even in cases of rape, executions of white men were rare. Thus, the Washburn and Farrell prosecutions are not merely historical anomalies; they are true enigmas.[6]

At other times, before and after the prosecutions of Farrell and Washburn, New Englanders knew and tolerated similar sexual transgressions. In Chapter 1 we pointed out the case of John Adams's second cousin and pillar of the Braintree church, Deacon Savil, who had become an embarrassment to the community when he not so secretly sought out sexual relations with boys. Though Savil's wrongdoing was known to townspeople, he was never formally accused or prosecuted.[7] Based on the extreme paucity of prosecutions for sodomy and buggery in New England, Braintree's calm response to noncoercive sexual transgressions must have been widespread. It is revealing that a century later, when the Massachusetts physician Charles Frederick Winslow learned of bestial misbehavior his response was matter-of-fact, showing no impulse to inform the authorities of the forbidden act. He noted:

I have today been called upon professionally for aid in a very strange case. The man concealed his name & residence. He is a shoe maker & farmer – aged 53 – has been a widower two years—& has had several children, one of whom is living. . . .

After informing me that he 'had been directed to me as an eminent doctor for curing unlawful diseases,' he with great secrecy, piety & self-abasement, came to the professional points of his story. . . . He took his cow to a neighbouring farmer's to receive the male. . . . Her actions were such he said as to excite him, & in a moment of unguarded weakness he attempted to satisfy her desires by having criminal intercourse with her himself. He said he completed the act of copulation with the cow & almost immediately afterwards he was seized with pain in his own organs of generation & had become afflicted with disease which he supposed was of a dangerous & unheard of character.

After a recital of these circumstances . . . I thought I would comfort him with the information that I had cured several very pious persons of high standing in the church, of unlawful diseases in the course of an extensive practice.[8]

Dr. Winslow regarded the case as "very strange," but not alarming. When the patient confessed to bestiality, the physician not only declined to report the crime, he minimized its seriousness. We are impressed that in the century that brackets the Farrell and Washburn episodes—1760 to 1860—acceptance, not severity, normally prevailed. Nevertheless, just as enlightened republicanism and Beccarian reform were sweeping over the United States in the late 1790s, in Hampshire County, Massachusetts, and Litchfield County, Connecticut, as in seventeenth-century New England, the harsh Mosaic sanction of the Puritans ruled.

We cannot believe that the gentry of the New England interior were in fact intensely worried by the threat of bestiality in their midst. There were pastures and barns all over the region, and in all probability the occasional young man engaged improperly with animals. Certainly somewhere, sometime—as in the New London County cases of the 1770s—someone saw something. Yet these behaviors were almost never raised to the level of public scandal and legal action, let alone capital punishment. In passing, one twenty-five-year-old convicted murderer confessed in 1805 that over the years he had made "repeated attempts to commit filthiness with beasts"; but Connecticut officials and clergymen expressed no particular alarm at this admission, viewing it as merely further evidence of the criminal's deeply sinful character. The fact is that young men's sexual misbehavior did not raise a hue and cry in the eighteenth century; but in 1796 and 1799 two men who were ancient by current standards, Farrell and Washburn, were prosecuted to the fullest extent of a scarcely defensible, harsh, and antiquated biblical law. Why?[9]

There is no simple answer to the question, and to explain the seemingly inexplicable we must turn toward a multilayered exploration of the cultural, social, and political circumstances that led some members of the local elites in New England's interior to pursue these merciless sexual prosecutions. To enlightened men and women the proceedings against Farrell and Washburn recalled the worst excesses of their seventeenth-century forefathers. To plumb this mysterious and irrational paradox we must analyze the multiple influences shaping the culture of western New England at the end of the eighteenth century. The decisions to enforce the letter of the law, we believe, were less the calculated judgment of high officials than they were a reflexive commitment to the traditional status quo. The well-being and equilibrium of New England did not require the execution of two harmless and eccentric old men for a crime that ordinarily was punished by nothing more than gossip. Instead we believe officials acted sternly, rigorously— ultimately aggressively—because social and cultural circumstances trig- gered profound internal conflicts and anxieties within the elite as well as in the broader society.

The Enlightenment, after all, had unleashed a sexual revolution in the Western world. In urban centers in Europe and the United States belief in personal autonomy, privacy, and individual choice took hold, giving rise to a sexual culture that was unthinkable before the age of reason. Indeed, the freedoms enjoyed by some women and men in cities threatened the tradi- tional sexual order in more traditional peripheries. To understand this response our analysis turns to the sexual tensions of the latter part of the eighteenth century and to the manner in which the New England hinter- land experienced the sexual revolution of the eighteenth century.[10]

In 1793 the most famous American physician, Benjamin Rush, received an alarmed letter from a Massachusetts colleague. The doctor reported that his patient, a seemingly healthy twenty-five-year-old married man com- plained of gloom, restlessness, "bad countenance, and a lax state of bow- els." As the physician investigated the strange malady more thoroughly, he discovered that though the patient felt "disgusted with his strong venereal propensities," the man felt unable to resist his sexual urges. The patient

had tried a series of cures, even separating himself from his wife by travel-
ling, but to no avail. So desperate was he that he asked the physician to
"render him impotent." Determined to get to the root of the disease, the
physician asked the patient "whether the gratification of his appetite was
equal to his desires." The response was too shocking to express in English:
"*Dixit, per annos tres, quinque vices se coitum fecisse in horis viginti quatuor,
et semper semine ejecto.*" For three years, the patient reported, he had
masturbated five times in twenty-four hours, and always with semen
ejaculated.[11]

Rush reported the case in his diatribe against the "Morbid state of the
Sexual Appetite," which formed a chapter in his treatise on the diseases of
the mind. Rush declared that "onanism" caused "impotence, dysury, tabes
dorsalis, pulmonary consumption, dyspepsia, dimness of sight, vertigo, epi-
lepsy, hypochondriasis, loss of memory, manalgia, fatuity, and death." This
scientific testimony belongs to a growing sexual anxiety literature on masturbation of the late eighteenth century that, as Thomas Laqueur has written,
"mixed medicine with moral pedagogy." Earlier in the century, the Enlightenment's critique of traditional conventions and superstitions had effectively
democratized sexual impulses. Erotic and pornographic forms of expression,
previously considered the exclusive domain of the "degenerate" aristocracy,
circulated up and down the social ladder. Novels and broadside depictions of
royal orgies unleashed the subversive power of sexuality and undermined the
established order. In addition to the rising interest in the curious and
deformed as well as hermaphroditism and other sexual curiosities, scientists
tried to understand the causes of the rising plague of syphilis.[12]

Many Enlightenment figures initially welcomed the liberation of desire
from repressive religious morality. Benjamin Franklin, for example, scarcely
concealed his libertine life in London and Paris. And Voltaire's *Candide*
(1759 and 1762) mocked Catholic sexual morality, openly discussing all sexual acts, even including the taste for bestiality of Candide's South American
captors, the Oreillon women. Yet these free and easy sentiments soon gave
way to a growing anxiety over the potentially destructive power of male
passions. Sexual pleasure could become an indiscriminate, subversive force
undermining, as it had in ancient Rome, the foundations of the social and
political order. Lust surged beneath the façade of civilization—explosive,
lascivious lust—ready to attack and reclaim its animalistic hold on humanity. The pursuit of individual sexual freedom risked the ruin of civilized
society.

The natural history approach, articulated by philosophers of the Scottish Enlightenment, devised a model that combined the progress of freedom with the taming of desire. Accordingly, societies moved through distinct stages of hunting, grazing, agriculture, and commerce. Through this civilizing process the "primitive" societies' enslavement to animalistic sexual cravings was transformed into a delicate, beautiful sentiment honoring the virtue of women. In contrast to the immorality of the countryside with its promiscuity and illegitimacy, civilized societies elevated the status of women and transformed lust into love. The culture of self-control that flourished in refined society made progress possible; it required that desire be checked.[13]

Sexual discourse in the late eighteenth century rejected Christian ideals, in the words of Michel Foucault, "without being truly independent of the thematics of sin." Moral censorship of sexual expression can itself be a titillating form of public sexual performance. The didactic anti-vice works of William Hogarth, for example, invoked a pornographic subtext that allowed Hogarth and his viewing audience to engage simultaneously in prurient pleasures and sanctimonious posturing. As Foucault argued, "What is peculiar to modern societies, in fact, is not that they consigned sex to a shadow existence, but that they dedicated themselves to speaking of it ad infinitum, while exploiting it as *the* secret." Talk of a breakdown in ideal sexual behavior generated a powerful reaction of restraint and prudery in late eighteenth-century England. A culture that had openly celebrated sexual pleasures in best-sellers like *Fanny Hill* (1748 and 1749) and salacious guides to London's prostitutes, now saw the resurgence of moralizing anti-lust vocabulary even in erotic narratives. As Dror Wahrman asserts, tolerance and the acceptance of varieties of gendered speech "were superseded by ones of anxiety and disbelief." A panic over gender transformed the English public sphere so that all forms of gender transgressions came to be regarded as grave political challenges. Simultaneously the modern conception of the individual emerged as one who judged morality in relation to *self*-control rather than obedience to the divine, thereby fostering the cultural hegemony of heterosexual gender roles and behaviors.[14]

This era saw the emergence of a new biological paradigm that gave scientific backing to the heterosexual gender division. Since antiquity, the reigning biological model assumed that women and men were anatomically and physiologically cast from the same body. According to this one-body model, the female body was simply a developmentally inferior version of the male body. But in the eighteenth century, as Thomas Laqueur has shown, a new paradigm took over, asserting that men and women were fundamentally different because their reproductive organs were different. This new approach led to sharpening of the boundaries of proper conduct for men and women—adding the backing of natural philosophy to rigid prescriptions of gendered sexual behavior. The sexual drive came to be seen as an exclusively male form of aggressive heterosexual desire; and women were understood to be the only legitimate objects of this desire. This changed the way society viewed intercourse. Before the modern age, male sexual behavior belonged to the broader spectrum of social relations of dependency and inequality. In antiquity the penetration of dependents not related by blood—women, servants (male or female), and children—was within the prerogative of the male head of household. During the medieval and early modern periods such actions had been proscribed, but their commission did not lead to a singular identity. For example, male-male sexual intercourse did not lead to a homosexual identity. But in the eighteenth century the development of a cultural requirement that male desire be associated exclusively with heterosexual masculinity meant that those who did not fit the model threatened the entire social order.[15]

Cultural critics, often clergymen, bemoaned the rise of solitary reading because they argued it fed the vice of masturbation. The new sentimental novels that became so popular in the second half of the eighteenth century underscored traditional Christian hostility to sexual pleasure. Their message was the same. Desire threatened society because men by their very nature were predatory, duplicitous, and rapacious. Women who succumbed to temptations would pay dearly for momentary pleasures. These novels taught readers that those who resisted desire would be rewarded. Three of the most popular seduction narratives, penned by Samuel Richardson, Susanna Rowson, and the American Hannah Foster, convey precisely this message. In Richardson's 1740 popular novel *Pamela*, a working-class servant rejects aristocratic seduction and ends up marrying the seducer, who is tamed by her virtue. In Rowson's *Charlotte Temple* (1791) and Foster's *The Coquette* (1797), both best-sellers in the United States, successful seductions are followed by the heroine's humiliation and death. Women in these sentimental novels were expected to direct aggressive male sexual desire toward sentimental love, a process that mirrored the movement toward refined society as proposed by Scottish Enlightenment philosophers. Failure to do so spelled personal doom, and by extension social doom.[16]

The blending of moral, scientific, and sexual rhetoric proved an effective weapon in English political battles during the second half of the eighteenth century. The renegade politician John Wilkes fashioned a public personality founded on libertine masculinity. His notorious 1763 *Essay on Woman* embraced the predatory masculine identity that declared that sexual pleasure was all that life could offer before death. This was in contrast to his political enemies—sexually voracious women and the submissive sodomites who controlled the sexually inverted court of George III. Wilkes denounced the supposed homoerotic features of his political rivals, spreading rumors that they engaged in sodomy. And Wilkes's rhetoric found a highly receptive English political culture, one that turned to brutal prosecution of sodomy in the late decades of the century. So powerful were English repugnance and repression that when Edmund Burke rose in Parliament in 1780 to criticize the cruelties of the pillory he was roundly criticized for "insinuating" that sodomy "deserved a milder punishment than ignominious death." To his critics Burke was "an advocate of the guilty, and displaying his talents to obtain mercy for *sodomites!*"[17]

Burke had not in fact challenged sodomy as a criminal offense; but after two convicted sodomites suffered excruciating deaths as a result of the pillory, he argued that Beccarian principles should forbid further resort to the pillory for this crime. Lawmakers should "proportion the punishment so that it should not exceed the extent of the crime, and . . . it should be of that kind, which was more calculated to operate as an example and prevent crimes, than to oppress and torment the convicted criminal."[18]

It is no wonder that his contemporary, the utilitarian philosopher Jeremy Bentham, suspected that political motives were the true drivers of the campaigns against sexual transgressors. In a daring 1785 critique of the persecution of homosexuals, Bentham challenged existing laws against bestiality. Though expressing his own distaste for the "abomination," he urged tolerance because "distress will force a man upon strange expedients." Whereas laws against buggery could do little to halt the practice, he believed they opened the door to political abuse. "The more of these sorts of prosecutions are permitted," Bentham warned, "the more scope there is given for malice or extortion . . . upon the innocent." Bentham, however, chose not to publish his critique; and though some of his contemporaries must have shared his skepticism toward sexual prosecutions, we have not found such writings.[19]

The laws in Britain against sodomy and the deadly penal code of the past ruled. Buggery remained a capital offense in Britain until 1861, although for much of the eighteenth century courts and communities did not commonly punish sodomy according to the letter or the spirit of the law. In 1781 a high court decision requiring proof of emission as well as penetration made convictions harder to obtain. But although the barrier to a guilty verdict was thus raised, the records of the Old Bailey court in London show a marked increase in the number of indictments for homosexual acts as the turn of the century approached. The single year of 1798 saw fourteen such indictments, the highest number in the century. The nature of criminal proceedings against sodomites also changed. Whereas most cases brought before the British courts around midcentury prosecuted older men for rape-like sexual assaults on children and young adults, prosecutors now targeted consenting adults.[20]

Britain was not typical. No place was. Across the Western world in the eighteenth century, the patterns of change in relation to sexuality were uneven. In some countries laws became more oppressive, and in others less. Greater tolerance and outright sexual freedom could be followed by moralistic repression. Conservative Englishmen associated French revolutionaries with promiscuity and sexual deviance, even as the French revolutionaries were associating conservative Englishmen with the same vices, as had John Wilkes. But what is clear is that English and Continental approaches to the prosecution of sodomy headed in opposite directions. In the second half of the century, and following the principles enunciated by the enlightened Italian Count Beccaria, France, Russia, Prussia, and the Habsburg Empire ceased to treat sodomy as a capital crime. In Bavaria the 1802 penal reforms reduced the penalty for bestiality from death to three or four years' hard labor and for male-male sodomy from death to hard labor for less than three years. In France the Revolution's initial penal code of 1791 did not punish private individual homosexual acts at all, though Napoleon would later punish sodomy as an offense against decency. In sharp contrast, Great Britain reinvigorated its deadly campaign against sodomites. Whereas no one was apparently executed for sodomy on the Continent in the nineteenth century, in Britain some sixty men were hanged in the first three decades of the century and another twenty were executed aboard vessels of the Royal Navy.[21]

In England it is evident that anxiety over sexual norms fluctuated synchronously with other social tensions. Concurrent with the imperial uprisings in America in 1776 and in Ireland in 1798, authorities launched raids against "molly houses" (homosexual brothels) in London. When Americans declared their intention to sever their ties with the British Empire, officials and journalists rocked London with highly publicized trials over the supposed bigamy of the Duchess of Kingston and the sodomy of actor Samuel Foote. And these prosecutions were merely precursors for the flood that followed during the wars of the French Revolution. Prosecuting sexual transgressors during the titanic battles against revolutionary French imperialism became part of the national war effort and evidently provided a measure of righteous catharsis for the fears and frustrations of the age. Indeed, the wars of the French Revolution ushered in a full-blown sex panic in England. English critics of the Revolution charged that the French Enlightenment's supposed assault on sexual restraint had unleashed the violent aggression that was now drowning Europe in blood. England's public sphere was inundated with various sexual scandals. Since sexual promiscuity had supposedly led France down the revolutionary road, many leading Britons believed that combating licentiousness at home was essential to the preservation of English civilization. Indeed, the concern became so central that in 1800 Parliament seriously considered a bill making one of the most common sexual transgressions, adultery, a criminal offense punishable by a prison term and a fine.[22]

That was too much. Many gentlemen agreed that duels, the extralegal honor ritual, should curb adultery—not criminal courts. Not so for sodomites. In the eighteenth century Englishmen linked sodomy with European and antique Roman corruption, so the humiliating prosecution of sodomites in the "participatory manner afforded by the pillory," writes Arthur Gilbert, "was an act of communal piety, an affirmation of the traditional moral code of the community as well as an offering for its sins." Indeed, of Britain's long list of hanging crimes, sodomy alone witnessed an absolute increase in executions during the Wars of the French Revolution— culminating in the year 1806 when more men in England were actually executed for sodomy than for murder. Both the trials and punishments— whether pillory, flogging, or hanging—intensified the homophobic political culture that designated sodomites as a particular threat to the British nation in a time of crisis. What had begun as revulsion toward the effeminate and passive behavior of those penetrated in homosexual acts now turned to severe condemnation of both the penetrator and the penetrated as sodomites. The participants were now branded as threats to the honor and moral fiber of the British nation. Indeed, by the end of the eighteenth century England set out to erase not just the crime of sodomy but the lives of sodomites.[23]

The hysteria took its most deadly turn in the Royal Navy, where the isolation of long voyages made situational male homosexual contacts commonplace. But until the crisis of the Napoleonic Wars, what had been largely an accepted fact of life, so long as it did not disrupt discipline, came to be treated as the most dangerous of vices, a breach of conduct worse even than deserting the service. During the Napoleonic Wars sailors convicted of sodomy received, on average, double the number of lashes of those convicted of desertion. And in the last four years of the century, coinciding with the Farrell and Washburn trials, hangings of sodomites became so common that they were far more frequently executed than murderers and mutineers.[24]

This newly aggressive prosecution of sodomites in England is particularly relevant to our New England inquiry. As in England, statutes in the United States did not distinguish between bestiality and sodomy. In September 1787, for example, Joshua Clark of Granby, Massachusetts, was accused of having "a venereal affair" with a mare. The authorities, however, did not charge him with bestiality, but with the "detestable and abominable crime of Sodomy." And the conflation of the two offenses found its way into both cases. Farrell was convicted of sodomy, not bestiality; and though Washburn was convicted of bestiality, some newspapers reported his crime as sodomy. Indeed, prosecutors and the press employed the terms "sodomy" and "bestiality" interchangeably during and after their trials.[25]

The New England proceedings took place in the interior—a region that retained strong personal, cultural, and even, in the case of Federalists, political affinities with England, so much so that during the War of 1812 leaders contemplated secession from the Union and making a separate peace with England. By 1794 the Federalist elite that would prosecute Farrell and Washburn had come to embrace the British view of the French Revolution and, panicked by threats to Christianity, they denounced Thomas Paine's Age of Reason. Moreover, we believe that just as Federalists followed the British lead in suppressing internal dissent with repressive laws against aliens and sedition, they, like their English counterparts, feared sodomy and "libertinism" as assaults on their social order.

To provincial Federalists the threat was all too immediate. In American ports sexual propriety seemed to unravel. Urban centers like Boston, New York, and most prominently Philadelphia—the new nation's capital—were witnessing the emergence of an urban pleasure culture where theaters, mostly prohibited in New England, ballrooms, and dancing assemblies were promoting unprecedented personal freedom. In urban America the political claim for individual rights was connected to assertions of personal autonomy and sexual freedom. In cities, young men and women could remove themselves from the watchful eyes and judgmental gossip of family and neighbors, so it was feared they were freely pursuing pleasure for its own sake. Casual sexual relations that crossed accepted boundaries of race and class seemed all too common, and nothing worse than gossip punished marital infidelity. Some women even deserted their husbands and households in acts of autonomous divorce. If a woman bore a child out of wedlock there was no penalty and, as in the past, women and men of the working class could dissolve marriages on their own without sanction. Even prostitution was moving from marginal waterfronts toward the heart of the cities. This emerging culture of pleasure in urban centers demonstrated that some Americans, as Clare Lyons noted, "embraced connections between Enlightenment-inspired quests for self-knowledge and human perfectibility, and self-directed choices in personal life and sexual practices."[26]

For such urban people concern about homosexual transgression was also in decline. While press reports of sodomy in the United States and abroad appeared occasionally, they were sensational stories unaccompanied by sanctimonious ruminations about the broader moral, social, or political significance of the vice. Same-sex relationships and even cohabitation were tolerated in the port cities of Philadelphia, New York, and Boston. Unlike Britain, not a single prosecution for sodomy took place in Philadelphia in the second half of the eighteenth century and the city's religious and secular leaders made no effort to demonize sodomites. Bookstores and libraries carried homoerotic literature without controversy. Even in Boston one printer sought to profit by republishing the prurient London work *Cuckold's Chronicle*, which included lurid illustrated accounts of adultery, rape, and incest.[27]

In America prosecutions of homosexuals were rare and the punishments light. Of the 115 prisoners housed at the Walnut Street Penitentiary in Philadelphia in 1795, the only convicted sodomite was a thirty-seven-year-old mulatto, serving a ten-year sentence for committing buggery. New York's state penitentiary similarly listed just one prisoner imprisoned for sodomy. Even the American military imposed relatively mild punishments. John Anderson, convicted of sodomy in 1792, for example, was sentenced to running the gauntlet three times in front of his army comrades during evening roll call. The ordeal was painful and humiliating to be sure, but a far cry from what would have awaited him had he served in the Royal Navy.[28]

When the United States won its independence, sodomy was a capital crime in every state. Pennsylvania, notwithstanding its long Quaker tradition of opposition to the death penalty, executed a man for bestiality in 1785, but in the following year it was the first state to reduce the punishment, from hanging to ten years' imprisonment and forfeiture of estate. In 1793 William Bradford, whom President Washington appointed as the U.S. attorney general the following year, published *An Inquiry How Far the Punishment of Death Is Necessary in Pennsylvania*, which echoed Enlightenment criticism of capital punishment. Executions should be reserved only for the worst offenses. Sodomy, he argued, was not one of them:

> This crime, to which there is so little temptation, that philosophers have affected to doubt its existence, is, in America, as rare as it is detestable. In a country where marriages take place so early, and the intercourse between the sexes is not difficult, there can be no reason for severe penalties to restrain this abuse. . . . The experiment that has been made [in the Pennsylvania penal code], proves that the mildness of the punishment has not encreased the offense. In the six years preceding the act, and while the crime was capital, there are on record two instances of it: in the same period since, there is but one.

Pennsylvania had not suffered any ill effects by ending capital punishment for sodomy. Empirically, Bradford argued, "these facts prove, that to punish this crime with death would be a useless severity." He concluded the facts "may teach us, like the capital punishments formerly inflicted on adultery and witch-craft, how dangerous it is rashly to adopt the Mosaical institutions. Laws might have been proper for a tribe of ardent barbarians wandering through the sands of Arabia which are wholly unfit for an enlightened people of civilized and gentle manners." Bradford's position expressed the enlightened cosmopolitan judgment on sodomy, and in 1794 Pennsylvania moved from experiment to abolition of the death penalty for sodomy. Soon after, even as Farrell and Washburn were being sentenced to hang, four other states followed suit: New York, New Jersey, Rhode Island, and Virginia. Massachusetts would take the same step in 1805—on the eve

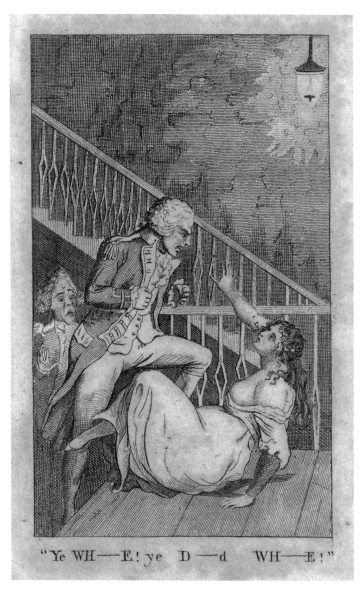

"Ye WH—E! ye D—d WH—E!"

Figure 14. The "Trial of Major Hook, for Adultery with his own Niece, Mrs. Campbell, Wife of Captain Campbell, before Lord Kenyon and a Special Jury, at Westminster, February 26, 1793," uses the form of a trial report to appeal to prurient aggressive tastes. *The Cuckold's chronicle: being select trials for adultry* [*sic*], *incest, imbecility, ravishment, &c.* (Boston, 1798), between pages 48–49. Courtesy of the Trustees of the Boston Public Library.

of the election of a Jeffersonian governor. Connecticut, the last bastion of
Federalism, retained the death penalty for sodomy until 1821.[29]

The fact that the legislatures of Massachusetts and Connecticut lagged
a decade or two behind states to their south was not, we believe, because
their political leaders were less enlightened or cosmopolitan than those of
other states. Nor was it because their states faced a surge in unbridled sexuality or sodomy in particular. In fact their port cities like Boston, and to a
lesser degree Salem and New Haven, lost the energy to prosecute illegitimacy, adultery, and fornication, and most alarmingly to evangelicals, prostitution. An anxious writer lamented in 1791 that every town or village in
Massachusetts "affords some instance of a ruined female, who has fallen
from the heights of purity to the lowest grade of humanity." And to some,
New England's great metropolis, Boston, became synonymous with idleness
and debauchery after that town—over the opposition of Lieutenant Governor Samuel Adams—narrowly approved theatrical performances in 1793. In
the very next year Boston's new Federal Street Theater "made allowances
for a whores' section, and they provided a discreet exit to those patrons
busy with assignations."[30] A character in Hannah Foster's The Coquette
called the performance of Shakespeare's Romeo and Juliet frivolous, asking:
"Are there not enough real woes . . . sufficient to exercise our sympathy
and pity, without introducing fictitious ones into our very diversions?" The
local circus was even worse: "The circus is a place of fashionable resort of
late, but not agreeable to me. I think it inconsistent with the delicacy of a
lady, even to witness the indecorums, which are practised there; especially,
when the performers of equestrian feats are of our own sex. To see a woman
depart so far from the female character, as to assume the masculine habit
and attitudes; and appear entirely indifferent, even to the externals of mod-
esty, is truly disgusting, and ought not to be countenanced by our atten-
dance, much less by our approbation." Such anxieties found their way into
law. In May 1800 Connecticut banned the theater outright. "Theatrical
entertainments" declared the preamble to the statute, "tend to the depriva-
tion of manners and impoverishment of the people." The legislature therefore forbade "any Tragedies, Comedies, Farces, or other Dramatic P[ie]ces
or compositions, or Pantomimes" from performance anywhere in the
state.[31]

The people of northern Connecticut and western Massachusetts did not
face immediate threats to sexual propriety in their own neighborhoods

because strictures against the pleasure culture as well as same-sex intercourse still ruled their counties. Yet as they witnessed barriers against sexual
transgression collapsing in not-so-distant urban centers, leaders in the hinterland came to see themselves as the final guardians of morality. Some
regional leaders believed the Republic was sliding into corruption and they
feared the Godless contagion was infecting their communities. As early as
1790 a Franklin, Massachusetts, pastor, Nathaniel Emmons, responding to
"the particular request of a number of respectable men" in his parish, had
raised an alarm against the progress of vice by calling for the creation of a
"Society for the Reformation of Morals." The Bible itself, he said, showed
the "shocking picture of the lusts and corruptions which ruined the old
world," and especially "the enormous vices, which finally destroyed Sodom,
Egypt, Babylon, Ninevah [*sic*], and many other . . . kingdoms." Consequently he called on everyone "to restrain the licentiousness of the times."
Reverend Emmons assigned first responsibility to seniors—to elders—even
before clergymen, magistrates and parents. "Let the Aged lead in this good
design," he declared, because they could "by their own observation and
experience . . . warn the young and inexperienced."[32]

Much the same call was repeated a decade later by the Reverend Lyman
Beecher, the New Haven blacksmith's son chosen by Litchfield magnates to
lead their village church in 1810. Beecher was a disciple of Yale's zealous
evangelist Timothy Dwight, whose extended 1788 verse *The Triumph of
Infidelity* had attacked the anti-Calvinist treatise of Litchfield native Ethan
Allen, *Reason the Only Oracle of Man, or a Compenduous* [*sic*] *System of
Natural Religion* (1784). In 1803 Beecher, an ardent spokesman for the New
Divinity, was pastor in the Connecticut Yankee enclave at Easthampton,
Long Island, when he proposed a broad movement to create local societies
for "suppressing vice." Inspired by England's very first society for the reformation of morals, created in 1697 to attack London's "swearing and cursing,
drunkenness, and open lewdness," Beecher cited its successes as a model
for his own time now that "debauchery had diffused itself through the
whole body of the nation." In 1697, as in Europe and in America in the
present day, "the champions of debauchery put themselves in array, to
defend their infamous liberties." Though earlier reformers faced "prevailing dissoluteness, countenanced by men in high stations" and "vice
intrenched, bold, open and daring," Christian gentlemen had "brought to
justice . . . multitudes of drunkards, profaners of the Lord's day, besides

hundreds of disorderly [prostitution] houses." Community leaders and public officials especially, Emmons and Beecher agreed, shared primary responsibility for suppressing vice.[33]

The Reverend Emmons had been especially sharp in calling officials to account. "It is," he admonished, "the proper business of executive Officers, to employ their power and authority in suppressing those public vices, which corrupt the morals and disturb the peace of society." The legislature had already done its part, Emmons noted, because "we have strict and severe laws" against a catalog of vices, including "lewdness and debauchery." But, Emmons asked, "have these laws against these public and pernicious vices been duly executed?" Over the previous twenty years, the Massachusetts clergyman noted there had been hardly a single prosecution "for swearing, Sabbath-breaking, drunkenness, or gaming," although everyone agreed that was not "owing to the scarcity of offenders" or any lack of evidence. No, Emmons scolded, there was both "a neglect of informing" by citizens and a reluctance to act by "executive officers." He blamed "silent magistrates" for "negligence." The Reverend Beecher's tone was gentler than Emmons's, but his assignment of responsibility echoed the Massachusetts preacher. Employing biblical rhetoric he asserted that "magistrates are under great obligations, and enjoy peculiar advantages to co-operate in the suppression of vice. They are appointed for this very thing: are invested with the authority of the law, and intrusted with the sword of justice, to be a terror to evil doers, and a praise to them that do well."[34]

Neither Emmons, Beecher, nor any others, to our knowledge, believed New England's rural crisis approached that of London or the American cities. But they feared a contagion was under way that could, if tolerated, reach epidemic proportions. Emmons particularly blamed the Revolutionary War for introducing "almost every species of vice and corruption among us." Unlike New England's well-ordered communities, "our army contained a collection of the loosest characters, who being free from their usual restraint, soon corrupted the minds of many" otherwise moral men. "Most of our youth," Emmons acknowledged, "were necessarily called in the course of the war, into this corrupt and dangerous school"; and after the war ended and the troops disbanded, "they mixed with the mass of the people, and, greatly increased . . . the corruption of morals." A decade later Beecher, still in his twenties, was more optimistic. In rural New England, he believed, "the body of the people are [sic] sober, honest and moral," and no one stood up as "the hardened, open champion of vice . . . to contend for licentiousness." Indeed Emmons, though he warned of the dangers of vice, had quoted the English Unitarian, Richard Price, who said the Americans had "fought with success for themselves and for the world; and in the midst of invasion and carnage, established forms of government favourable in the highest degree to the rights of mankind." Precisely because the Lord had assigned a providential mission for the United States it was impossible to overstate the threat posed by "the decay of virtue and the corruption of morals."[35]

Neither Emmons nor Beecher had visited London; indeed, Boston was probably the only city Emmons knew. But the elites of Hampshire and Litchfield Counties were conscious of the sexual discourse and culture in the rapidly growing cities of New York and Philadelphia, as well as Boston. Most had visited or worked in these cities and witnessed the libertine culture and "vicious" sexual practices that challenged Christian morals. In fact, some of the players in Farrell's and Washburn's courtroom dramas had themselves spent significant time in Philadelphia when it served as the nation's capital. Farrell's attorney, the Federalist Caleb Strong, had been resident in Philadelphia for years and as a member of the U.S. Senate he was present in 1794 when Pennsylvania reformed its criminal code. Washburn's prosecutor Uriah Tracy served there as U.S. congressman from 1793 to 1796 and afterward as a senator. Washburn's defense attorney John Allen had also served in the House of Representatives. The court clerk in the Washburn trial, Frederick Wolcott, was the brother of Alexander Hamilton's ally, Secretary of the Treasury Oliver Wolcott, Jr. Moreover, both Northampton and Litchfield were regional political and cultural centers where people and news frequently came to and from the leading cities. Federalist New Englanders, who proudly claimed English descent, supported Britain's battle against revolutionary France. Federalists in New England like those elsewhere followed the British model for suppressing opposition by supporting the Sedition Act in 1798. But although they never pursued sodomites with British zeal, their refusal to acknowledge that sodomy did not warrant hanging—as did Federalist legislators in other regions—suggests the lingering persistence of a phobia rooted in English masculinity.

The conversation over the legitimate boundaries of sexuality that engaged cosmopolitans in Europe and urban America was too threatening for a rural New England culture and society that was already anxious over the apparent decline in Christian virtue and sexual morality. Public officials maintained positions of power and prestige only with the support of clergy-men and parishioners, and to soften the penalty for the "detestable and abominable Crime of Sodomy (not to be named among Christians)," in the words of Farrell's indictment, would have signaled public rejection of New England's first principles and founding fathers. Since many recognized the ongoing, present-day relaxation of patriarchal controls in their own families as well as their neighbors' increasing acceptance of premarital sex, sexual morality was a matter of immediate concern. Marriage ages for both sexes rose in the second half of the eighteenth century and, not surprisingly, premarital sex became more prevalent, with over 30 percent of first children being born less than eight months after their parents' marriage. Bastardy rates, always higher in cities, rose even in rural towns, and among the jurors who decided Farrell's and Washburn's fate there were those who if they had not themselves married women they had already impregnated, certainly knew such cases were common. Indeed, the rising tide of premarital sex—where young people were taking control of matrimony away from their parents—was so radical that historian Joan Hoff Wilson argues it symbol-ized "a generational conflict and a revolt of the young."[36]

In recognition of these realities legislatures had begun to relax enforce-ment of sanctions against premarital heterosexual sex. Before the Revolu-tion, prosecutions for sexual immorality, especially fornication, had been the most common category of all criminal offenses prosecuted in both Con-necticut and Massachusetts. But the last criminal prosecution against forni-cation in Massachusetts came in 1784, when Priscilla Warfield was declared guilty of "negro fornication" in Hampshire County, and then, after spend-ing an hour on the gallows and being lashed with twenty stripes, was ordered "forever hereafter to wear a capital A of two inches long, and pro-portionable Bigness, cut out in Cloth of a contrary colour, to her cloaths and sewed upon her upper garment on her back in open view." Signifi-cantly, Warfield's worst offense was crossing not the sexual but the color boundary. Two years later, in 1786, Massachusetts revised the statute under which Warfield was prosecuted so that women charged with fornication need only pay a fine rather than face criminal prosecution and brutal cor-poral punishment. Indeed, all such courtroom proceedings became rare. Fornication was turned over to churches, which typically demanded confes-sion and repentance for expiation of the sin. Even women who bore illegiti-mate children escaped punishment. Moreover, responding to the values that Beccaria had proclaimed and Voltaire popularized, prosecutions for infanticide, the means that single mothers had traditionally used to conceal illegitimate births, dropped sharply. Even though public monies might be required to support a bastard child, the coercive apparatus of the state turned to more humane responses to this consequence of sexual transgression. Whereas Massachusetts executed two mothers for murdering their newborns in the 1780s, though there were similar prosecutions later, there were no more hangings. Indeed after 1780, except for the two Massachusetts cases no one was executed for this crime from New Jersey north to Maine.[37]

The relaxation of sexual policing among the states reflected officials' newly charitable response to social realities; but it appears that in the interior local elites in New England were not so tolerant. They worried that this new acceptance of sexual transgression was opening the way to sexual license. The prosecution of nonviolent sexual offenders showed a distinctly geographic pattern in Massachusetts. After 1776, though the actual reality of nonviolent sexual misbehavior must have persisted throughout the state, in the eastern counties prosecutions virtually ceased. Not so in the central and western parts of the Massachusetts, where in the 1780s and especially the 1790s citizens backed a wave of prosecutions for adultery and a variety of other nonviolent criminal sexual offenses. Such proceedings, if not commonplace, became frequent. In Hampshire and Berkshire Counties, with just 24 percent of the state's population, accusations led to 62 percent of the state's proceedings (thirty-three cases), while the central Massachusetts county of Worcester, with 15 percent of the state's people, accounted for an additional 19 percent (ten cases). In contrast, the eastern counties of Essex, Middlesex, Plymouth, and Suffolk, where 46 percent of the Massachusetts population lived, saw only 19 percent of the nonviolent sex prosecutions (ten cases). The climax came during the 1790s when Hampshire County officials pursued twenty-three nonviolent criminal sex cases, those in Berkshire conducted eight more trials, and Worcester County officials heard seven cases of adultery, unlawful cohabitation, and lewd and lascivious conduct. Though in the 1790s adultery was the most frequently prosecuted offense against the sanctity of marriage (64 percent), authorities in the hinterland also brought cases of incest, sodomy, lascivious behavior, lewd and lascivious cohabitation, and mere cohabitation before the Supreme Judicial Court.[38]

While their parishioners consumed the new romantic novels, New England clergymen condemned this, to them, disturbingly popular genre.

The novels, they warned, would forever corrupt young readers by putting dangerous ideas into youthful minds, democratizing and normalizing London-style libertinism. In a time when acceptance of premarital intercourse was growing, moralists saw a crisis. The Reverend Jonathan Edwards, Jr., brother of Washburn's attorney, Pierpont Edwards, warned his niece Sally Burr against the essential predatory nature of men: "our sex seems naturally to take a pride in gaining any advantage over yours; & the more we can bring you [into] a compliance with our desires the more do we boast & glory in it." Young men, he continued, "have a strong ambition to subdue the virtuous resolutions of chaste young women. . . . Men will flatter & sooth you, & yet aim at nothing but your ruin. Thus (greater part of men are) proper enemies of the female sex."[39] Among clergymen, Edwards's views were typical.

Elders fretted and admonished. They wanted young men of the Republic to fulfill the ideal of a masculine virtue shaped by restraint. They must discipline their passions. Gentlemen and elders must set the example because the people at large were "much disposed to vice." But the young increasingly asserted their autonomy in matters of love, even in conservative Litchfield. Aaron Burr was hardly the only law student who shelved his books so as to pursue local women. Though community leaders criticized such behavior, they had come to expect it from young men. Natural philosophy—science—as well as sentimental novels taught that it was men's nature to pursue sexual conquests. Even more alarming was the assertiveness of some elite young Litchfield women. Whereas the novelist Hannah Foster considered a flirtatious character a tragic flaw leading first to shame and then death, some young women refused to bow to conventions. Mariah Wolcott, for one, declared, "*Coquette* is the least odious epithet they bestow upon me." A few years later she asked her sister to inform a suitor that "being '*obedient*' and '*dutiful*'" was "not in my creed." Courtship centered on a ritual of maneuvers. New England maidens were not passive vessels. When Mariann Wolcott Goodrich instructed her brother about how to unlock the "mysteries of the female heart," she confessed women enjoy "to see our Lovers unhappy; at least, we love to think that it is in our power to make them so. Believe me, the Lover, even the highly favoured Lover, ought frequently to complain of his Mistress's cruelty. We love to have you feel and feel ourselves, as if we were doing a mighty, benevolent, disinterested act, when we recompense your sufferings." Ultimately, as daughters and wives women might have to submit, but in courtship they possessed new powers.[40]

Litchfield earned the reputation of being an elite marriage market—provincial Connecticut's version of Jane Austen's Bath. According to local lore, "a handkerchief waved from the rear windows of Miss Pierce's establishment would have been at once perceived in Judge Reeve's recitation room, nor could the Romeos and Juliets of the day have met by a few obstacles [sic] in arranging their stolen interviews." The staid Catharine Beecher recalled some years later that "while Judge Reeve's law school attracted the young men from all quarters, the town was radiant with maidens both indigenous and from abroad." Mariah Wolcott, from a local family and a student at the female academy, proudly noted "that it had always been an established practice with the Litchfield Ladies to steal the hearts of all the Gentlemen who came there, and that I thought a New Haven Lady must have a degree of modest assurance to expect to keep her sweet-heart after he had seen the Litchfield beauties!" This kind of female self-assertion in the volatile arena of romance and sexuality did not frighten Jane Austen's gentry, but in Hampshire and Litchfield Counties, where the tide of evangelical Christianity was running strong, guardians of families and communities shuddered.[41]

Their concern with the loose sexual morals of youth intensified as the turn of the century approached. James Morris recalled that when he opened a school for both boys and girls in 1794 in the South Farms section of Litchfield, some in the local elite accused him of being "too familiar with the ladies who were pupils in my school," and others condemned him for bringing into the community urbane "fashions repugnant" to the culture of the local ecclesiastical society. The girls at Pierce's Female Academy—future gentlewomen—took boat rides on a pond, competed in bowling matches, enjoyed recreational rides in carriages and sleighs, and played a kissing game with young men called "button." In 1798 a Litchfield publisher reprinted a tiny book of advice to women that could easily fit into a lady's pocket and it echoed Edwards's message to his niece. Entitled *The Whole Duty of Woman*, it provided a morality tale of a woman who after going astray made her way back to respectability so that she became eager to help others avoid similar mistakes. The author warned the daughters of Eve to avoid "the bewitching charm of Curiosity . . . the first of all evils, as the source of calamity, as the source of all pain." The following year, Julia

Cowles, a Litchfield pupil at Pierce's Female Academy, joined her friends on a field day and was "shocked to see the indelicacy with which some of my sex appeared in. One, perhaps a woman of 40, went far enough to use very vulgar expressions and even to strike a gentleman who sat upon his horse, with whom she was [an] entire stranger. It wounded my delicacy to see girls of 17 encircled in the arms of lads; what a pity that their reason could not have taught them better! . . . Girls who perhaps would have made (with a little education) fine women, good mothers, and happy wives, will now make neither, entirely destitute of the common rules of decency." Here Cowles articulated the prudery of many parents who saw youthful impropriety sliding into immorality and threatening ruin. While Washburn awaited his trial in jail, the *Connecticut Courant* printed an amused report of many young men swimming "naked in public view" in the Connecticut River during the heat of the summer. In mock alarm the item read: "No Ladies can look from a window near the river, walk its banks, or cross it at the ferry, without exposing themselves to be insulted with the sight of these sansculottes." That this risqué behavior would be associated with *sansculottes* was no coincidence. The writer satirized the hyper-Francophobia of evangelicals and Federalists who linked sexual transgression to the French Revolution.[42]

Much attention focused on sexual impropriety at dancing balls, even as they became fashionable in 1790s New England. James Morris noted that whereas the cost of having a party in mid-eighteenth-century Litchfield "did not exceed one dollar; out of which the fiddler was paid," the ball of 1798 "with all the customary entertainment and variety of music, cost about $160, and nothing was said about it." The elegance and gentility of Europe was worthy of emulation, the American gentry believed—but they felt guilty about adopting models that threatened to violate what they saw as vital boundaries of sexual respectability. For a girl who relied on marriage to provide for her future, her chastity was her most essential attribute, to be protected at all costs. The wrong move at a ball could forever compromise a young woman's reputation. In 1781, for example, Thomas Goodwin and his daughter Mary sued Elihu Harrison for spreading rumors about Mary's behavior at a dance held in Goodwin's house. The defendant reportedly said that Mary had allowed three men to "debauch her chastity." Not so, charged the plaintiffs. The young men, "instigated by . . . shear malice . . . put into a Bowl of Toddy a quantity of Cantharides or Spanish flies and gave the same to the Plt [plaintiff] to drink of . . . to deprive [her] of her reason that they might accomplish the vile purposes of their Heart." Evidently the young men had hoped the aphrodisiac would enable them to "debauch her chastity," but their scheme failed.[43]

Despite worries over their impropriety, balls became popular. After the Revolution dancing masters, often from Italy or France, set up classes in all the major cities, and it did not take them long to extend their fashionable instruction to the countryside. In 1787, for example, a dancing master moved from New York to set up classes in Hartford, where he almost immediately attracted over ninety students eager to learn the latest European court dances. By the 1790s, students at the new, orthodox trinitarian Williams College in western Massachusetts held two annual dancing balls: one in January and one in the summer as part of commencement. This in spite of the fact that the Williams trustees had created their college so that the gentry of western Massachusetts would not have to send their sons to the distant, morally compromised Harvard College. Similarly, students at Pierce's Female Academy regularly attended balls where they could meet eligible and promising young men, preferably from the Law School down the street. Julia Cowles's sanctimonious outrage at the improper behavior of some women at the field day proved brief. The very same evening she attended a ball in which she was "agreeably surprised" to see one such eligible gentleman. While Gideon Washburn sat in jail awaiting trial, Pierce's Academy held an elaborate ball, with over sixty guests, including the four daughters of one of the richest families in town.[44]

The anthropologist Mary Douglas pointed out that social and sexual taboos protect "the local consensus on how the world is organized," shore up society's sense of itself, and reduce "intellectual and social disorder." But when social and cultural ambiguities threaten the social order to its foundations, the protection of taboos becomes the arena in which social tensions are acted out. As the region's young enjoyed their dances, flirted, and seemed to turn their back on the traditional sexual order, the local elite began to rail against the emerging pleasure culture, canonizing their Puritan forefathers afresh, and dreaming of a return to the good and simpler old days, when temptations were, they imagined, effectively restrained, religious doubt was suppressed, and disbelief banished.[45]

CHAPTER 4

Fearful Rulers in Anxious Times

In the late 1790s Massachusetts and Connecticut bore little resemblance to either revolutionary Paris or Georgian London; but developments in those trendsetting capitals—political, religious, social, and sexual—ignited alarm and even panic in the minds of the region's self-styled guardians. Vices, they knew, were contagious; and if virtuous men did not fortify defensive battlements and guard them vigorously, the nation's newborn state republics would fail. These were the lessons taught by the Bible, by ancient and modern history, and by the frightful news they read in the press. Given the Protestant diversity that now pervaded their states, and the political partisanship that divided their communities, the law had become the sole pillar of order that all gentlemen could support. Custom, tradition, and their Revolution had sanctified their statutes and their judicial procedures as the bulwarks of both liberty and order. So in anxious times, they hugged them closely.

But this tight embrace of statute law and correct procedure could lead in unexpected, even doubtful directions. First in Massachusetts, then in Connecticut, the machinery of justice determined that an ancient man should hang for the crime of sodomy with animals. In both cases a jury seated before the state's highest tribunal and operating precisely according to law proclaimed a guilty verdict; and the judges, as directed by statute, ordered death for the convict. Still, the ark of safety and reason, the law, allowed for one last remedy—the pardon. All was not lost for the condemned men if they could only win mercy. Both Farrell and Washburn could appeal to a higher political authority for a pardon, or at least a stay of execution. In Massachusetts this authority rested with the governor and council, whereas in Connecticut the state legislature possessed the power to overturn convictions, commute sentences, and pardon offenders. Given the

ages of the convicted men, the oddity of the charges, and the growing sentiment in both states against all forms of corporal punishment, especially the
death penalty, pardon remained a possibility for both.

In Massachusetts the penal code was moving away from its harsh
Puritan roots during the post-Revolutionary era. To be sure, the old criminal penalties survived in many statutes. But the policing of "moral" and
religious offenses such as fornication and blasphemy had already declined
sharply, and a Beccarian spirit of measured punishment in proportion to
the severity of the crime dominated public discourse. Thus, for example,
in the 1780s the state ended capital punishment for the crimes of polyg-
amy, concealment of a bastard child, and larceny. And while the legislature renewed the statute ordering death for sodomy and bestiality, this
was more a case of legislative caution than a fresh assertion of Puritan
values. Beccarian reform was making headway, and within the decade
following Farrell's sentencing, the state would end branding, whipping,
and cropping ears. Most importantly for this study, the legislature would
remove sodomy and bestiality from the capital list. As of the 1790s the
governor could pardon Farrell, a seemingly harmless old man, or at least
commute his sentence to an hour standing on the gallows followed by
whipping and imprisonment.

Nine years earlier Governor John Hancock had pardoned several Shaysites convicted of treason—the gravest of all crimes—so as to gain a measure of political reconciliation. Hancock and the Governor's Council had
also pardoned three of the five other capital criminals who petitioned for
mercy in the preceding decade. Though their crimes, burglary and manslaughter, were grave (and Massachusetts did hang a full dozen burglars in
the 1780s), their offenses, like Farrell's crime, did not pose the most violent
threats to society. In fact analysis of death sentences, executions, and pardons (see Table 2) demonstrates that the number of executions per capita
declined sharply in the early republic: from 6.5 executions per hundred
thousand inhabitants in the 1780s to 1.3 executions per hundred thousand
people in the 1810s, one-fifth as many on a per capita basis. In the 1790s in
particular, the rate fell from 6.5 to 2.7 executions. Indeed pardoning for
capital crimes peaked between 1790 and 1799. Given this trend, if Dr. John
Farrell petitioned for mercy he could conceivably escape the gallows.[1]

To Caleb Strong, Farrell's conviction was deeply troubling. Like other
learned and cosmopolitan Massachusetts leaders, Strong knew that enlightened penology condemned the use of capital punishment for victimless

Table 2. Massachusetts Death Sentences (Excluding Treason), Executions, Pardons, 1780–1819

Aggregate Data

1780–1819	Death Sentences	Executions	Pardons/Commutations (% of death sentences)	
Men	63 (9 Black, 1 Indian)	55 (8 Black, 1 Indian)	8 (1 Black)	12.7%
Women	4 (1 Indian)	3 (1 Indian)	1	25.0%
Total	67	58	9	13.4%

Data by Decade

1780–89	Death Sentences	Executions	Per 1000	Pardons/Commutations (% of death sentences)	
Men	25 (1 Indian, 1 Black	23 (1 Indian, 1 Black)		2	8.0%
Women	3 (1 Indian)	3		0	0.0%
Total	28	26	.065	2	7.1%

1790–99	Death Sentences	Executions	Per 1000	Pardons/Commutations (% of death sentences)	
Men	18 (3 Black)	15 (3 Black)		3	16.7%
Women	0	0		0	0.0%
Total	18	15	.029	3	16.7%

1800–1809	Death Sentences	Executions	Per 1000	Pardons/Commutations (% of death sentences)	
Men	8 (2 Black)	7 (1 Black)		1 (1Black)	11.1%
Women	1	0		1	100%
Total	9	7	.011	2	22.2%

1810–19	Death Sentences	Executions	Per 1000	Pardons/Commutations (% of death sentences)	
Men	12 (2 Black)	10 (2 Black)		2	16.7%
Women	0	0		0	0.0%
Total	12	10	.013	2	16.7%

Compiled from records of the Supreme Judicial Court and the Governor's Council at the Massachusetts Archives, Boston; Daniel Allen Hearn, *Legal Executions in New England: A Comprehensive Reference, 1623-1960* (Jefferson, N.C.: McFarland, 1999); and United States Bureau of the Census, *Historical Statistics of the United States* (Washington, D.C.: Government Printing Office, 1976), 1: 28-29, 2: 1168. The table was first presented at the annual Meeting of the American Historical Association, Boston, 2001, by Irene Quenzler Brown and Richard D. Brown in "Pardons Won and Pardons Lost."

crimes like sodomy or bestiality. Moreover, from his experience in national politics he knew the stigma that Massachusetts carried owing to its brutal prosecution of Quakers and the Salem witches a century earlier. Strong also believed that Farrell had been wrongly convicted despite his own and his son-in-law's courtroom arguments to persuade the jury otherwise. So he tried to avert Farrell's execution in the only way the law still provided to save his client's life. Petitions to the governor and council for a pardon might not only save Farrell's life but also the reputation of Massachusetts.[2]

Could a petition by Farrell succeed? It would depend. In the 1780s five nonpolitical criminals had won pardons, and more recently three more had won mercy. But each case was different as to the exact nature of the crime, its degree of aggravation, the nature of the evidence, and the character and record of the convict. For Farrell's case there were no precedents; his conviction was essentially *sui generis*. Strong knew that when Farrell's pardon petition came to Governor Samuel Adams and the Governor's Council, comparisons would be difficult. For one, Anglo-American jurisprudence did not distinguish the specific crimes of sodomy and bestiality. English law classified both bestiality and homosexual intercourse as buggery, and in the preceding century judicial moralists like Sir Edward Coke denounced both equally, expressing society's fear that the temptation to commit both acts was ever present. Massachusetts's most recent precedent for the Farrell case—that of Benjamin Goad in 1674—was so distant, and the circumstances so different (Goad was seventeen years old) that it could not supply much guidance. In that case the final word had been delivered by the Reverend Samuel Danforth, who told the crowd assembled to watch the execution that the youth was guilty of "Sodomiticall wickedness."[3] The suitability of the punishment directed by Leviticus and English law was then unquestioned.

Whether hanging was equally legitimate in 1796 remained to be seen. So Caleb Strong instructed his client to petition the governor and council and, as lawyers often did, helped his client draft his pardon plea. In the meantime Farrell would sit in the Hampshire County jail, not knowing whether the governor in Boston would actually issue a pardon or, more likely, the death warrant specifying the date and time when the state would launch the old man into eternity at the end of a rope.

Strong hoped that Hancock's successor, Governor Samuel Adams, together with the Governor's Council would respond to a direct plea for mercy from a piteous old man. In the petition Strong drafted for Farrell's

Figure 15. Farrell's defense attorney Caleb Strong, by Gilbert Stuart (n.d).
Photograph by David Bohl. Courtesy of Frederick S. Moseley III.

signature, the old man noted his birth year, 1711, and his "weak and decrepid [sic] State," as well as the fact that he was "a Stranger and friendless," who was "wholly innocent of the Crime." Relying on Strong's language, Farrell challenged both the evidence and the outcome of the trial. It was impossible, he argued, "that he or indeed any other man could be guilty in the Manner described by the Witnesses," men who were themselves "prompted by . . . interested motives." These facts he had hoped would have blocked "the Resentment of his Persecutors & refuted their accusations." Yet as he had been convicted, Farrell begged for "Compassion" so that "his few remaining days may not be cut off for a Crime which it would have been impossible for him to commit & which he could never have thought of in any period of his Life without Abhorrence." In all probability this direct, almost confrontational appeal echoed arguments Strong and Hooker had used in court to defend Farrell. This October 1796 petition sought to exonerate the convict, not just commute his sentence.[4]

But the executive branch was not easily moved by Farrell's plea. The governor and council could assume that everything Farrell claimed in his petition had already been argued before the Supreme Judicial Court. The jurors had found Farrell guilty and the justices had communicated no reservations about that verdict—as they occasionally did—to cast doubt on it or their sentence. Though such a trial and such a conviction was unheard of in eastern Massachusetts where no one had even been prosecuted for sodomy, buggery, or bestiality in years, Governor Adams and the council declined to act on Farrell's petition. The death sentence stood.[5]

In contrast to the forty-one men and women Massachusetts hanged between 1780 and 1799, Connecticut had executed only six people during those decades—two for rape, both black, and four for murder, including a twelve-year-old Native American-mulatto girl. But the tradition of pardoning condemned criminals that was well established to the south and west of Connecticut (half of all condemned criminals in eighteenth-century New York were pardoned) and was developing in Massachusetts seemed to have skipped the land of steady habits. Perhaps the difficulty lay in Connecticut's legal process. Only the state legislature could pardon criminals or commute sentences. Success depended on persuading majorities in both houses to reverse a decision by a jury composed of voting constituents.[6]

Nevertheless the Connecticut legislature was amenable to forgiving noncapital offenders, and regularly pardoned men convicted of lesser crimes. In May 1796, for example, it pardoned Stephen Fox, convicted of theft, and in October it pardoned Lewis Goldsmith Stanbrough for horse stealing. Both white men were already incarcerated in the state's New Gate Prison, so the pardon amounted to shortening their sentences. No such mercy was shown to those condemned to hang. Two petitions in capital cases came before the legislature in its May 1797 session. The lawyers for Thomas Starr, sentenced for murder, persuaded the lower house to postpone his execution to August so he could prepare an appeal, but the upper house objected and the lower house reversed course, so Starr, denying his guilt to his dying breadth, was executed at Haddam in June 1797. At about the same time Richard Doane suffered the same fate. Condemned for killing a fellow artisan in a drunken melee, the Scottish immigrant won a commutation in the lower house. But as in Starr's case, the upper house refused to pardon and the lower house reversed itself. In June 1797 Doane was hanged in Hartford in front of thousands of spectators.[7]

But these were murderers. With the exception of a notorious burglar whose repeated convictions left him branded and earless when he went to the gallows thirty years before Starr and Doane, no white person had been hanged for an offense other than murder or treason since the execution of William Potter for bestiality in 1662.[8] Perhaps a carefully crafted petition that combined a plea for mercy with arguments that echoed appeals by successful petitioners in nonlethal cases could sway the legislature.

On October 14, 1799, eleven days before Washburn's scheduled execution, his lawyers, John Allen and Pierpont Edwards, petitioned the legislature to pardon the old man. Four years earlier the horse thief Lewis Goldsmith Stanbrough won an appeal after his attorneys presented evidence that he was "in a deranged State of Mind, and not being in the perfect possession of his understanding." Washburn's lawyers employed a similar argument. They argued that the "debilitated and deranged" old man was "utterly ignorant of his guilt in that respect and is insensible of having ever done the facts charged before him." This denial of criminal responsibility offered a pathway to mercy. If legislators were persuaded by his claim of no memory of the events and by the petition's assertion that Washburn was "debilitated and deranged," they might grant him a pardon.[9]

In addition, attorneys Allen and Edwards invoked a procedural loophole. In his 1795 treatise *A System of the Law of the State of Connecticut* Zephaniah Swift recalled witnessing a trial of a man accused of bestiality "who escaped conviction from the circumstance, that no two witnesses saw him at the same time, tho sundry saw him at different times separately. The jury supposed that there must be two witnesses at the same time, to the same act, to comport with the statute, requiring the testimony of two or three witnesses, or that which is equivalent, to take away the life of a man." Washburn's case was similar. Although four separate witnesses testified against him, no two witnesses testified to any one particular act and therefore the prosecution had failed to provide corroboration for any one of the charges. Consequently Allen and Edwards argued the conviction failed the legendary common law standard of two witnesses per incident and "the Jury erred and mistook the Law."

Washburn himself, like Farrell before him, pleaded for mercy on account of his old age and poor health, explaining he "will be eighty four years of age on the day appointed for his execution, and is very infirm in mind and body." He could not expect to live much longer and begged the delegates to allow him to "prepare for death and immortality" as he approaches "the throne of Grace and Mercy" as "the horrors of despair seems to await him." He asked the legislature "to grant him your full and free pardon of the offense of which he stands convicted; or at least to post-pone the day of Execution that he may have some further opportunity to prepare for his fate."[10]

Washburn's petition stirred much debate in the legislature. The legislature discussed the matter on six different sessions in October 1799, though no record of what was actually said was preserved. The lower house voted to grant Washburn a delay, but the upper house, as it did in the murderers' petitions of 1797, insisted that "the said sentence be executed in manner directed by said Superior Court" and the lower house, as in the cases of Starr and Doane, now concurred. Washburn won only a brief postponement. He would not be executed on his eighty-fourth birthday; instead the legislature ordered that he be hanged in Litchfield on the third Friday in January 1800.[11] Officials were not in a forgiving mood.

Neither the evidence against Farrell and Washburn nor the proceedings against them explain why public officials and the political community that sustained those officials—the ruling establishments of Massachusetts and Connecticut—insisted on pursuing these prosecutions to their ultimate consequences. Such deadly outcomes seem contrary to the enlightened spirit of the early republic. How, we wonder, could responsible, conscientious, and experienced officials—learned men—follow this path? They were, after all, rulers who normally exercised discretion. In the past they had often relied on their own judgment—whether in the War for Independence and the formation of state and national governments or in the suppression of rebellion. Massachusetts's and Connecticut's leaders were no mere "literalists" who mindlessly or mechanically followed the letter of the law. Confronting the use of the death penalty for Farrell and Washburn did in fact bring some of them to have grave doubts. Caleb Strong, surely a representative member of the Yankee elite, felt such powerful reservations that he was driven to pursue the petition process more actively than ever before. And while the lawyers defending Washburn did not match Strong's energy and commitment, the Connecticut House of Representatives debated Washburn's fate during six straight sessions. Clearly some rulers questioned the severity of his punishment.

To make sense of the prosecutions it is instructive to go beyond the particular circumstances of each case and the immediate tensions connected to them. We must consider whether the proceedings against Farrell and Washburn did in fact illustrate the outlook of New Englanders in the early republic and their deep-seated Puritanical reaction to the Enlightenment. Alternatively, if these death sentences were not mere accidents, perhaps they expressed something more modest and transitory in New England. Conceivably the convictions of the two old men may have embodied a last gasp of the expiring Puritan penal culture.

We thus turn to exploring the array of forces and tensions stimulated by late eighteenth-century neo-Puritanism. The strange and deadly prosecutions of Farrell and Washburn coincided with this movement and, superficially at least, were clothed in the language of the Puritan era. Desire and aspiration lay at the heart of the late-century awakening, and it was the stresses propelled by desire and aspiration that combined to create an explosive mixture of partisan politics, religious anxiety, and conspiracy fantasies. The cultures of common Yankees as well as aspiring gentlefolk were shaped by these tensions in varying ways. This was especially true for those who saw themselves as defenders of Puritan traditions. In the wake of the French revolutionaries' attack on Christianity, the victories of French armies, and the dissemination of Paine's *Age of Reason*—the era's most incendiary book, according to orthodox clergymen—the Puritan heritage and the order it sustained appeared to be collapsing.[12]

For anyone with English affinities in the late 1790s, anxiety gripped the imagination because spectacular French battlefield conquests seemed to herald the victory of the Jacobins' godless, blood-soaked, anti-Christian message. According to overheated Federalists, American allies of the French terror, led by the free-thinking Thomas Jefferson, were steadily gaining power. Indeed the Virginia apologist for the French Revolution came just a few electoral votes short of gaining the presidency from a Yankee in 1796; and Jefferson, who was both feared and hated, seemed poised to win the office in 1800. More practically, New England shipping suffered from the French campaign to seize American vessels trying to bypass France's blockade of England.

In the very heartland of orthodox Congregationalism religious apostasy mushroomed: Deism, Unitarianism, Universalism, and "Nothingarianism" were all gaining converts rapidly. Even the once forlorn Anglican Church was resurgent, shedding its association with the Tories as it reestablished parishes throughout the region. At the same time Baptists and Methodists mounted their own fresh competition with the orthodox Congregational Church. Literate culture itself seemed to be debased when increasing numbers of daughters and wives embraced the fashion of reading novels. Most clergymen believed these sentimental fictions exerted a pernicious, self-indulgent moral influence.[13] Moreover, connected to these cultural developments, the economy was changing rural society in unsettling ways. Where markets had often been local, now the national and international market economy, long familiar to those who dwelled in coastal areas, was coming to displace the traditional face-to-face ways of business among inland farmers, artisans, traders, and merchants. In port towns an influx of immigrants, often affiliated with the Jeffersonian movement, diluted the region's generations-old English lineage: foreigners were even turning up in the countryside.[14]

For newspaper readers the reports from Europe were alarming. Revolutionaries were mounting assaults on Christianity and hierarchy—indeed the entire social order—and they were winning one bloody victory after another on European battlefields. To the consternation of New England's Federalist elite, public sentiment in most of the United States was cheering for republican France. Jeffersonians welcomed vivid press accounts of the guillotine-fed Terror aimed at aristocrats; but Federalists dreaded this vengeful revolutionary republicanism. To them, anarchy and apostasy seemed so contagious that violent revolutionary rituals might jump across the Atlantic. When the Washington administration signed a commercial accord with Great Britain in 1794 (the Jay Treaty), protests by Jeffersonian

Republicans evoked the spectacle of Parisian terror. Pro-French crowds burned effigies of the New York Federalist John Jay, they stoned Alexander Hamilton, and they shattered windows at the genteel homes of treaty supporters. Federalists shuddered at the reported toast of New Jersey Republicans on July 4, 1795—"The guillotine: May it maintain its empire till all crowned heads are laid in the dust." And in Anglophile New England, Jonathan Maxcy, the president of Rhode-Island College (now Brown) extolled the success of revolutionary armies: "Brave Frenchmen! Your cause is the cause of all nature: your victories the liberties of the world!" The twenty-seven-year-old Baptist president ecstatically proclaimed, "the shining car of freedom will soon roll over the necks of kings, and bear off the oppressed to scenes of liberty and peace." When he finished his 1795 Independence Day oration to the dignitaries and townspeople in the fifteen-hundred-seat First Baptist Meeting-House, the town of Providence paid to publish the speech, so Maxcy's declaration of solidarity with France reached thousands more in no fewer than four printed editions.[15]

Nothing seemed to be going according to Federalists' plans for the United States. Trade with Britain, the pillar of New England's economy, was now hazardous, and the French assault on American vessels in the West Indies threatened to draw the new nation into the European war. Federalists themselves were divided, and the presidential campaign of 1796 exposed their alarming rift when one of the party's most powerful men, Alexander Hamilton, concocted a last-minute scheme to defeat his party's candidate, New England's John Adams, in favor of the South Carolinian Thomas Pinckney. As a last, desperate resort, alarmed New England Federalists, led by the Secretary of the Treasury, Litchfield's Oliver Wolcott, Jr., saved Adams's election. They persuaded their region's electors to submit ballots to the Electoral College in support of Adams, and Adams alone. This victory, though crucial, was only partial, since this Federalist infighting allowed the Francophile Deist Thomas Jefferson, to gain the vice presidency. Upon hearing this news, the usually tolerant minister of Litchfield's Congregational church, Judah Champion, announced he would pray for the Lord to "bestow upon the Vice-President a double portion of Thy grace, for Thou knowest he needs it." Moreover, to the most doctrinaire Federalists the prudent President Adams proved a disappointment because in 1798 he chose to respond to French assaults not by a manly defense of America's honor, but by sending a conciliatory peace commission to Paris that included the leader of New England's French party, Elbridge Gerry.[16]

Though some Federalists took these setbacks in stride, many more convinced themselves that a treasonous grand conspiracy threatened the nation. The French faction in the United States, which had so warmly greeted the French emissary, Citizen Genêt, was now, they imagined, preparing to emulate the republican fifth columns that aided France's conquest of Switzerland and Holland and set the table for a French takeover of the United States. As Litchfield's Uriah Tracy charged in 1797, "certain characters who compose the French faction in the United States" were behind "the unjust and injurious measures of the French Republic towards our commerce." The following year the arrival of the United Irishmen as refugees—after the failure of their French-assisted rebellion—reinforced their fears. And some of the Federalist rhetoric turned sexual. From the mid-1790s onward the English immigrant journalist William Cobbett in Philadelphia launched vicious attacks on the legacy of Benjamin Franklin by following the model John Wilkes had used against rivals a few decades earlier in London. Drawing a direct connection between Franklin, France, and the French party, Cobbett condemned the deceased sage as a libertine, the father of illegitimate children, and, paradoxically, an effeminate courtier tainted by the suggestion of sodomy. Cobbett publicly claimed Benjamin Franklin was guilty of such perversions and—by association—so, too, were the Jeffersonian politicians and printers who promoted his legacy.[17]

Close to home, the character of the vile seducer in the era's most popular American novel, *The Coquette; or, The History of Eliza Wharton* (1797), was said to be modeled on Connecticut's leading Republican. Many gossiped that the villain of this "true-life" story of a woman seduced and abandoned to die in childbirth was in reality Pierpont Edwards, the New Haven lawyer who led Gideon Washburn's defense in the Litchfield courtroom. And the conjecture was far from flattering since that villain, and by extension Edwards, though handsome and charming, was the "disgrace of humanity and virtue, the assassin of honor; the wretch, who breaks the peace of families, who robs virgin innocence of its charms, who triumphs over the ill placed confidence of the inexperienced, unsuspecting, and too credulous fair." One reason for the novel's remarkable appeal was its timely juxtaposition of French sexual immorality, freethinking American Francophiles, and the utter ruin—moral and physical—caused by libertine conduct.[18]

Federalists—and Yankee farmers—might have shrugged off some of these cultural concerns if they had not also been struggling for years to adjust to new and unsettling social and economic realities. At the beginning of the 1780s the inflated farm prices of the Revolutionary years had led to a brief era of farmhouse prosperity; but when the peace in 1783 brought an influx of eagerly sought consumer imports, prices and the economy fell. Private indebtedness soared just at the moment when the governments of Connecticut and Massachusetts raised taxes to pay off their states' Revolutionary debts. By 1786 the result was a wave of farmer discontent throughout New England; and especially in central and western Massachusetts, where a pro-debtor, anti-foreclosure movement culminated in the courthouse closings and armed confrontations of the Shays Rebellion. In Litchfield County establishment leaders proved capable of containing this discontent, but not easily. In Salisbury (in the state's northwest corner) the town's representative to the legislature, Hezekiah Swift, had proclaimed the "righteousness" of the uprising and defended "the insurgents recourse to arms." When hundreds of Litchfield County farmers flocked to the cause, Governor Samuel Huntington sent a committee of four notables—including Uriah Tracy, the prosecutor in Washburn's trial—"to quiet the Disorders that appear to be prevalent among the People, and for the establishment of Government and good Order." Simultaneously the Connecticut legislature sent the militia to the neighboring town of Sharon so that local officials would enforce the law and prevent "any Insurrections of the People." When the militia mobilized, Tracy and his colleagues jailed the leaders of the protest and squashed active resistance. But the gentlemen who weathered this storm of hostility from their farmer neighbors were scarred by the experience. Never again could they take for granted the deference of their less educated neighbors. No wonder Federalists shuddered a few years later when the *sansculottes* and their Jacobin allies destroyed France's established church and turned the guillotine on France's aristocrats.[19]

On a practical level at home other forces were subverting social stability. At the end of the 1780s, following ratification of the new U.S. Constitution, prosperity returned, bringing new perils. Indeed by the 1790s many in Hampshire and Litchfield Counties came to enjoy more affluence than ever before. For even as the size of farms was shrinking and the scarcity of land propelled family members to depart for distant settlements and cities, rural New Englanders were consuming more and more comforts and ornaments. Because the national union promoted the expansion of regional and national markets at the same time that European warfare was propelling unprecedented demand for American farm and forest products, towns like

Northampton and Litchfield that enjoyed access to urban markets were flourishing.

Signs of this new, more cosmopolitan order were conspicuous. Newspaper publication, for example, had been limited to ports and capitals before the Revolution, but in the 1780s print shops spread to county seats, where growing commerce and more affluent readers were eager to support them. In Litchfield two printers founded the *Weekly Monitor, and American Advertiser* in 1784; and two years later the *Hampshire Gazette* set up shop in Northampton, just as the crisis of taxation and debt provoked the rural insurrection. Both the *Weekly Monitor* and the *Hampshire Gazette* weathered this storm; and when it passed they filled their pages with advertising for all sorts of trade. Merchants offered everything from imported china and flatware to looking glasses and wine in exchange for the countryside's furs, lumber, meat, and produce.

In the villages of Northampton and Litchfield, as in villages throughout New England and on prosperous farms, new, white-painted two-story dwellings were rising, complete with central hallways, two or three chimneys, and elevated ceilings. These larger, newly arranged houses enabled their residents to enjoy greater privacy and refinement than the colonial central chimney houses had permitted. While the new prosperity and comfort never included everyone, many did climb the social ladder from artisan to owner and from shopkeeper to merchant. Men who had, in their boyhood, callused their hands splitting wood and soiled their clothes butchering livestock now dressed in ruffled linen shirts and velvet smallclothes. Women who grew up tending fires, kitchen gardens, and younger siblings now took time to embroider and to read newspapers and novels. Village gentry even went so far as to dress in their finest clothes to have their portraits painted by the itinerant limners. Most of these painters were self-taught men whose "primitive" two-dimensional canvases and panels adorned parlors in the new dwellings, but a very few, such as Ralph Earl from central Massachusetts, went on to become professionally trained artists.[20]

The region's elite was divided. Although Federalists held power, their control was somewhat precarious. In many towns, including Litchfield and Northampton, Republicans competed for office; and sometimes they won elections. Republican newspapers published in towns across the region enabled activists to challenge the privileges of the Congregational establishment and to reject the vision of a unified organic community that was

Figure 16. Elijah Boardman, by Ralph Earl, 1789. Courtesy of the Metropolitan Museum of Art / Art Resource, NY.

so central to New Englanders' traditional self-image. Republicans, unlike Federalists, accepted conflicts among interests and social groups as inevitable. Their highest aim was not unity but the assertion of individual liberties and recognition of the equal rights of freemen, regardless of property or religious preference. The prosperous Elijah Boardman, for example, followed the Episcopal faith, and so could see himself as an outsider to the standing order—one reason, no doubt, why he would become a Jeffersonian Republican, ultimately being elected by the Connecticut legislature in 1820 to serve in the U.S. Senate. Some New Englanders—we cannot say in Boardman's case—even subscribed to the most inflammatory Jeffersonian newspaper, the *Philadelphia Aurora*, which regularly featured attacks on the region and its culture. Henry Adams believed that local Federalist elites panicked, coming to believe that every "dissolute intriguer . . . every harebrained, loud talking demagogue; every speculator, scoffer, and atheist . . . [was] a follower of Jefferson." Perhaps Adams exaggerated, but if one reads Federalist rhetoric literally, calling some Federalists hysterical is a simple statement of fact.[21]

All these political, economic, and social developments took place against the backdrop of a profound crisis of the region's defining culture and identity—its Puritan heritage embodied in the established Congregational Church. When the first shots were fired at Lexington and Concord, New England's founding faith, Congregationalism, was the largest denomination in the young nation and its future seemed promising. Congregationalists led the Patriot cause; in contrast Anglicanism, the largest and most powerful competing denomination, was associated with Great Britain and treason. But much to the chagrin of Congregationalist leaders, their own connection to victory in the Revolution did not launch a golden age for their church.[22] Though Congregationalism remained the established tax-supported church in both Massachusetts and Connecticut, and although their clergymen continued to deliver election-day sermons to their governors and legislatures, some citizens challenged Congregational hegemony.

As a result contests over control of church buildings and tax revenue divided both states and, as the historian Jon Butler notes, "drained away the grandeur that state support for Christianity was designed to provide." In 1784 Connecticut followed the Massachusetts compromise and freed dissenters from having to pay the Congregational tithe, but only if they could present a certificate proving tithe-paying membership in another legally recognized church. This gave local Congregational officials the power to decide which denominations and practices were legitimate. No wonder, then, that dissenters objected to being required to satisfy their Congregational neighbors—who coveted their church-tax revenues—that their own somewhat different Christian beliefs were acceptable. In a republic that proclaimed all men equal before the law, the New England establishment was branding religious dissenters—whether Protestant or Catholic—with second-class citizenship.[23]

In Litchfield and Hampshire Counties the Congregational establishment enjoyed broader support than in coastal regions. These counties had few Episcopal churches and virtually no Catholics, and though ministers complained of competing Baptists and Methodists, their own Congregational voters dominated town and parish meetings. Still, Congregationalists fretted over the growing number of rival churches as well as their own neighbors' declining commitment to Congregational piety. By the 1790s ministers preached to aging and increasingly female audiences. Townspeople—tending toward "Nothingarianism"—skipped services, balked at paying their ministers' salaries fully, and turned to the church only when they needed to baptize children, to marry, and to bury the dead. With young people departing for cities and frontier settlements, families worried that their own sons and daughters together with other emigrants to urban America, western New York, northern New England, and the Ohio country would fall away from the old New England way. Worst of all, in the mid-1790s they detected the rise of home-grown infidel challenges to the orthodox interpretation of the scriptures.[24]

When politics and religion combined they nourished explosive rhetoric. Widespread Congregational fears of Christian decline blended with partisan Federalist warnings about the wave of international revolutionary radicalism. In parlors and law offices in Northampton and Litchfield—as well as Boston, Hartford, and New Haven—the New England elite understood partisan struggles and the erosion of traditional hierarchy as the consequences of religious apathy and pro-French radicals' anti-Christian crusade. Their rejection of Christ was the core problem. Deist treatises, by Litchfield-born Ethan Allen and the Englishmen Joseph Priestley and Thomas Paine, circulated widely and young men, often gentlemen, embraced this dangerous Enlightenment rationalism. Federalists believed Thomas Jefferson, the Republican hero, was a confirmed Deist or even an atheist. At the shrine of orthodox Congregationalism, Yale College, during the presidency of Reverend Ezra Stiles in the 1780s and early 1790s, students were avidly reading Rousseau and Voltaire more enthusiastically than sacred Christian texts. By 1795, when Yale's trustees appointed the evangelical Northampton native Reverend Timothy Dwight, some students were even skipping church. Establishment leaders saw calamity approaching.

Only a few years earlier Congregational ministers had sympathized with the cause of French republicanism. But in 1794 when they learned of the Terror and when Thomas Paine's *Age of Reason* arrived in their communities, they turned against France. Paine's book—published in Massachusetts in both Worcester and Boston—connected the cause of freedom to tolerant Deism—orthodoxy's most dangerous and insidious enemy. This was a false religion and emblematic of the era's evils: France's revolutionary terror in Europe and the agents of apostasy at home, Paine and Jefferson. Deist writers, as Timothy Dwight protested, exchanged the profound teachings of true Christianity for lukewarm social conventions of "decency" judged exclusively by what was "agreeable to men." Deists were "[I]nfidels without knowing it," who ultimately "renounced scripture entirely"—an utterly damning accusation for orthodox Christians.[25]

Religious anxiety fed xenophobia. Fears centered on transatlantic radicals who threatened to turn the United States into the New World's France—where Robespierre's Cult of the Supreme Being reigned. In 1797 Congressman Harrison Gray Otis of Massachusetts warned that foreigners coming to America's shore, "after unfurling the standard of rebellion in their own countries, come hither to revolutionize ours." Most European immigrants, a writer for the *Gazette of the United States* declared, were convicts of the worst kind, guilty of murder, rape, and sodomy. In May 1798, Litchfield's John Allen warned Congress that the new restrictions on foreigners should not merely apply to French citizens, because "citizens of several other countries are as dangerous." They possessed "dispositions equally hostile to this country with the French." At Litchfield, 1798 Fourth of July orator James Gould who was recently made Tapping Reeve's associate at the law school, told the gathering that the French Revolution has brought forth on the nations of Europe "evils, which without experience, cannot be known." Immigration must be checked because "*the fortune of every community must depend upon the character and conduct of its members.*" And Senator Uriah Tracy

concurred. In Pennsylvania, he claimed, where unworthy European multitudes had been allowed to settle, these people had embraced the Jeffersonians, so as to elect every "scoundrel who can read and write into
office." Traveling through Pennsylvania, this Litchfield lawyer and politician was disgusted by the "very many Irishmen, and with a very few
exceptions, they are United Irishmen, Free Masons, and the most God-
provoking Democrats on this side of Hell." As for "the Germans," he
found them "stupid, ignorant, and ugly, and [they] are to the Irish what
negroes at the south are to their drivers." These immigrants must never
flood into New England because they posed political, cultural, and sexual
threats. As for the author of *The Rights of Man*, Federalists denounced
Paine not only for religious blasphemy and transatlantic revolutionary
troublemaking but for being "a wretch without character . . . devoted to
the most *bestial* intoxication." Picturing events in Europe and in American cities, orthodox ministers of the New England interior believed, as a
recent historian of sex put it, that "sexual toleration grew out of religious
toleration."[26]

Under siege, Congregational preachers rose to defend the faith furi-
ously. Coming together as advocates of the New Divinity, they cast themselves as protectors of New England orthodoxy and stewards of American
virtue. They took on the new philosophies and lambasted the degenerate
morals and the conspiratorial influences of groups associated with the
French Revolution—from America's Democratic-Republican societies,
implicated by President Washington in the 1794 Whiskey Rebellion, to the
secret order of Bavarian Illuminati that Reverend Jedidiah Morse charged
with fomenting a global conspiracy against Christianity a few years later. In
contrast to many urbane and secular Federalist gentlemen dwelling in port
towns who were coming to terms with the prosperous new era, many Federalist leaders in New England's interior believed their society stood at the
precipice in its battle against the forces of unbelief. In this crisis, the Reverend Azel Backus of Bethlehem in Litchfield County declared, "let us cleave
to our religion, and our constitution as the refuge of our hopes." New
Divinity pastors like Backus pledged loyalty to the tradition of their forefathers. They would rejuvenate orthodoxy, truly the sole alternative to the
rising tide of infidelity.[27]

The ghost of Jonathan Edwards hovered over the region. His son and
namesake, Reverend Jonathan Edwards, Jr., born in Northampton and
trained by the New Divinity champion Joseph Bellamy, led the church in

Colebrook in Litchfield County. Following the teachings of Jonathan Edwards, Sr., whose fierce theology first awakened the Connecticut River valley in the 1730s, the younger Edwards (with his student Jedidiah Morse) was part of the generation of clergy that idealized the senior Jonathan Edwards as the model of correct Christianity. Under their leadership the reprinting of old Edwards sermons, haphazard at first, became a project of the New England Tract Society and its successor, the American Tract Society.[28]

Edwards's grandson Timothy Dwight led orthodoxy's charge from his position as Yale's president, a post he accepted in 1795 intent on building "up a ruined college."[29] A Northampton native, he was raised by a mother who neither forgot nor forgave the Northampton church for driving her father out. By beating back the forces of corruption and secularism Dwight determined to succeed where his grandfather had been thwarted. Dwight traveled the region taking stock of religion and engaging local ministers and congregations in the project of revitalizing orthodox Congregationalism. A shrewd and gifted intellectual, familiar with many of the philosophical and religious texts of the age, Dwight armed graduates of Yale with the learning necessary to combat unbelievers. Always self-confident, he inspired his students to become driving forces in the Congregational revival. When Dwight died in 1817 he was mourned as a popular preacher whose "powers natural and acquired were eminently displayed in clear and expressive exhibitions of evangelical truth," and for the "great revivals of attention to religion" he aroused, as well as the many students he placed in New England pulpits.[30]

Dwight set orthodoxy's intellectual and psychological foundation of the late 1790s upon two pillars—the threats from the French Revolution and its American agents and the general decline of Christianity in America. His writings and sermons were calls to arms against the infidelity and apostasy that led to moral bankruptcy and the dissolution of social bonds. He bemoaned the introduction of a "multiplicity of loose doctrines" that, "under the pretence of enlarged philanthropy, and of giving mankind liberty and equality," actually encouraged poisonous plans for spreading atheism, "exterminating Christianity, . . . rooting out of the world civil and domestic government, the right of property, marriage, natural affection, chastity and decency; and in a word[,] for destroying whatever is virtuous, refined or desirable, and introducing again universal savageness and brutism . . . [and] reduc[ing] the whole human race under the complete subjugation to these Philosophers, a subjugation of mind as well as body."

Figure 17. Timothy Dwight, by John Trumbull, 1817. Courtesy of the Yale University Art Gallery.

Extreme words, to be sure, but Dwight and his followers feared the apocalypse, not only for New England but for the entire United States and for mankind.[31]

In Connecticut and much of New England these calls to arms reinvigorated the old faith. Renewed interest in scripture coincided with the outbreak of war in Europe—the number of treatises on the Bible published in the four years from 1793 to 1796 was many times greater than for all the years since 1760. Suddenly and seemingly independently, religious revivals erupted in the second half of the 1790s in the New England interior, shaping Christianity for a generation. Some ministers shed the cool, intellectual preaching style of their Puritan forefathers and aggressively embraced revivals, while in other congregations a new generation of evangelical pastors entered the pulpit. The result was transformative. What began as a "succession of heavenly sprinkling" turned into a flood sweeping over the interior of southern New England. In contrast, Boston and its eastern Massachusetts hinterland embraced liberal Unitarian Christianity; but inland the "old time religion" flourished. By 1799 Litchfield County pastor James Russell recalled, he could stand on his porch and "number fifty or sixty contiguous congregations laid down in one field of divine wonders, and as many more in different parts of New England." Here Dwight's followers came to lead one parish after another, dominating countywide ministerial associations.[32]

The religious revival joined with economic, political, and cultural upheavals to create a crisis of confidence among many in the ruling class. Established institutions—the church, the state, the law—they were sure, provided the strongest ark of security. Acting in light of these anxieties and governing according to these assumptions, justices of the peace like Simeon Strong in Amherst and Lynde Lord in Litchfield, as well as the jurists who sat on the highest courts, felt compelled to adhere to the law and to their states' penal codes when householders came to them with accusations of bestiality against two old men. In other times officials had temporized, allowing delay and procedural obstacles to permit such bizarre accusations to fade. But now they responded to their neighbors forcefully, bringing into play the full power of government so as to prosecute these nonviolent sexual transgressors.

Farrell's affair coincided with the first revivals that followed the start of Dwight's evangelical missions across New England. Because town and church records for Leverett are sparse, it is impossible to know whether a revival was coursing through that community in the mid-1790s. We do know that the pastor, Reverend Henry Williams, was an evangelical and that when the Congregational clergy of the county organized a missionary society in 1802 it raised contributions of $1,163.77 in the first year and pledges of $4,130 for the following six years. So there is no question that the county elite embraced Christian revivals. But whether or not the people of Leverett were especially imbued with evangelical fire at the time of Farrell's accusation and trial is beyond reach. Leverett's clergyman, who held no college degree, published only a single sermon, an evangelical "call to thirsty souls" that admonished listeners to "give yourselves no rest until you can be sure you are fleeing from the wrath to come"; but that was a dozen years after the Farrell episode.[33]

The evidence from Litchfield, however, directly connects the broader developments in the region with local conflicts and the prosecution of Gideon Washburn. Dwight and his followers had transformed Litchfield County's religious landscape. For nearly a half century, from 1753 to 1798, Judah Champion, a moderate traditionalist who "held the doctrines of grace, as they were understood by the early Reformers," had led the Litchfield Congregational Church. Champion was a friend of Dwight's predecessor at Yale, Ezra Stiles, a vocal defender of the American Enlightenment. Indeed when Stiles visited Litchfield and stayed with Champion, Stiles recalled, Champion had confronted the evangelical Bellamy. As Stiles put it, Bellamy was "slaying and turning out Ministers in Litchfield in his mistaken Zeal," but Champion "stood it out manfully and supported by Gov. Wolcott stood his ground." Like Stiles, Champion was tolerant of other denominations. In 1796, for example, he welcomed local Methodists to hold their quarterly meeting in his church. But by then the sixty-seven-year-old Champion's health was declining and the town was already looking for a replacement. One year earlier Frederick Wolcott had asked his father, Lieutenant Governor Oliver Wolcott, Sr., to "inquire of Doctr Dwight & of other Gentlemen what respectable young Candidates they are acquainted with. If Mr. Champion remain unable to preach, it is of consequence that we endeavour to find a character we shall all be willing to settle." In 1798, a year before the Washburn prosecution, the church found their man, installing Dwight's evangelical protégé Dan Huntington to replace Champion, who in fact remained active in Litchfield's public life until his death in 1810. The moderate Champion, it appears, was a casualty of the revivalism of the late 1790s.[34]

Huntington's ordination sermon, delivered by the Reverend James Dana, pastor of the First Church in New Haven, and author four years

Figure 18. Litchfield's Congregational minister Judah Champion, by Ralph Earl, 1789. Courtesy of the Litchfield Historical Society.

earlier of *The Folly of Practical Atheism*, foretold the coming evangelical crusade. Dana warned against sins, elaborated on divine punishments, called for obedience and repentance, and reiterated the Calvinist argument about the radical otherness of God, whose choices are "above human discovery or comprehension." He called on the congregation to fight for Christianity, declaring: "Modern infidels, with arrogance unparalleled, have combined to establish atheism, and prostrate human society. . . . Our age and country furnish speculative characters, who, instigated by Lucifer, . . . spurn the government of him who sitteth on the throne of the universe. Christianity is honored by the contempt and detestation of the atheists." By installing young Huntington, Dana pronounced that the Litchfield congregation was raising the evangelical message to "a conspicuous part of the vineyard." Dana praised Litchfield leaders for making their town an inspiring example and, echoing John Winthrop's shipboard sermon of 1630, he proclaimed: "A city that is set on an hill cannot be hid. Let your light shine, that men may glorify God in you." Litchfield would proclaim salvation; so it must banish sin.[35]

The young preacher was determined to change a town that was, he claimed, known for having "voted Christ out of their borders." In nearby towns revivals were already taking place, but Litchfield, Huntington later reflected, "was originally among the number of those decidedly opposed to the movements of former revivalists." So with the support of his congregation Huntington determined to make certain that Litchfield would no more be "like the barren heath in the desert;" and he succeeded. In a dozen years hundreds of converts joined the church. When Representative Benjamin Tallmadge in Philadelphia learned of Litchfield's awakening, he wrote, the new conversions "feast my Soul." By the time Lyman Beecher replaced Huntington in 1810, in twelve tumultuous years the young evangelist had converted Litchfield's Congregational Church into a revival center.[36]

Evidently Huntington excelled at delivering "a handsome & moral discourse" that moved many to return to Christ; but his political instincts were less inspired. Arriving in 1798, he was full of hope. Litchfield, he noted, was "a delightful village on a fruitful hill, richly endowed with schools both professional and scientific, with its venerable governors and judges, with its learned lawyers, and senators both in the national and state departments and with a population both enlightened and respectable, Litchfield was now in its glory." But Huntington's optimism was short-lived after the fiery and combative preacher aligned himself with the town's Federalist elite.

Litchfield Jeffersonians charged that the new pastor "devotes himself wholly, to a *few individuals,* whose dupe he has become and under whom he acts the part of a most busy arrant retailer of slander."[37]

Huntington promptly alienated the town's leading Republican, Ephraim Kirby. This distinguished lawyer, who published the first collection of court cases in America in 1789, stood outside the town's elite. When he ran for the state's Council of Assistants in 1791, Frederick Wolcott wrote his father Oliver that everyone they knew was "violently oppos'd" to Kirby. No wonder that Kirby did not win a place on the council; but he won a majority of the town's voters and so gained a seat in the state legislature for most of the decade. When the Republican opposition formed, Kirby became its primary leader in northwest Connecticut. In 1794–95, writing under the alias of Cassius, he published a series in Hartford's Jefferson-slanted *American Mercury* that strongly condemned the political machinations of the state's "established aristocracy." In effect, he attacked his neighbors; and they repaid him in kind. The following year the writer who exposed Kirby's authorship of the Cassius essays called him "a Lawyer; who for cool and deliberate cunning and intrigue stands unrivalled in the dark catalogue of false patriots of the day." By 1796 Kirby was so alienated from Litchfield's elite that he described his town as "the hotbed of envy, malice and every other dissocial feeling of the mind." The following year he sent his daughter to be educated at a school in neighboring Bethlehem, rather than at the more prestigious local Pierce's Female Academy.[38]

For much of the decade, then, Kirby and his rivals engaged in bitter, though essentially secular, disagreement over politics. But Huntington's arrival in 1798 added a religious dimension to the mixture. Now Kirby stopped attending church, leading his rivals to declare him an "infidel," "open scoffer at all religion," and a "disgrace to this town." Kirby blamed the new minister. Huntington, he complained, was speaking out of both sides of his mouth. Among the "republicans in *Litchfield*" and among Kirby's friends, Huntington "spoke of [Kirby] even in terms of superfluous and exaggerated recommendation." But when the pastor moved among Federalists, he denounced Kirby as trying to prove that "republicanism and infidelity are in alliance." Kirby described himself as a believer; but he refused to attend a church whose minister he "found acting the part of a *rancorous, overheated, political partizan*; attempting to destroy the confidence of the people in their chief magistrates, exciting discontent, speaking lightly and contemptuously of the officers of government, slandering and backbiting individuals, to aid the base intrigues of a party." And while Kirby had earlier hoped "to strip the imposter of his false dress, and to expose him to the world in his true character," his conflict with the town's minister would put an end to his own political and professional career in Litchfield. After Jefferson's election as president he appointed Kirby judge of the newly organized superior court of the territory of Mississippi in 1803, where Kirby died the following year.[39]

Huntington's attacks were not limited to Litchfield; he denounced ministers elsewhere who dared join the Republicans. In 1801 he took aim at Stanley Griswold, minister of the First Congregational Church of nearby New Milford. Previously Huntington had supported Griswold when the Association of Litchfield ministers censured the latter for unsound doctrine in 1797. But when Griswold joined Connecticut Republicans and sermonized against ministers' slandering political rivals, which Griswold said "has crept into public Gazettes, Magazines and Pamphlets and swollen their impure pages, branding the worthiest men with infamy," Huntington turned on him. When visiting friends in western Massachusetts in 1800, Huntington spread word that Griswold now "*believed, that the whole system of the Christian Religion was a mere piece of mummery.*" When Griswold learned of it, he confronted Huntington to deny or to retract the charge. But Huntington would not retreat, declaring Griswold to be a clergyman who had cast his lot with "the large proportion of reputed Infidels." He accused Griswold of Episcopalian tendencies, of baptizing avowed infidels, and doing away with family prayers in his home. Worst of all, Huntington claimed Griswold sided with supporters of French apostasy "who by their sorceries and witchcrafts, are endeavoring to turn the world upside down."[40]

The New Milford pastor believed these charges aimed at "the murder of my reputation." Huntington had betrayed their friendship by spreading malicious accusations without checking to see if they were true. Griswold denied he had abandoned Congregational doctrine, but acknowledged his support of toleration because "*a man ought not to be injured for his religious opinions.*" He argued that the "bigots and hot-headed partisans" who attacked his character did "more to wound the cause of Christianity than all the Infidels that ever wrote." The claims of blasphemous slanderers like Huntington were pernicious because, instead of defeating infidelity, Huntington actually encouraged it; and he would witness "an unusual crop of deists spring forth in the country." To Griswold the skepticism of Deists was "the natural produce of that bigotry, intolerance, and sacrilegious abuse of the name of religion." Griswold may have bested Huntington in argument, but like Kirby, he lost the war. Griswold's parishioners forced him out within the year. Required to leave New England, he spent the rest of his life moving from one republican patronage position to another.[41]

There is no clear link between Huntington and the prosecution of Gideon Washburn; however by installing a preacher determined to revive the rigid moral standards of the old Puritan way—in contrast to his predecessor—Litchfield's rulers and the broader community positively declared their outlook. We suppose their newfound Puritanism shaped their response to the accusations against Washburn when, in 1799, witnesses recalled that they saw the old man engaged in a bestial act as early as 1796, although they had held off their accusations. Washburn's offense had not changed; it was the community's response that was new. This Litchfield episode allows us to examine the impact of the Puritan flashback at a critical moment for New England Federalists. We believe that by momentarily slipping the reins of prudence and reason that usually guided Federalist officials, the threats to Christian orthodoxy and the simultaneous wave of Francophobia opened the way for the bestiality trials—giving legitimacy to such unthinkable proceedings.

In Litchfield County the revivals turned harsh and censorious when, in addition to their other fears, many New Englanders came to believe that a secret cabal of Freemasons and Illuminati were conspiring to take over America's civil and religious institutions. In 1798 Jedidiah Morse, the Yale-trained Congregational minister of Charlestown, Massachusetts, warned of a secret plot to "prepare the way among us, for the spread of those disorganizing opinions, and that atheistical philosophy, which are deluging the Old World in misery and blood." Reinforcing the explosive rhetoric of the religious and political controversies of the moment, Morse's report of the Masonic-Illuminati conspiracy resonated with an anxious clergy and with a public that relied on their pastors not only for spiritual guidance but for information about the world beyond local borders. Nevertheless Republicans, especially, were skeptical. "Since the days of the Salem Witchcraft," wrote the editor of the New London *Bee*, "no subject perhaps, has so much affected minds of a certain cast in New England as this pretended conspiracy against religion and government." Indeed when challenged, Morse could not cite any concrete evidence of the Bavarian Illuminati society in America. To Republicans, Morse appeared ridiculous. The conspiracy, one wrote, was "a subject which has stricken many a venerable gentlewoman with marvel, and more than one rev. Dr. [Morse] with horrors—a subject that seems to have dried up the last drop of moisture of our eagle eyed Dr.'s brain." In Massachusetts, Republican editors printed letters from European experts that debunked the whole conspiracy theory.[42]

On the other hand, the popularity of the secret society of Freemasons—another European import tinged with Deism—was exploding. In Massachusetts alone, local elites created some forty-three lodges in communities outside of Boston in the 1790s and fifty-one more in the following decade.[43] No illuminati clubs could be found, but one scholar estimates that masonry was so popular in the United States at the turn of the nineteenth century that roughly 3 percent of white men belonged to Masonic lodges. Because the order was secret and possessed foreign origins and rituals, outsiders suspected a connection to Enlightenment-inspired atheism. So anti-Illuminati zealots also turned against the Freemasons. Litchfield's Oliver Wolcott, Jr., supplied his correspondent Reverend Morse with a list of the lodges and their French and American members in 1798, and Morse went on to claim the Masonic order was the agent of the Illuminati in America.[44]

This charge against the Masons smeared the local Republican opposition with treasonous intentions. The fraternal association that had earlier numbered many of the nation's leaders—including George Washington—among its members now became associated with the Jeffersonian opposition. In Connecticut the Freemasons coalesced as the organization for people alienated by the aggressive orthodox hegemony. Pierpont Edwards was one of Connecticut's leading Republicans as well as the state's first Masonic grand master. In Massachusetts a similar drama was enacted. By attacking the Masons and Illuminati, the orthodox clergy merged their campaigns against Republicans and infidelity. This fanatical, fantasy-based campaign against the Masons and Illuminati attacked not only the legitimacy of the opposition but their institutional base. To Litchfield Federalists the conspiracy seemed all too real when they considered that Ephraim Kirby, the local Republican leader, also became the first general grand high priest of the Royal Arch Masons of the United States in 1798.[45]

Litchfield's Masonic chapter, the lodge of St. Paul, had been founded in 1781, with Ephraim Kirby, its secretary, writing and signing its official charter. Until the mid-1790s many of the town's Federalist elite joined the fraternity; John Allen was the senior warden, and other prominent Masons included the merchant Julius Deming, Washburn's jailer Lynde Lord, and

Peter Collier, publisher of the Federalist *Litchfield Monitor*. But after 1795 the political and social profile of Litchfield's Masonic lodge changed. Whereas earlier meetings featured prominent Litchfield residents, now leaders like Deming and Collier absented themselves. Among the town's leading citizens, only Kirby and Moses Seymour, like Kirby a Republican, and an artisan as well as an Episcopalian, remained with the order. Consequently a lodge that had been politically ecumenical became the meeting place for men who shared the Jeffersonian resentment of the town's self-styled aristocratic elite. The record of the meeting on the first Sunday of 1794 includes for the first time the listing of Gideon's son, William Washburn, as a member of the lodge. Washburn attended meetings regularly in 1795 and 1796, and sporadically in 1797 and 1798. When the lodge met on December 27, 1799, William Washburn was absent. His father was in jail awaiting execution. The direct involvement of the state's leading Republican and most prominent Mason in Washburn's defense suggests that from the perspective of Jeffersonians and Masons, Washburn's trial was political. Why else did Pierpont Edwards travel from New Haven to Litchfield? Edwards was not, after all, part of the Litchfield bar, and we find no evidence of his participation in any other Litchfield trial.[46]

The focus on the Masons also added a sexual dimension to the supposed conspiracy. Freemasons imported rituals that made the organization susceptible to conspiratorial anxieties centering on sexual transgression. One ritual, steeped in secrecy and homosocial bonds, and expressing a nonsectarian appeal, corresponded to groups of sodomites whose hidden sociability appeared to outsiders as founded on similarly immoral principles. Critics wondered what actually transpired among men secreted behind closed doors. Some suspected that members engaged in unnatural practices including sodomy and sadomasochistic rituals. In 1751, for example, the *Boston Evening-Post* accompanied an anti-Masonic piece with an illustration of a Mason hammering a nail into the buttocks of another—while a donkey (no less) calls, "Trunil [nail] him well brother." Some writers alleged that members performed enemas for one another in addition to spanking with whips, rods, and nails.[47] Freemasons could not easily dispel such fantasies since they were pledged to secrecy.

In their longing for a mythic half-remembered Puritan order, anxious leaders opened the door to the bizarre prosecutions of Farrell and Washburn. On the same day the Superior Court sitting at Litchfield tried and sentenced Washburn it also considered two additional cases of sexual

To Mr. CLIO, at North-Hampton,
In Defence of MASONRY.

PRAY Master *CLIO* now take care,
    And write against us if you dare.
For if you do, the World will know it,
And call you *Fool*, instead of *Poet*.
For we walk'd in Order as we shou'd,
And look'd as sober as we cou'd do.
If you think to scare us, you're mistaken,
For we stand firm and unshaken.
'Tis true, I own it may be objected,
That our proper *Musick* was neglected;
An *ASS* to bray and *Kettle Drum*,
Which I must own makes up the Sum
Of all the Musick of a *MASON*,
And all allow'd us by our *JASON*.
But instead of Braying we'd *Luke's* Mortars,
Which draw'd Men to us from all Quarters;
And Stock eno' of right good Powder,
Which made a Noise full ten times louder.

Figure 19. Sexualized mockery of Freemasonry was not unknown in the eighteenth century. From *Boston Evening-Post*, January 7, 1751, "To Mr. Clio, at North-Hampton: In Defence of Masonry." Courtesy of the American Antiquarian Society.

misconduct, and here the impact of the Puritan legacy was mixed. Rape victim Phoebe Thomson was charged "for Felony, on the Statute which prescribes Death for the illicit birth and concealment of a Bastard Child, under circumstances of violence." This was the Puritan statute, but the jury took just ten minutes to acquit Phoebe Thomson. Without knowing the facts of the case one cannot say unequivocally that the jurors deliberately rejected Puritan-style severity; but that conclusion is likely since the verdict reinforced and extended Connecticut's generation-long aversion to hanging women.[48]

The court then turned to consider the case of Jesse Clark, "a Soldier in the Army of the United States" who pleaded guilty to bigamy. Here, where capital punishment was not an issue, the court enforced the letter of the Puritan-inflected statute, sentencing Clark "to be whipped ten stripes on his naked body and branded . . . with the Letter A, on his forehead on a hot iron and to wear a halter about his neck on the outside of his garments during his abode in this State of Connecticut."[49] This penalty, like Washburn's sentence, recalled a Puritan era even more severe than Nathaniel Hawthorne imagined fifty years later in *The Scarlet Letter*.

The policing of sexual transgression, then, intertwined with religious, political, and cultural anxieties. And when it came to "the unnatural connection between the human being and a brute," Federalists like Swift were appalled: "I should hardly have thought it possible, that a human being could be so vile and depraved, as to commit this crime, had I not been present at the trial of a man indicted for it, and against whom the most explicit and convincing proof was adduced." In that particular case owing to the jury's misunderstanding of the law, Swift complained, "this atrocious offender escaped that punishment which he richly merited." As to sodomy between men—"repugnant to every sentiment of decency"—the statute prescribed death. Speaking of the earlier case, Swift noted that sodomy "is very prevalent in corrupt and debauched countries, where the low pleasures of sensuality, and luxury, have depraved the mind, and degraded the appetite below the brutal creation."[50] Evidently the Supreme Court justice who sentenced Washburn, Jesse Root, shared similar views.

Puritan justice seemed to be back, and with a vengeance. In 1796 Massachusetts condemned Farrell to hang, and in early 1797 Governor Samuel Adams and the Governor's Council twice denied the old man's petition for a pardon. And when apocalyptic partisan rhetoric was coming to a climax in 1799, Connecticut authorities sealed Washburn's doom. Mercy for violators of Leviticus' strictures seemed to be missing from awakened Christianity. The late eighteenth-century descendants of the religious enthusiasts who created the Puritan communities of New England reached back to the cultural world of their forefathers in their determination to protect themselves and their posterity from the enlightened cosmopolitan ways that were encroaching on them, their families, and their communities. The sacrifice of two old sinners would merely be collateral damage.

CHAPTER 5

Puritan Twilight in the New England Republics

In second half of the 1790s highly placed New Englanders believed that forces beyond their grasp had launched a broad assault on their world. They watched the resurrection of the old Gallic peril, and this time it was even more menacing than it had been in papist garb; for now it was spreading vicious anti-Christian ideas by musket, sword, and cannon. They suspected that the American fifth column, the Jeffersonians, or as they called it, the French party, was poised to deliver New England's old bastions of the true faith to the ranks of apostasy. Simultaneously they saw their communities threatened by impersonal demographic and economic forces. And so some of them panicked. They resolved to protect their homeland from debauchery and disbelief. They detected conspiracies. They persecuted political dissenters. They launched religious revivals. Moreover they revived the Mosaic code of their ancestors as they set out to hang two men in their eighties for a strange, victimless crime for which no one had been sentenced to hang in their region for well over a century. As a result the two octogenarians languished gloomily in their cells counting the days to their executions. Yet their strange stories each took an unexpected final twist.

In November 1796 Governor Adams and his council had denied the petition Caleb Strong had drafted for his client, most likely because it rehearsed courtroom arguments and sought to exonerate John Farrell. So the determined Caleb Strong had drawn up a second, less confrontational petition for Farrell, "humbly" seeking "the Mercy of the Government" and "compassionate Attention to his unhappy Case." Again lamenting that he, the convicted man, "has no Friends," this petition seemed to admit some culpability, inasmuch as Farrell now declared, "he is not guilty in the Manner which one Witness against him testified." Here Farrell opened the door to the possibility that he had behaved improperly with the dog, but that the testimony against him was flawed. Now, instead of repeating courtroom arguments that the jury had rejected, this second petition stirred compassion by stressing Farrell's declining health and begging "your Excellency and Honours to commiserate a poor, friendless & distressed old Man."[1]

But however piteous, this second petition of Farrell's was no more successful than his first; and on the day after Christmas, December 26, 1796, Governor Samuel Adams, with the advice and consent of the council, issued Farrell's death warrant for February 23, 1797, at Northampton. Nevertheless there would be another chapter—wholly unexpected—in the chronicle of the old man's life. Caleb Strong, Farrell's senior defense attorney, a Federalist, a man known for his compassion and one whose leadership would later be recognized by his election as governor of Massachusetts eleven times, would invent a novel republican remedy to save his client. First he would seek a delay in the scheduled execution and then, if Farrell won a postponement he would use the time to mount a petitioning campaign to save the old Irishman's life. Though Quakers and other foes of slavery in Britain and the United States had recently been using popular petitions to end the slave trade, such petitions had not been aimed at saving the life of an individual criminal and certainly not a man convicted of such a crime as bestiality.

In Massachusetts, certainly, and perhaps everywhere, the strategy Strong invented was unprecedented. He began by drafting yet another appeal for Farrell to sign. But though Strong drafted this third petition, here John Farrell's voice, pathetic and personal, is more resonant than his attorney's; and the plea—perhaps reflecting the convict's growing realization of his fate—is both more modest and impassioned:

I am sorry to trouble your Excellency, and Honors with another petition,—but life is sweet, although I enjoy but few of its comforts—one consolation I have, which is, that I never saw a person in distress, without releaving [sic] him, if it was in my power; and what little property I have been possessed of, has been spent in that way;—but alas! no one appears to releave me: I am quite confounded at the Providence, that reduces me to this distress and ignominy—for I must now declare, in the presence of that God, before whose Bar, I must shortly stand, that I am not guilty of the charge for which I am to die: and that it is a wicked combination to destroy me. I believe there is a God—I believe there is a day of retribution, nor should I dare to appeal to that God—with a lie in my mouth: under these impressions I cannot forbear to mention my innocence—and might I be permitted, should state the impossibility of my guilt under the charge upon which I am convicted—was I in the forenoon of life—it might be more probable—but in the frosty night of old age, it must appear altogether unaccountable.

Farrell concluded his appeal: "I beseech you, extend your compassion to me, and give me time to prepare for my dissolution; restore me to the world, and what little time yet remains of my life, shall be spent in doing good to mankind—and preparing for eternity. I pray your Excellency & Honors to grant me a full Pardon, *or at least for a short time longer than the* [execution] *Warrant gives.*"[2] This time the governor and council responded. Though they refused to overturn the Hampshire County jury by pardoning Farrell, on February 2, 1797—just three weeks before his execution date— they agreed to suspend his hanging for seven weeks to April 13, 1797. They gave the old man ten more weeks to prepare for his doom.

By this time Caleb Strong had come to recognize that Farrell's appeals for mercy and declarations of innocence could not win a pardon. The executive would not reverse both a jury verdict and a Supreme Judicial Court sentence merely on the strength of a convict's assertions of innocence and victimization. To do so could be seen not only as rebuking the Supreme Judicial Court and the Hampshire jury but also as repealing the Massachusetts death penalty for sodomy. Strong knew that the governor and council were mindful of the Enlightenment movement against capital punishment and that they could also be merciful. By granting a delay to allow an offender to prepare his soul, Strong reasoned that the executive could show compassion without compromising the authority of Massachusetts criminal justice.

What Strong had also come to realize was that John Farrell might not in fact be friendless. It was true that no one from Leverett or the adjacent towns had come to his defense or testified as to his character; but before Farrell had come to Leverett he had practiced medicine in Worcester and Hampshire Counties, including a number of the hill towns along the Worcester-Hampshire border. There, Strong discovered, Farrell possessed grateful patients—beneficiaries, perhaps, of Farrell's openhanded practice of relieving people in distress and expecting no fee if his treatment failed.

Figure 20. The Massachusetts governor who weighed Farrell's petitions, Samuel Adams, mezzotint by George Graham from a lost 1795 painting by Major John Johnson. William V. Wells, *The Life and Public Services of Samuel Adams*, vol. 3, frontispiece (Boston, 1865). Courtesy of the American Antiquarian Society.

Using the time won by Farrell's third petition, Strong took advantage of the wintertime pause in farm labor to circulate petitions so that men who knew Farrell could join his plea for mercy.[3]

The result was, according to the records in the Massachusetts Archives, unprecedented in the state's history. Before Strong's petitioning campaign was finished, four new petitions were delivered to Governor Adams and the council, signed by 445 voters and marked by one more. We assume that the weak and distressed John Farrell supplied some key names; but it was Strong, who had earlier drafted Farrell's own petitions, who took the lead. Indeed the petitions that garnered the most signatures—282 and 84 names, respectively—were written in Strong's hand and repeated Strong's arguments from Farrell's first and third petitions, petitions that were also in Strong's hand. Evidently, Caleb Strong believed not only that his client was innocent of the crime for which he had been convicted but that to execute Farrell would disgrace Massachusetts justice.

Yet what is most remarkable in these new, citizens' petitions are not Caleb Strong's words but the personal testimonials supplied by men who knew the ancient physician. One hundred five men from Worcester County, eleven from the town of Boylston (population 839 in 1790), attested that they "have been acquainted with . . . John Farrel for about four Years past, and have never known of his behaving himself in an Obscene manner but on the contrary has behaved Himself as a peaceable member of Society—and that He has been peculiarly successful in the cure of that Fatal disease the Cancer." One petitioner was the former pastor and sometime physician Ebenezer Morse, expelled from his pulpit as a Loyalist in 1775, though he later served in the Continental army. Now this seventy-nine-year-old Harvard graduate and his son joined their ardent Patriot townsman and recent representative in the legislature Major Ezra Beaman to seek Farrell's pardon. Together with the locally powerful tavern-keeping Bush family, and others who had helped suppress Shays's Rebellion, these men asked that Farrell be spared "as a Blessing to Society."[4]

Farrell's advocates also included prominent former Shaysites, for the next largest group—seven signers—came from Daniel Shays's Pelham, a community of eleven hundred people in the Hampshire County uplands not more than ten miles south of Leverett. Here Farrell had practiced his medicine before coming to Leverett, and here ten men, virtually all of Protestant Irish origin, stood up for Farrell the Irish immigrant. One was the same John Conkey who had been called as a witness at Farrell's trial.

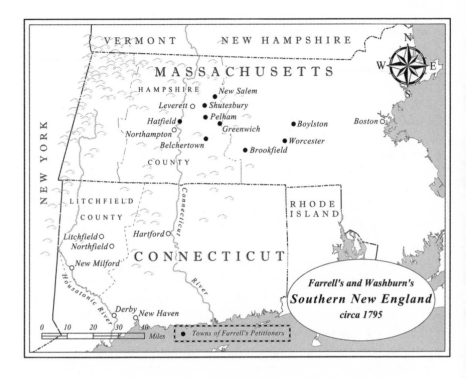

Figure 21. Caleb Strong found supporters for John Farrell in neighboring towns in Hampshire and Worcester Counties in western and central Massachusetts. Created by Brian Perchal, Cartographer, University of Connecticut Libraries, Map and Geographic Information Center (MAGIC).

Perhaps Conkey regretted his testimony; or he may have believed the trial had wrongly led to Farrell's conviction. Whatever Conkey's reasoning, he added his signature to those of men from Belchertown, Boylston, Greenwich, Hatfield, New Salem, Shutesbury, and Worcester.

Since about 40 percent of Pelham men had been Shaysites, according to the best estimate, it is not surprising that at least one of Farrell's petitioners can be confirmed as an insurgent who took the state's oath of allegiance in 1787. Indeed he with seven others had petitioned to save the life of fellow rebel Henry McCulloch when he was sentenced to hang. Moreover, the selfsame McCulloch now joined the petition to Governor Adams to save

Farrell's life, asking clemency for the old Irishman just as ten years earlier Governor Hancock had spared his life with a pardon.[5]

An even more detailed testimonial came in from Brookfield (population thirty-one hundred in 1790), a Worcester County town about thirty-five miles east of Pelham. Here, David Thomas headed a list of eighteen voters who wrote:

> He [Farrell] is already far advanced in age, said to be 85 years: according to the common course of nature he cannot long continue. Since our knowledge of him, his usual business has been the administration of relief and affecting [sic] the cures of cancers. Of his abilities we cannot entertain a doubt. One of your excellency's memorialists . . . David Thomas, had long been afflicted by a formidable cancer. It had already destroyed one of his eyes and he had every reason to expect a period must soon have been put to his life. Every effort had been made, every experiment tried, which was and could be devised by a great number of physicians. . . . But all were fruitless and unavailing till providentially he heard of Farrell's skill and success in combatting [sic] the direful malady. To him application was made & (under God) to him your memorialist attributes the preservation of his life and the restoration to comfortable health. Skill and talents of this man in curing cancers are conceived to be great indeed, and we earnestly wish that he might be preserved for the relief of those in society who are or may unhappily be afflicted by that terrible disorder. Short, at the longest, must be the remainder of the poor old man. Being spared he may however render some further services. He may be made the instrument of saving some other lives and possibly may communicate a knowledge of his art to some other physician and thereby render a service to the human race. The memorialists are therefore induced most respectfully to solicit your excellency that . . . John Farrell may receive a pardon and escape ignominious death to which he is now sentenced.[6]

This disinterested plea appealed to the enlightened interests of the community; and it came from people who were convinced that just as the condemned man had served the public in the past he could do so again. The citizens of Massachusetts, these petitions argued, had a stake in saving Farrell from the gallows.

In contrast to Farrell's own petitions, the four new petitions coming from 446 men evidently weighed powerfully against the judgment of the twelve trial jurors. Collected in the space of barely one month, together these petitions supported three principles that traditionally sustained pardons: the convict possessed a reputation for good character, the evidence against him was tainted by malice and self-interest, and finally if his life were spared he would serve the community as he had done before. Interestingly, though many New Englanders doubted the wisdom of punishing sodomy with death, and indeed eight years later the legislature would vote to reduce the penalty to life in prison, none of the petitions challenged the existing law. Apparently it was more effective to provide reasons to justify a pardon than to confront the Supreme Judicial Court and ask the executive to nullify the statute by arguing against the verdict.

The deliberations of Governor Adams and the council are not recorded, but they voted to reverse their decision. On March 8, 1797, in consideration of the humble supplications of "John Farrell & also a number of the good Citizens of the Commonwealth," the seventy-four-year-old Revolutionary hero Samuel Adams erased the aged physician's death warrant with a full pardon. At a time when other states had reduced the penalty for sodomy—action Massachusetts would finally take in 1804—the state's highest officials decided to accede to the pleas of so many of its citizens. As a result Farrell's story has a happy ending.

But if in the region where the Puritan flashback was most powerful one of Massachusetts's most prominent leaders had not taken up Farrell's cause and pursued it vigorously, the state would have hanged Farrell on the gallows at Northampton on February 23, 1797. Notwithstanding the doubts of Jeffersonians and qualms among the cosmopolitan Federalist elite, almost exactly one century after the Salem witchcraft debacle, Massachusetts criminal justice would have again distinguished itself for injustice and cruelty. In 1797 as in 1692, Massachusetts law and society stood poised between old values and new ones—and in 1797 as in 1692 old ways embedded in old law possessed a lingering legitimacy reinforced by inertia. In such a time of unrest, where religious and partisan divisions were shaking New England's elite, officials and ordinary citizens had found safety in adhering to law rather than departing from it or quietly ignoring it. The same could certainly be said in England where in the generation after Massachusetts's 1805 abolition of the death penalty for Farrell's crime no fewer than fifty men were hanged for sodomy.[7] But the Puritan flashback in Massachusetts was only a brief echo of the counterrevolutionary fervor that overtook the mother country. Yes, as late as 1796 there were citizens ready to accuse and officials ready to prosecute an old man, not for witchcraft, but for an almost equally improbable crime. Farrell found enemies in Leverett, but his earlier work as a doctor had made him so many friends in central Massachusetts that their signatures saved his life. The citizens of Massachusetts approached the edge of the Puritan abyss. But at the last moment their reason and mercy prevailed.

Would Gideon Washburn be equally fortunate? Washburn's attorneys appealed to the Connecticut legislature to reverse the old man's conviction and sentence, declaring he was "utterly ignorant of his guilt . . . and is insensible of having ever done the facts charged before him." This argument, which did not challenge the factual testimony of the courtroom, allowed Washburn to plead for mercy on a *non compos mentis* basis, while also showing repentance. This approach was time tested, for if pardon claims were to succeed in the early republic, convicted offenders could rarely claim complete innocence for fear of appearing unrepentant and therefore undeserving of mercy. Nor could they admit their guilt openly for fear of confirming court decisions. If, as Washburn's attorneys hoped, the legislature were persuaded by his claim of no memory of the events, the representatives could pardon him as not having criminal responsibility; moreover, if the legislature were persuaded that Washburn was in fact guilty, they could reward the old man's contrition with a merciful pardon. The petition described Washburn as "debilitated and deranged"; surely an octogenarian who was *non compos mentis* could not be held criminally responsible for his actions.

In the meantime, as he awaited the decision of the Connecticut House of Representatives and Council of Assistants, Washburn's five months in the Litchfield jail—August through mid-January—undermined the old man's health. The conditions of his Litchfield confinement were notoriously pitiful. During the Revolution the last royal governor of New Jersey, Benjamin Franklin's son, William Franklin, had spent long months locked in the selfsame jail: "a most noisome filthy Room . . . the very worst Gaol in America. In this Dungeon, for I can call it no other, it having often been appropriated to condemn'd Criminals, I was closely confined for about eight Months, overrun and molested with the many kinds of Vermin, debarred of Pen, Ink, and Paper and of all Conversation with every Person,

except now and then, a few Words with the Sheriff, Gaoler, or Centries. . . .
My Victuals was generally pok'd thro' a Hole in the Door."[8] Indeed as the
weeks passed Washburn's health deteriorated. Reuben Webster, his jailer,
charged the state $25.66 for boarding Washburn for twenty-three weeks and
three days, adding additional health-related costs: $0.34 for going to get
Litchfield's physician, Daniel Sheldon, to make two jailhouse calls at $2.50
each; and $4.00 more for "Tending Sd Washburn in his sickness." Webster
also charged the state an additional $11.50 to supply some heat for the jail
and to "lighte Candles in the Night," explaining that Washburn was "un-
well moste of the time."[9]

In preparation for the hanging, Sheriff Lynde Lord ordered construction of a gallows in Litchfield. For the first time the town would provide
the stage for a dramatic public execution of a sexual offender. But Litchfield
County residents did not finally share in the moral instruction and psychological catharsis promised by the execution of Gideon Washburn. Instead,
just five days before the old man was scheduled to pay for his sins on the
scaffold, he died in jail. As the *Litchfield Monitor* reported, "*Death* . . .
suddenly stepped in" on January 12 to visit the man who "was to have
expiated his crimes at the gallows." Though the *Monitor* commented that
"the unreflecting and pitiless" would be disappointed to miss a hanging,
the town of Litchfield would be spared the "bustle, pain and expense of a
public execution."[10]

The *Monitor* injected a note of mystery by reporting that two days
before Washburn died, when his family visited him in jail, they "discovered
no unusual gloom or debility." His collapse had been sudden. Only when
jailer Reuben Webster came to feed him Saturday morning, January 11, did
he discover Washburn, "stupid and insensible," a condition that persisted
until he died the next day. In his official report Sheriff Lord noted that
"Gideon Washburn being confined in Litchfield County Gaol until the 11th
day of January 1800, When the said Gideon was found in the Room in
which he was confined (Speechless & Supposed to be in a fitt) in which
state he remained until the 12th day of said January when he Expired." The
next day, Lord commented further, "(being fully convinced he was dead) I
delivered the Body of the said Gideon, to his Son William Washburn to be
buried as his friends and Connections thought Proper." The *Monitor*
invited readers to ask whether Washburn's "solitary, *night reflections*,
produced agitations of mind too mighty for human frailty,—or whether
he was precipitated into eternity by any criminal desperate means." That

question, it concluded, "will probably remain unsettled speculation." Washburn's "mysterious exit," the *Monitor* opined, was "an apt counterpart to his life and character."[11]

Sheriff Lord turned Washburn's body over to his family for burial; but there is no record that he was interred in one of Litchfield's cemeteries. In the past men executed for bestiality had been buried ignominiously with the carcasses of their sexual partners, not in cemeteries but in out-of-the-way locations, a stigma marking that they did not deserve to be buried among humans. Since society had considered the animal to be a partner in sin, authorities had often followed the biblical command, "if a man lie with a beast, he shall surely be put to death: and ye shall slay the beast." Young Benjamin Goad had to witness the mare he had penetrated "knocked in the head under the Gallows," before his own execution in 1674. Cotton Mather reported in the late seventeenth century that authorities required a man from Weymouth, Massachusetts, to witness the hanging of his sexual consorts: three sheep, two sows, two heifers, and a cow, before he himself was put to death. A century later the laws were virtually unchanged. Zephaniah Swift commented in 1796 that "the statute inflicts the punishment of death on the offender, and to inspire the deepest detestation of the deed, directs that the very beast shall be slain and buried." In other times and places officials had consigned the offending beast to fire. Burning the animal served the threefold purposes of punishing bestial lust, cleansing by fire, and removing all physical remains of the transgression. As Jeremy Bentham wryly noted, "Some persons have been for burning the poor animal with great ceremony under the notion of burning the remembrance of the affair. A more simple and . . . more effectual course to take would be not to meddle or make smoke."[12] Yet notwithstanding the statute there is no record of ritual killing of Washburn's barnyard partners, nor of a joint burial of the old man and the animals. The sheriff delivered the corpse to William Washburn's family and he must have found a private way to inter the corpse—perhaps on his Northfield farm. If William still possessed the animals in question there is no evidence that he destroyed them, so they probably lived on at his farm since they would have been hard to sell locally.

The trial and its aftermath tainted the Washburns and hastened the family's departure from Litchfield. A little over a year after Gideon's death, in March 1801, William Washburn sold his entire property to four buyers for a total of £788. Now aged forty-four, he moved north to make a fresh start. Two years later, on February 25, 1803, his mother, Gideon's wife,

Esther Alling Washburn, died; and later that year Washburn's final effort to retain the Sanford property failed when the Connecticut Supreme Court of Errors rejected his appeal of a lower court ruling that had awarded the land to yet another man. Discredited in Litchfield, the Washburns settled in Middlebury, Vermont, a hilly town settled mostly by migrants from the New England interior. William Washburn's name appears on the town's census in 1810, but soon after he went west to scout for a new home and his name disappears from the record, perhaps owing to his own death. His wife, Rachel (McDonald), remained in Middlebury until her death on April 20, 1841. Buried among McDonalds, Gideon's daughter-in-law was the only Washburn in the town's cemetery.[13]

The prosecution and punishment of Gideon Washburn remains puzzling. On the surface Washburn's guilt—and hence his trial and punishment—seems undeniable. Washburn was observed committing the crime and he was given a fair trial according to contemporary standards. Highly respected lawyers defended him and no procedural error tainted his conviction by a jury of his peers. Yet the accusations, the proceedings, the verdict, and the sentence leave questions. Washburn steadfastly denied the allegations to the end. Unlike many criminals who pleaded "not guilty" in court, after his conviction the old man never did acknowledge guilt by confessing and seeking God's pardon. Moreover, though his family must have felt shamed by their connection to a man dishonored by an unspeakable crime, they stood by him to the very end.[14]

Remarkably, Washburn's indictment charged that he had engaged in bestial sexual acts over a period of four years, prompting the question as to why behavior that had been overlooked for years demanded prosecution in 1799. Why would neighbors apparently tolerate the crime for several years and then join together to go to the justice of the peace to make accusations? If bestiality was as heinous as the indictment declared, then the first or second witness should have come forward years earlier to report the old man who was mounting Northfield cows and mares. It is possible the recurrence of incidents led to the decision to accuse; but we doubt that repetition was critical since bestiality is such a singular crime—having always been treated as so "unnatural" as to be unlike other nonviolent sexual offenses. Nor is there reason to suppose Litchfield people experienced a radical transformation in sexual attitudes between 1796 and 1799. More likely Litchfield leaders, like those throughout New England in the eighteenth century, would have quashed such an outlandish capital indictment in times past; but in 1799 they felt compelled to enforce the old bestiality law to the letter. Washburn's jailhouse death raises additional questions. The fortunate timing of his demise may well have been coincidental—after all, the old man had been failing throughout his incarceration, and anticipation of his immanent trip to the gallows must have put him under extraordinary stress. Yet skeptics at the time recognized that preempting the hangman as Washburn did made a better end for the condemned man, his family, and the community. By dying in jail Washburn evaded the public humiliation and prolonged pain of hanging; and his wife and family were not only spared that ordeal but also escaped some of the shame his punishment brought. Thomas Collier, publisher of the *Monitor*, as noted, pointed out that the Litchfield community was spared the expense of execution, an occasion that would have brought to the village thousands of spectators from neighboring towns to join in the ominous proceedings. Although Collier lacked evidence, he raised the question of whether Washburn's death was natural. He invited his readers to speculate, as to whether a member of the shamed family poisoned the old man, or whether, as James Morris reported fifteen years later, Washburn had committed suicide. Certainly, the sheriff's affidavit reporting the death said nothing to suggest suicide or murder. In our judgment it is more likely that, because Washburn was an ailing eighty-four-year-old living in conditions that made healthy men sick, and since the jailer had to call the town's physician twice to attend to Washburn in jail, the old man died of natural causes "in a fit"; nonetheless, the possibility of foul play remains.[15]

The court described Washburn as a vicious old man who had squandered God's gift of "long life and many days," who had instead chosen to "grow gray in the vile drudgery of sin and Satan." Newspapers broadcast this official portrait. Nevertheless Washburn's case had attracted the attention—and participation—of some of the state's leading politicians. Aligned on both sides, none feared that participation in this bestiality trial would tarnish their prestige. U.S. Senator Tracy lined up against Congressman John Allen and the renowned Pierpont Edwards, perhaps the most prominent Republican in Connecticut. That the Jeffersonians' distinguished leader would join with a Federalist just back from Congress so as to defend an unsavory old man reveals the importance of capital cases and this one in particular.[16] It appears the Connecticut elite recognized that a capital trial for bestiality demanded their best talent so as to assure that the conduct of the trial would not dishonor their state. To cosmopolitans, it was bad enough that the trial was proceeding at all; the least they could do was make certain it was conducted according to the highest legal standards.

Court day in Litchfield usually attracted "an uncommon number of strangers" from neighboring towns, and Washburn's case spurred popular curiosity. This trial spectacle enabled elite gentlemen to win attention and respect, one reason, perhaps, men of such eminence took part. The Washburn case was not a simple reenactment of the partisan conflict of the 1790s. Prominent Federalists were part of both prosecution and defense. And yet partisanship was at play. Tracy, one of the prosecutors, was a leader of the establishment, whereas Washburn's defender, Allen, though a Federalist, was now an outsider on a steep downward slide. When the Federalist prosecution argued in favor of the death penalty for Washburn and the Jeffersonian Edwards opposed such severe seventeenth-century-style punishment, each was expressing the prevailing tendency of his party in Connecticut. Indirectly the trial provided another stage for political positioning at a moment when bitter partisan conflict in Litchfield, in Connecticut, and in New England tore at the fabric of republican society.[17]

Gideon Washburn was not, as we understand the facts, an innocent victim or in any sense a martyr. More likely Washburn became demented in his old age and turned to a not-so-covert expression of bestiality until finally, besieged by the complaints of neighbors angered by William Washburn's land grab, officials arrested and indicted the old man. Still, lacking the witnesses' specific testimony, evidence is limited to the claims of the indictment; so Connecticut's insistence on executing this marginal eighty-four-year-old man invites further reflection. Surely it is significant that although the legislature did not end the death penalty for sodomy or bestiality for another generation (1821), no Connecticut judge ever again sentenced anyone, young or old, to die for committing such an act. Evidently the divisions in the Connecticut legislature concerning Washburn's execution were emblematic of the ambivalence some leaders felt regarding the severity of the Puritan-era sanctions.

Had it not been for the petitioning campaign that generated such broad citizen support for Farrell's pardon, providing the Massachusetts governor and council with a republican justification for granting clemency, Massachusetts, like Connecticut, would have insisted on executing an old man for a scandalous but nonviolent, victimless crime. Even so, many did not have the stomach to execute Farrell. Three years later, at the peak of apocalyptic Puritan flashback, Connecticut authorities erected gallows to execute Washburn. However, even if the state had hanged Gideon Washburn as planned, there is no reason to believe die-hard Federalists and Congregationalists thought such a performance would restore the old New England way. Apart from Washburn's family, no one seemed to care about Washburn's fate, so memories of his trial, condemnation, and death faded; they did not survive even in local lore. As with Farrell's trial, Washburn's condemnation never found its way into local history.[18]

Although some Federalists invoked the Puritan legacy, they did so selectively and inconsistently. Puritan Connecticut had punished the crime of adultery with death in 1650, but since that date no such sentence had ever been carried out, and gentlemen—even Zephaniah Swift—now agreed such a penalty was unreasonable. In his 1796 treatise this oracle of Connecticut law wrote that the state's capital list was too long. It still included homicide, treason, rape, sodomy, bestiality, dismemberment, and arson leading to fatality. In his view "the dreadful punishment of death ought only to be inflicted on treason and murder."[19] Swift also condemned adultery, but he qualified his censure in terms that would have scandalized Connecticut's founders. According to Swift "there are frequent instances of men, who disregard the principles of chastity, but in other respects conduct with propriety." No wonder, then, that he explicitly criticized "the spirit of puritanism" when he explained Connecticut's statute proscribing lewd and lascivious behavior. Swift opined that "the gloominess of their [Puritan] manners was heightened by the singular opinions they entertained respecting social pleasure." Puritans were so wrongheaded, Swift claimed, "they considered the joys of love, to be in a great measure inconsistent with the grace of God; they reprobated the appetites of men, and many entertained the whimsical idea, that the husband should not indulge in the conjugal act in the arms of his wife, with any other view than procreation." Without recognizing the Puritan tendency of his own thinking Swift went even further—referring to the "blue laws, respecting which so many laughable stories have been told." By striving for "the greatest purity of manners," Puritans had gone too far—embracing "such whimsical ideas, respecting the impurity of the sexual passion."[20]

Remarkably, Swift in his unconscious way displayed the conflicting tendencies affecting New England's rulers. By embracing Beccarian reforms the elite deliberately narrowed the scope of capital punishment. As Swift's remarks suggest and as the record of prosecutions confirms, criminal trials for nonviolent sexual offenses were fading out. Consequently by the late 1790s the Farrell and Washburn trials were possible only in jurisdictions where, due to extraordinary strains, the Puritan cultural heritage outweighed Beccarian enlightenment. As we have seen, the people of both Hampshire and Litchfield Counties were living through a fundamental shift away from traditional, semi-subsistence farming and toward market-oriented agriculture, where commerce and industry, once subordinate to farming, were now becoming dominant. Simultaneously consumption-centered standards of respectability and the intensification and democratization of genteel expectations were undermining their traditional values.

In Hampshire and Litchfield Counties cosmopolitan urbanity was gaining the upper hand, challenging rustic, old-fashioned ways of life. Ultimately these deep cultural conflicts pitted a backward-looking, "restorationist" Puritanism against the commercial and cosmopolitan values expressed in Enlightenment ideology and liberal Protestantism.[21] Even the most provincial Federalists pursued commercial prosperity and experienced the tension between desire and self-discipline in an acute personal way. The challenges to the society they regarded as literally their own—communities bequeathed to them by their fathers—were not merely worrisome; it was alarming. When the rising Jeffersonian party avidly embraced radical ideas inspired by the French Revolution and advocated them throughout the nation, the Federalist elite panicked. They were convinced they faced an existential threat. In Hampshire and Litchfield Counties especially, epicenters for the Puritan revival, this traditional elite believed legal procedures provided the only barrier against disorder.

In Massachusetts and Connecticut, two republics threatened by rural uprisings as recently as 1787, the rule of law—enforced to the letter—appeared to be the only ark of safety. It was in these exceptional circumstances that in 1796 and 1799 they prosecuted bestiality as a capital crime. Anxious over religious decline and their own diminishing political power, worried by the seeming corruption of morals, and troubled by geographic mobility, ethnic diversity, and the destabilizing effects of capitalism on the social order, officials could not deny, resist, or shelve accusations brought by their neighbors. No, they must follow the law, even if the statute was a Puritan holdover that contradicted the enlightened Beccarian principles that were sweeping over New England and the whole United States, principles that they themselves mostly embraced. In our judgment, prosecuting two octogenarians who dwelled at the margins did not represent a full-scale rejection of the Enlightenment; instead it was a nostalgic spasm, a gesture toward an imagined New England past they felt slipping away as their region joined in the bourgeois gentility of the new order.

Unlike the notorious case of Jean Calas, the French Protestant whose brutal torture and execution by Catholics in 1761–62 Voltaire made into an Enlightenment *cause célèbre*, neither John Farrell nor Gideon Washburn would gain recognition as a martyr to the Puritan revival. Federalists found nothing to trumpet as victory in either case; they preferred to make an issue of France and the XYZ diplomatic affair. And for Republicans neither of the two old convicts could be fashioned into a useful hero. For Republicans the Sedition Act of 1798 was far more productive as the epitome of Federalist tyranny. Political freedom, after all, was an issue far more resonant and respectable than the draconian prosecution of sodomy. The Puritan flashback of the 1790s faded quickly.

Regardless of the fears that worried so many of interior New England's residents and notwithstanding the rhetoric of their clergymen and politicians, New England in the 1790s was vastly different from a century earlier. Four generations and a Revolution had made the entire region a much larger, more cosmopolitan society—one that was more thoroughly commercial, secular, and enlightened than in the era of witchcraft and sodomy trials and executions. Population statistics are revealing: the combined populations of Connecticut and Massachusetts barely approached 100,000 people in 1700, whereas by 1800 they had grown to over 825,000 people.[22] In 1800 most people were still descended from Puritan migrants, but now there were many whose families had arrived more recently, chiefly from the British Isles, including Scotland and Ireland, but there were also Huguenots directly from France and via England, as well as Germans, Africans, and others from around the Atlantic world; some were Catholics and there were even a few Jews. Whereas late seventeenth-century Puritans could imagine that criminal enforcement could restore John Winthrop's vision, where they could "worke as one man" and "entertaine each other in brotherly Affection," not even the most vigorous rearguard warriors like Jedidiah Morse could imagine such a restoration in the 1790s.

Moreover, however reluctant the orthodox clergy had been to accept different faiths, by the 1790s the region had become pluralistic in religion, both in fact and in law. Even the most retrograde Trinitarian reactionary recognized that a measure of religious tolerance was legitimate. Now everyone agreed that the execution of four Quakers by Massachusetts authorities in the previous century had been wrong, as had been the execution of witches in both colonies. Though the Congregational churches still fought for a privileged position in both states, taxes now supported several denominations; even the once-proscribed Roman Catholics could practice their religion openly and proselytize freely. Indeed the intensity of fears over Deists and freethinkers was fueled by the fact that by the 1790s some leading men embraced such ideas and they could be found almost everywhere. Already the seeds of the Unitarian and Universalist movements, which would flower in the next two decades, especially in eastern Massachusetts, were sprouting.

Social customs, too, in the 1790s bore little resemblance to those of Cotton Mather's Boston or Solomon Stoddard's Northampton. As in Litchfield and Northampton, elegant balls and assemblies proliferated all over New England, supplying platforms for the new and growing elite to display their refined manners and elegant dress. They reveled in precisely the worldly vanity condemned by Puritans and New Divinity evangelicals. They even went further. The people who joined and promoted this outward-looking, cosmopolitan mind-set created and enrolled in a host of institutions to supply a foundation for their new customs—shouldering aside the preeminence of the meetinghouse. The beginnings of this shift in society started decades before independence when enlightened gentlemen founded academies, social libraries, and Masonic lodges: but it was not until the 1790s that groups like these were multiplying rapidly all over southern New England and in newly settled parts of northern New England. Now almost everywhere there were nondenominational organizations that bore only the slightest tinge of religion.

Consequently prosecutions like those against Farrell and Washburn had become anachronistic because the cultural outlook of the early republic was so profoundly different from the Puritan era. When one considers the reading matter now widely available and widely consumed—by women as well as men—the contrast with the prior century reveals a changed outlook. Whereas religion had been virtually the only subject of New Englanders' reading matter a century earlier—theology and religious disputation for learned men and devotional works for everyone else—now newspapers and a flourishing market in pamphlets and books supplied everything from current events and diplomatic affairs to history, political theory and law, and natural sciences, *belles lettres* and poetry as well as novels. The newspapers, which were now operating in county seats such as Northampton and Litchfield, were vehicles of cosmopolitan commerce, providing advertisements for a wide array of imported consumer goods, from French brandy and Indian spices to English and Irish textiles, glassware, crockery, brassware, looking glasses, hardware, and wallpaper. Clergymen warned from time to time that luxury was corrupting the morals of parishioners, and some of their parishioners nodded in agreement. But the very same people came to the meetinghouse dressed in their finest broadcloths and linens, and entertained pastors in their drawing rooms with tea served on china as they sat on mahogany chairs and settees upholstered in silk.[23]

New Englanders' outlook was not only far more cosmopolitan and worldly, it was also more widely and variously informed. Everywhere the Federalist press competed alongside Jeffersonian papers. And while the reading of secular books did not reach into every household, book sales and the formation of libraries demonstrated a substantial eagerness to reach beyond the local clergy for knowledge of the world. Enlightenment optimism—so heavily criticized by Calvinists—buttressed much of this activity. In the 1760s John Adams had demanded in the newspaper to "let every sluice of knowledge be opened and set a-flowing"; by the time he became president his command had become a reality.[24]

When the Presbyterian pastor Samuel Miller came to write his *Brief Retrospect of the Eighteenth Century* (1805) he reported that "printing presses have not only become numerous in the populous cities . . . but also in remote parts of the country"; and he went on to extol the "unprecedented and wonderful multiplication of books," which "has rendered the means of information more easy of access, and more popular." While Miller, as a good Calvinist, had some misgivings—he called this "The Age of Superficial Learning"—he judged "there never was an age in which knowledge of various kinds was so *popular* and so generally *diffused*." Indeed he was as optimistic as a Calvinist could be, concluding that the eighteenth century witnessed "a larger portion of human society enlightened, polished, and comfortable, than ever before."[25] John Adams would sum up this perspective when he remarked to Thomas Jefferson, "we may say that the Eighteenth Century, notwithstanding all its Errors and Vices has been, of all that are past, the most honourable to human Nature." Like Miller, he celebrated advances in secular affairs: "Knowledge and Virtues were increased and diffused, Arts, Sciences useful to Men, ameliorating their condition, were improved, more than in any former equal Period."[26] Jefferson shared Adams's "eulogies on the eighteenth century," believing "it certainly witnessed the sciences and arts, manners and morals, advanced to a higher degree than the world had ever before seen."[27]

Adams and Jefferson were, of course, quasi-Unitarians; but even orthodox Christians like Yale's Ezra Stiles shared a similar, millennial-inflected optimism. His sermon to the Connecticut General Assembly on Election Day in 1783, *The United States Elevated to Glory and Honor*, expressed enthusiasm for America's political transformation and the progress it heralded. Certainly there were skeptics who did not share Stiles's or Adams's hopefulness. Stiles was, after all, succeeded at Yale by the fiery Dwight; but New Englanders no longer thought of themselves as "sinners in the hands of an angry God" who must direct their thoughts to prepare for an immanent "day of doom." Evangelical revival sermons strove to revitalize acute religious anxieties, but even Dwight and his followers also sought to energize converted sinners with the optimistic message that salvation might come to every true believer.

In hard times the legislatures of Connecticut and Massachusetts still turned to days of "fasting and prayer" for the well-being of their communities. But by the 1790s the fast-day sermons and messages no longer expressed the old Puritan conviction that God would visit destruction on communities that failed to strike down violators of the Mosaic code. In the first place the belief in collective responsibility had given way to a more individualistic belief system, in which offenders, not their communities, possessed exclusive responsibility for violations. This Lockean, liberal individualism did not permeate everyone everywhere, but it was an underlying assumption of elite cosmopolitan leaders. These were the people whose views toward the punishment of violations of social codes—shaped by the ideas of Montesquieu and Beccaria—were guided by humanitarian values and practical outcomes rather than Leviticus. Like Montesquieu, New England political leaders in the early republic came to believe that policing sexual misconduct—adultery, fornication, even sodomy—by social sanctions like scorn and contempt were more appropriate than legal proceedings, the whipping post, and gallows. Though Federalists worried that radical politics and religious apostasy threatened the republic, few believed that prosecuting sexual misbehavior would save the nation.

Under these circumstances the seemingly sensational bestiality cases in Northampton and Litchfield proved sensational for those communities only. In contrast to the Jay Treaty controversy of 1794–95 and the XYZ Affair in 1798 that led to a quasi war with France, neither case commanded substantial attention in the press. Nor was news of Farrell and Washburn widely disseminated. And after the two guilty verdicts were pronounced, no printer in Northampton or Litchfield published a trial report pamphlet to gratify the curiosity market. Though their trials required some graphic sexual testimony, a prerequisite for conviction in both cases, and though all capital cases were sufficiently rare and serious to generate unusual attention, printers evidently saw no commercial advantage in either of these extraordinary sexual misconduct trials. Indeed it is striking that even though the strains that wracked the interior of New England were powerful and profound, the cases of Farrell and Washburn did not generate any wider panic or scapegoating. The rhetoric of their time was, people recognized, inflated. In opposing the Jay Treaty the Jeffersonian Republicans had cried: "Damn John Jay! Damn everyone who won't damn John Jay!! Damn everyone that won't put lights in his windows and sit up all night damning John Jay!!!" And in 1798, the Federalist press cried: "Millions for defense, but not a cent for tribute!" The words were incendiary, but Federalist and clerical firebrands knew that Jeffersonians sprouted horns only in Federalist polemics; Satan, they knew, was not lurking in every dark corner. Using the law to enforce the boundaries of correct sexual behavior, frequent in the seventeenth century, now declined sharply across the eighteenth century and, though it lingered, it was finally subsiding. In counties where cosmopolitan and commercial values dominated, such criminal prosecutions had all but disappeared. Even in the interior region, where the orthodox revival most nearly paid homage to the Puritan era, prosecutions were in decline. In Massachusetts the record shows that accusers and justices of the peace chiefly prosecuted behavior, such as adultery, that not only disrupted social order but could also result in tax consequences in the form of town support for bastard children.

As the world seemed in the grips of French apostasy and the French faction in America was poised to take over, anxious citizens in the New England interior fought back by trying to revive the spirit of their Puritan forefathers. But the prosecutions of Farrell and Washburn demonstrate the limits of the Puritan flashback. Instead of signaling the return of the old order, the extraordinary proceedings turned out to have been isolated reminders of Puritan severity, possible only in the New England interior, where evangelicals were reimagining the Puritan way and where local elites, fearful of threats to their power from "Jacobins" and "Deists," decided that strict adherence to the law must be their bulwark. The 1790s sequel to the fierce Puritan project of the previous century featured paranoid outbursts and a readiness to take the lives of marginal old men who may indeed have committed bestiality. But just as the Federalist clergy's panic over the Bavarian Illuminati conspiracy swiftly collapsed and faded away, so, too, did the intensity of concern over bestiality and sodomy. The trials and convictions of John Farrell and Gideon Washburn were grotesque aberrations from the early republican commitment to enlightened justice. By the time the legislatures of both states abolished the death penalty for sodomy, Massachusetts in 1805 and the more conservative Connecticut in 1821, such a punishment for such a crime was only a memory.

Had Farrell and Washburn been executed they would have been, we believe, the oldest men executed in American history. Farrell was saved from the gallows by the shrewd and persistent efforts of Caleb Strong, the future long-time governor of Massachusetts—a man who, though a native of the very Northampton where Farrell was convicted and a Federalist, was nevertheless a leader of enlarged, cosmopolitan sympathies. Strong's petitioning campaign opened a republican path for Samuel Adams and the Governor's Council to allow enlightenment and mercy to override statute law and so save Massachusetts from reviving memories of its seventeenth-century atrocities.[28] In Connecticut, where no one mounted a similar campaign for Washburn, a man for whom no praise was ever publicly spoken, the question was settled in the political arena of the legislature, where the state's Court of Assistants overturned the lower house's temporary stay of execution. Evidently a majority of Connecticut's elite who gathered in the upper house were too fearful to follow the lead of a Caleb Strong; so they set their state up to become the last one to enforce the Puritans' bloody, "Mosaical" code by executing a man for bestial intercourse. That Washburn's natural death spared Connecticut this dishonor was, perhaps, an act of Providence.

NOTES

Introduction

1. At least from the time of the Greeks and in contrast to biblical proscription, tolerant sexual sensibilities have taught openness toward varied sexual tastes. Yet intercourse with animals—though very much part of ancient Greek mythology—has been regularly classified as a sexual perversion. Animal rights philosopher Peter Singer believes the reason sex with animals has remained a taboo through the ages originates in the persistent human anxiety, proclaimed in Ecclesiastes, questioning whether humankind is really superior to beasts. (Ecclesiastes, chapter 3, verse 19 notes: "Surely the fate of human beings is like that of the animals; the same fate awaits them both.") Singer argues that our doubts on this score have some foundation, since fundamentally human beings cannot help behaving like other mammals: "We copulate, as they do. They have penises and vaginas, as we do, and the fact that the vagina of a calf can be sexually satisfying to a man shows how similar these organs are. The taboo on sex with animals may . . . have originated as part of a broader rejection of non-reproductive sex. But the vehemence with which this prohibition continues to be held, its persistence while other non-reproductive sexual acts have become acceptable, suggests that there is another powerful force at work: our desire to differentiate ourselves, erotically and in every other way, from animals." Singer's insight suggests that some of those who engage in sex with animals are seeking to undo the ancient social, cultural, and legal taboos. Peter Singer, "Heavy Petting," *Nerve* (March–April 2001), http://www.utilitarian.net/ singer/by/2001----.htm, accessed March 3, 2011. Mark Matthews called for precisely such revision in *The Horseman: Obsessions of a Zoophile*, a 1994 autobiographical account of his lifelong passion for sex with horses. Mark Matthews, *The Horseman: Obsessions of a Zoophile* (New York: Prometheus Books, 1994). Campaigning for "Equality for All," practitioners of sex with animals claim they are merely following in the footsteps of the gay liberation movement, and that their struggle is the next chapter in the battle for sexual liberation. Though psychiatric classification treats attraction to animals as an aberrant pathology, some of those who practice bestiality have taken to calling themselves defenders of animal rights who "yearn to live with animals as partners and love them as equal creatures." Equality for All website, http://www.equalityforall.net/en/, accessed March 3, 2011.

We find such assertions outlandish, but we recognize that bestiality is in fact another, albeit extreme, alternative form of human sexual taste. Yet no fair discussion of the phenomenon can ignore the ethical questions raised by the practice. The contemporary porn industry, catering to the sadistic tastes of its audience, has produced horrific, dehumanizing, and humiliating images of women and men engaged in sex with animals, people performing acts that—leaving aside the wishes of the animals—call into question the free will of the human participants. Porn producers show little concern for their human actors and even less for the animals they use in bestiality features. The seemingly endless craving to titillate through ever more extreme transgressions can end quite horrifically. Gay-porn-actor Kenneth Pinyan, for example, died while filming an intercourse with a horse when the penis of the animal perforated his colon. Pinyan's strange career and gruesome death were preserved in a 2007 documentary, *Zoo*. "Enumclaw-area animal-sex case investigated," *Seattle Times*, July 15, 2005.

2. Charles-Louis de Secondat, baron de La Brède et de Montesquieu, *L'Esprit des lois* (*The Spirit of Laws*)) translated by Thomas Nugent (New York: Hafner Press, 1949), book 12, chapter 6, section 6. On the cultural meanings of sodomy, see Hanne Blank, *Straight: The Surprisingly Short History of Heterosexuality* (Boston: Beacon Press, 2012), 2; Cynthia B. Herrup, *A House in Gross Disorder: Sex, Law, and the 2nd Earl of Castlehaven* (New York: Oxford University Press, 1999), 38–46, 145; John D'Emilio and Estelle B. Freedman, *Intimate Matters: A History of Sexuality in America* (Chicago: University of Chicago Press, 1997), 30–31; Thomas Foster, *Sex and the Eighteenth-Century Man: Massachusetts and the History of Sexuality in America* (Boston: Beacon Press, 2006), 95–97.

3. Concern for the welfare of animals actually emerged in eighteenth century English culture, most famously with Anna Barbauld's poem "The Mouse Petition" in which she pleaded for the life of a mouse that scientist Joseph Priestley was planning to kill in a demonstration experiment. According to popular lore, Priestley was so moved by the poem that he spared the life of the mouse. Opposition to cruelty to animals became a prominent feature in some genteel English circles. Mary Ellen Bellanca, "Science, Animal Sympathy, and Anna Barbauld's 'The Mouse's Petition,'" *Eighteenth-Century Studies* 37 (Fall 2003), 48. Similarly, James Sullivan, attorney general of Massachusetts, prosecuted and convicted George Johnson in the late 1790s for physically abusing his horse. Irene Quenzler Brown and Richard D. Brown believe that the successful proceedings against Johnson indicate that "there were many in early republican Massachusetts who shared in the larger humanitarian outlook that was growing in societies touched by Enlightenment ideas." *The Hanging of Ephraim Wheeler: A Story of Rape, Incest, and Justice in Early America* (Cambridge, Mass.: Harvard University Press, 2003), 57–58.

Modern critics decry the physical abuse and suffering animals may suffer, even costing the animals' lives. Piers Beirne writes that bestiality is a form of sexual assault that "almost always involve[s] coercion, because such practices often cause the animals pain and even death, and because animals are unable either to communicate consent to us in a form that we can readily understand or to speak out about their abuse." Piers Beirne, *Confronting Animal Abuse: Law Criminology, and Human-Animal Relations* (Lanham,

Md.: Rowman & Littlefield, 2009), 13. Researchers study "the psychological consequences for bestiality for humans" but ignore "the internal bleeding, the ruptured anal passages, the bruised vaginas, and the battered cloacas of animals, let alone to animals' psychological and emotional trauma." Beirne, "On the Sexual Assault of Animals: A Sociological View," in Angela N. H. Creager and William Chester Jordan, eds., *The Animal/Human Boundary: Historical Perspectives* (Rochester, N.Y.: University of Rochester Press, 2002), 201. A newer form of criminalizing bestiality is shifting the legal concern from sin and community standards to the welfare of animals. There is, of course, a measure of hypocrisy in the modern concern for the well-being of animals when, simultaneously, we accept brutal treatment of the animals we slaughter and eat. Why should sex with animals be regarded as worse than killing and eating them? The novelist Jonathan Safran Foer posed the question pointedly: "Why doesn't a horny person have as strong a claim to raping an animal as a hungry one does to confining, killing, and eating it?" "Against Meat," *New York Times Magazine*, October 7, 2009, http://www.nytimes .com/2009/10/11/magazine/11foer-t.html?pagewanted = all&_r = 0 (accessed July 16, 2013). See also Christopher Hensley, Suzanne E. Tallichet, and Erik L. Dutkiewicz, "Childhood Bestiality: A Potential Precursor to Adult Interpersonal Violence," *Journal of Interpersonal Violence* 25 (March 2010), 557–67; Richard A. Posner and Katherine B. Silbaugh, *A Guide to America's Sex Laws* (Chicago: University of Chicago Press, 1996), 207.

4. That the episode from Woody Allen's *Everything You Always Wanted to Know About Sex* (But Were Afraid to Ask)* is the most frequently evoked image is probably reflective of our age.

5. Robert Darnton, *The Great Cat Massacre and Other Episodes in French Cultural History* (New York: Basic Books, 1984), 77; Sigmund Freud, *Jokes and Their Relation to the Unconscious* [1905], in James Strachey, ed., *The Standard Edition of the Complete Psychological Works of Sigmund Freud*, 24 vols. (London: Hogarth Press, 1966–74), 8: 170; Judith Butler, *The Psychic Life of Power* (Stanford, Calif.: Stanford University Press, 1997), 143.

6. Sexual interactions across species boundaries, and between humans and other animals, while not common, in contrast to the usual male-female attraction within species, have always been part of human imagination, or at least since our ancestors dreamed up centaurs and mermaids. Traditional science teaches us that two fundamental biological principles define the boundaries between different species: 1. Procreation must be a possible outcome of sex between a male and a female; 2. Animals born of such sexual unions must be able to reproduce their own sexually fertile offspring. Horses and donkeys, for example, can engage in cross-species intercourse with reproductive results, but they constitute separate species because mules are infertile. In reality, however, these scientific definitions are historically constructed. Paleontological discoveries challenge essentialist zoological classifications. Our DNA is a testimony to the fact that the evolutionary process involves breaking the seemingly impermeable boundaries between species. We thank Professor Richard Prum of Yale University's Department

of Ecology and Evolutionary Biology for helping us understand the fluidity of species classifications in modern science. For a discussion of the impact of recent paleontological discoveries, see Jill Neimark, "Meet the New Human Family," *Discover* (May 2011), 48–76.

7. Havelock Ellis, *Studies in the Psychology of Sex*, 6 vols. (Philadelphia: F. A. Davis, 1905–29), 5: 75, Project Gutenberg, http://www.gutenberg.org/ebooks/13614, accessed February 19, 2011; Sigmund Freud, *Three Essays on the Theory of Sexuality* [1905], in Strachey, *The Standard Edition*, 7: 148; Richard W. Bulliet, *Hunters, Herders, and Hamburgers: The Past and Future of Human-Animal Relationships* (New York: Columbia University Press, 2005), 6; Alfred Kinsey, *Sexual Behavior in the Human Male* (Philadelphia: W. B. Saunders, 1948), 261–62.

8. American Psychiatric Association, *Diagnostic and Statistical Manual of Mental Disorders*, 5th ed., rev. (Washington, D.C.: American Psychiatric Association, 2013), 705; Keith Thomas, *Man and the Natural World: Changing Attitudes in England, 1500–1800* (New York: Pantheon Books, 1983), 119; William E. Monter, "Sodomy and Heresy in Early Modern Switzerland," *Journal of Homosexuality* 6 (Fall–Winter 1980–81), 41–55. Occasional testimonies from men who grew up on farms confirm Kinsey's suspicions about the dimensions of the practice. Conservative activist Neal Horsley, for example, told host Alan Colmes on the Fox radio *Alan Colmes Show* on May 9, 2005: "When you grow up on a farm in Georgia, your first girlfriend is a mule." Horsley insisted the practice was widespread. On the farm, "you experiment with anything that moves when you are growing up sexually. You're naive. You know better than that . . . If it's warm and it's damp and it vibrates you might in fact have sex with it." Otto Kreider, "Georgia Candidate for Governor Says Sex with Mules, Watermelon Behind Him," *Examiner*, April 28, 2009, http://www.examiner.com/article/georgia-candidate-for-governor-says-sex-with-mules-watermelon-behind-him (accessed July 16, 2013).

9. Freud, *Three Essays on the Theory of Sexuality* [1905], in Strachey, *The Standard Edition*,7: 157–58.

10. Colin J. Williams and Martin S. Weinberg, "Zoophilia in Men: A Study of Sexual Interest in Animals," *Archives of Sexual Behavior* 32 (December 2003), 523–35; Ellis, *Studies in the Psychology of Sex*, 5: 75; Jens Rydstrom, *Sinners and Citizens: Bestiality and Homosexuality in Sweden, 1880–1950* (Chicago: University of Chicago Press, 2003), 77; Leon Shenken, "Some Clinical and Psychopathological Aspects of Bestiality," *Journal of Nervous and Mental Disease* 139 (Spring 1966), 137–42; Gerald H. Cerrone, "Zoophilia in a Rural Population: Two Case Studies," *Journal of Rural Community Psychology* 12 (Summer 1991), 29–39; Gary Duffield, Angela Hassiotis, and Eileen Vizard, "Zoophilia in Young Sexual Abusers," *Journal of Forensic Psychiatry* 9 (September 1998), 294–304; William A. Alvarez and Jack P. Freinhar, "A Prevalence Study of Bestiality (Zoophilia) in Psychiatric In-patients, Medical In-patients, and Psychiatric Staff," *International Journal of Psychosomatics* 38, spec. issue (1991), 45–47.

11. Peter Singer provides an illuminating illustration of the contextual, cultural and social construction of bestiality: "At a conference on great apes a few years ago, I spoke

to a woman who had visited Camp Leakey, a rehabilitation center for captured orang-utans in Borneo run by Birute Galdikas, sometimes referred to as 'the Jane Goodall of orangutans' and the world's foremost authority on these great apes. At Camp Leakey, the orangutans are gradually acclimatized to the jungle, and as they get closer to com-plete independence, they are able to come and go as they please. While walking through the camp with Galdikas, my informant was suddenly seized by a large male orangutan, his intentions made obvious by his erect penis. Fighting off so powerful an animal was not an option, but Galdikas called to her companion not to be concerned, because the orangutan would not harm her, and adding, as further reassurance, that 'they have a very small penis.' As it happened, the orangutan lost interest before penetration took place, but the aspect of the story that struck me most forcefully was that in the eyes of someone who has lived much of her life with orangutans, to be seen by one of them as an object of sexual interest is not a cause for shock or horror. The potential violence of the orangutan's come-on may have been disturbing, but the fact that it was an orang-utan making the advances was not. That may be because Galdikas understands very well that we are animals, indeed more specifically, we are great apes. This does not make sex across the species barrier normal, or natural, whatever those much-misused words may mean, but it does imply that it ceases to be an offence to our status and dignity as human beings." "Heavy Petting." For a legal theoretical debate of the victimless feature of the criminalization of bestiality, see Richard J. Arneson, "Liberalism, Freedom, and Community," *Ethics* 100 (January 1990), 368–85; Jonathan Schonsheck, *On Criminaliza-tion: An Essay in the Philosophy of Criminal Law* (Boston: Kluwer Acacemic, 1994), 215–26; and Bradley Chapin, *Criminal Justice in Colonial America, 1606–1660* (Athens: University of Georgia Press, 1983), 128.

12. Simeon Strong, a resident of Amherst, just south of Leverett, was the justice of the peace who heard the complaint against Farrell on June 25, 1796. This record and the indictment, Commonwealth v. Farrell, Northampton, September Term, 1796, are found in the Suffolk Files, no. 159835, Supreme Judicial Court records, Massachusetts Archives. Death warrant, December 26, 1796, Governor's Council, Pardon Files, John Farrell, located in Massachusetts Archives.

13. Litchfield County Superior Court, August Term 1799, bill of indictment against Gideon Washburn, Connecticut State Archives, Crimes and Misdemeanors, 2nd series, 2: 87a; "Preliminary Remarks of Judge Jesse Root at the Sentencing of Gideon Wash-burn," *Litchfield Monitor*, October 2, 1799; Litchfield Co. Superior Court Executions on Judgment Cases, box 1, 1798–1816, Litchfield Superior Court Executions 1798–1802 Inclu-sive, Litchfield Historical Society.

14. Indictment of John Farrell, Commonwealth v. Farrell, Northampton, September Term, 1796, is found in the Suffolk Files, no. 159835, Supreme Judicial Court records; "Remarks of Chief Justice Jesse Root," *Litchfield Monitor*, October 2, 1799.

15. John Murrin, " 'Things Fearful to Name': Bestiality in Early America," in Angela N. H. Creager and William Chester Jordan, eds., *The Animal/Human Boundary: Histori-cal Perspectives* (Rochester, N.Y.: University of Rochester Press, 2002), 16; Michael Mer-anze, *Laboratories of Virtue: Punishment, Revolution, and Authority in Philadelphia,*

1760–1835 (Chapel Hill: University of North Carolina Press, 1996), 21, 78–79. The data on hanging is compiled from Daniel Allen Hearn, *Legal Executions in New England: A Comprehensive Reference, 1623–1960* (Jefferson, N.C.: McFarland, 1999).

16. Count Cesare di Beccaria's *An Essay on Crimes and Punishments* appeared serially from March 2, 1786, to May 11, 1786. The April 27 issue carried the discussion of sodomy on p. 86. The work first appeared in Livorno in 1764. An English translation followed in 1767. John Adams's copy of the work (London, 1775) is held by the Boston Public Library. Within two decades of publication the work was printed from Spain to Russia.

17. Adam Jay Hirsch, *The Rise of the Penitentiary: Prisons and Punishment in Early America* (New Haven, Conn.: Yale University Press, 1992), ch. 2 ("The Ideology of Sanction"), esp. 25–26; Cesare di Beccaria, *On Crimes and Punishments, and Other Writings,* ed. Richard Bellamy and trans. Richard Davies with Virginia Cox and Richard Bellamy (New York: Cambridge University Press, 1995); Alan Rogers, *Murder and the Death Penalty in Massachusetts* (Amherst: University of Massachusetts Press, 2008), 31; Meranze, *Laboratories of Virtue,* 21; William Bentley, *The Diary of William Bentley* 4 vols. (Gloucester, Mass.: Essex Institute, 1962), November 11, 1794, 2: 112.

18. Murrin, "'Things Fearful to Name,'" 8–43.

19. In being both a study of sexual episodes in their own rights and an analysis of their significance to the broader historiographical issues of the early republic, *Taming Lust* tries to break from what Cynthia Herrup astutely called "the paradox of triviality" that plagues studies of sexual affairs. Herrup writes: "Because mainstream scholars consider histories of sex marginal, it has been difficult not to cast histories of sex as responses to that classification. . . . Historians of sex, in effect, collude with other historians in the belief that materials containing sexual discussions must be primarily understood in terms of sex. Yet if we challenge this assumption by arguing that sex is part and parcel of other sorts of histories, we still pay a considerable price. . . . So we point out echoes of sex where it physically is not and claim to find something more than sex where it physically is. . . . So either way we lose: histories of sex are trivial because they are of interest only to specialists, or histories of sex are trivial because their importance lies in the ways they illuminate something that is not 'merely' sex." Herrup, "Finding the Bodies," *GLQ: A Journal of Lesbian and Gay Studies* 5 (Spring 1999), 257.

20. John Farrell and Gideon Washburn were marginal men who did not leave a large body of documents behind. Farrell, in particular, was an immigrant without a family who moved from town to town and very few documents from 1790s Leverett survived. We had greater success tracing the life and career of Washburn and his family, and in contrast to Leverett's, Litchfield's archival records are very rich. Still, when it comes to the bestiality trial of 1799, the record is uneven. At a time when formal court records were limited to procedures and outcomes, and governments made no record of either the oral testimony of witnesses or the arguments of prosecutors and defense counsel, no printer in Northampton or Litchfield commissioned a transcript of either trial to print for sale. In light of the history of published trial reports in early America, this is

not remarkable. Trial reports were virtually a new genre for American printers in the 1790s, and though one had been published for a rape trial in New York in 1793, it was not until 1801 that a New England printer ventured into this genre with a report of the sensational murder trial of Jason Fairbanks in Dedham, Mass. Until then, almost the only supplement for the laconic official records was the occasional execution sermon or broadside, which might include a sketch of the convict's crime and biography. In rare cases an ambitious author and printer might undertake a criminal biography, as did the New Haven attorney David Daggett, who published the best-selling *Sketches of the Life of Joseph Mountain, a Negro, who was executed at New-Haven, on the 20th Day of October, 1790, for a Rape* (New Haven, Conn., 1790). But such publications did not report legal proceedings, and in any case the stories of Farrell and Washburn lacked the swaggering braggadocio that drew Daggett to recount Mountain's picaresque tale of criminal life in Britain. None of the many lawyers in Northampton or Litchfield stepped forward to write the lives of the two old sex offenders or to report their trials. Farrell's and Washburn's stories promised revulsion, not adventure. And as for the execution sermons that were usually associated with hangings, they were only published when a local printer believed the notoriety of the crime and the expected turnout for the execution, together with the stature of the preacher, would underwrite profitable sales. For many hangings both before and after 1800 the only printed record was a terse sentence in a newspaper. Scott D. Seay, *Hanging Between Heaven and Earth: Capital Crimes, Execution Preaching, and Theology in Early New England* (DeKalb: Northern Illinois University Press, 2009); Daniel A. Cohen, *Pillars of Salt, Monuments of Grace: New England Crime Literature and the Origins of American Popular Culture, 1674–1860* (New York: Oxford University Press, 1993), 26–31. Although the genre did not flourish until the beginning of the nineteenth century, Cohen points out (14) that trial reports were not completely new at the end of the eighteenth century, since "at least five accounts of piracy cases [were] issued by Boston printers and booksellers between 1704 and 1726." So in reconstructing these rare and seemingly idiosyncratic episodes, we have followed the approaches pioneered in local and community histories where town meeting, tax, voting, and probate records and wills supply particular facts as well as critical contextual data. Similarly, we have employed the scholarship analyzing the literature of crime, as well as actual records of executions and pardons. Even when primary source material is uneven and gaps exist in the record, the microhistorical approach makes inferential judgments reasonable. This is not, of course, remarkable since in nearly every historical explanation the absence of full and complete evidence, together with multiple interpretive possibilities, limit scholars to conclusions that rely on plausible inferences. And partial evidence is all the more salient in studies of sexuality since under the best of circumstances only the tip of the iceberg is visible. And yet, sexual secrets can be unpacked by close examination of the records within the broader social and cultural context. Richard D. Brown, "Microhistory and the Post-Modern Challenge," *Journal of the Early Republic* 23 (Spring 2003), 1–20.

21. Precise data on the octogenarian fraction of the adult male population is not available; however, analysis of the "Ages of White Males, Hartford [Connecticut], 1830"

showed one-quarter of 1 percent (0.24 percent) in the eighty-to-eighty-nine-years category, a figure that, owing to the declining birthrate would be slightly greater than the region a generation earlier. By contrast, males aged ten to twenty-nine years, and more likely to commit bestial acts, were 49.6 percent of the population, with 45.5 percent of adult males aged twenty to twenty-nine years. Paula A. Scott, *Growing Old in the Early Republic: Spiritual, Social, and Economic Issues, 1790–1830* (New York: Garland, 1997), 262, table 8.11.

22. Mary Douglas, *Purity and Danger: An Analysis of Concepts of Pollution and Taboo* (New York: Routledge Classics, 2002 [orig. 1966]), xiii.

Chapter 1. The Sisyphean Battle Against Bestiality

1. Kenneth James Dover, *Greek Homosexuality* (Cambridge, Mass.: Harvard University Press, 1978), 97; Richard W. Bulliet, *Hunters, Herders, and Hamburgers: The Past and Future of Human-Animal Relationships* (New York: Columbia University Press, 2005), 146–49, 159–63; Erik Gunderson, "The Ideology of the Arena," *Classical Antiquity* 15 (April 1996), 143; K. M. Coleman, "Fatal Charades: Roman Executions Staged as Mythological Enactments," *Journal of Roman Studies* 80 (1990), 63–64; J. Rainsnow, "Entertainment, Politics, and the Soul: Lessons of the Roman Games (Part Two)," http://www.rainsnow.org/wod_roman_games_part_two.htm (accessed March 2, 2011); Rashi, commentary on Genesis 2: 23; Luke 1: 35. Sixteenth-century Christian theologians, who in general approved of Rashi's commentary, censored this passage. Michael T. Walton and Phyllis J. Walton, "In Defense of Church Militants: The Censorship of Rashi Commentary in the Magna Biblia Rabbinica," *Sixteenth Century Journal* 21 (Autumn 1990), 397. Augustine's rebuttal of the theory, in which he declared that the snake "never physically defiled Eve," demonstrates that many others thought differently. Augustine, "Sermon 213," *Saint Augustine: Sermons on the Liturgical*, trans. Mary Sarah Muldowney (New York: Catholic University of America Press, 1959), 127; Midas Dekkers, *Dearest Pet: On Beastiality* [*sic*], trans. Paul Vincent (London: Verso, 1994 [orig. 1992 in Dutch]); Marina Warner, *From the Beast to the Blonde: On Fairy Tales and Their Tellers* (London: Chatto & Windus, 1994).

2. Jennifer Stone, "A Psychoanalytic Bestiary: The Wolff Woman, the Leopard, and the Siren," *American Imago* 49 (Spring 1992), 117–52; Wendy Doniger, "The Mythology of Masquerading Animals, or, Bestiality," *Social Research* 62 (Fall 1995), 751–73; David Frankfurter, "The Perils of Love: Magic and Countermagic in Coptic Egypt," *Journal of the History of Sexuality* 10 (July–October 2001), 480–500; Charles Knight, *The Literature of Satire* (Cambridge: Cambridge University Press, 2004), 71; Karin Calvert, *Children in the House: The Material Culture of Early Childhood, 1690–1900* (Boston: Northeastern University Press, 1992), 26; Wilhelm Stekel, *Patterns of Psychosexual Infantilism* (New York: Liveright, 1952). Sigmund Freud's study of the "Wolf Man" explores the tensions between sadistic and sexual animal-centered fantasies and phobias of adult life. Freud, *From the History of Infantile Neurosis* (1918 [orig. 1914]), in James Strachey, ed., *The*

Standard Edition of the Complete Psychological Works of Sigmund Freud, 24 vols. (London: Hogarth Press, 1966–74), 17: 7–122. For a psychoanalytic case study of the impact of Jonathan Swift's *Gulliver's Travels* on the zoophilic fantasies of a patient, see Ben Karpman, "A Modern Gulliver: A Study in Coprophilia," *Psychoanalytic Review* 36 (1949), 260–82.

3. William Butler Yeats, "Leda and the Swan." Poetry Foundation http://www.poetryfoundation.org/poem/172064 (accessed July 10, 2013).

4. *Ancient History Sourcebook: The Code of the Nesilim, c. 1650–1500 B.C.E.*, http://www.fordham.edu/halsall/ancient/1650nesilim.html (accessed February 19, 2011); G. M. A. Grube, trans., *Plato's Republic* (Indianapolis: Hackett, 1974), 220 (book 9, 571d); Clifford Geertz, "Deep Play: Notes on the Balinese Cockfight," *Daedalus* 101 (Winter 1972), 7.

5. Ian Frederick Moulton, *Before Pornography: Erotic Writings in Early Modern England* (New York: Oxford University Press, 2000), 185; Courtney Thomas, " 'Not Having God Before His Eyes': Bestiality in Early Modern England," *Seventeenth Century* 26 (April 2011), 152, 155; Jeremy Webster, *Performing Libertinism in Charles II's Court: Politics, Drama, Sexuality* (New York: Palgrave Macmillan, 2005), ch. 6; Dena Goodman, *Marie-Antoinette: Writings on the Body of a Queen* (New York: Routledge, 2003), 129; Marquis de Sade, *Juliette, or Vice Amply Rewarded*, trans. Austryn Wainhouse (New York: Grove, 1968), 426, 188. Pat Robertson has asked "if we take biblical standards away in homosexuality, what about the other? And what about bestiality. . . . You mark my words, this is just the beginning in a long downward slide in relation to all the things that we consider to be abhorrent." *Think Progress*, May 7, 2009, http://thinkprogress.org/2009/05/07/robertson-child-molestation/ (accessed March 28, 2011). Governor Michael Huckabee of Arkansas declared: "Well, I don't think that's a radical view to say we're going to affirm marriage. I think the radical view is to say that we're going to change the definition of marriage so that it can mean two men, two women, a man and three women, a man and a child, a man and animal." "Mike Huckabee: 'The Lord Truly Gave Me Wisdom,' " January 22, 2008, http://www.beliefnet.com/News/Politics/2008/01/Mike-Huckabee-The-Lord-Truly-Gave-Me-Wisdom.aspx?p = 2 (accessed March 28, 2011).

6. Exodus 22: 17–18; Leviticus 18: 23; Leviticus 20: 15–16; Deuteronomy 27: 21. The leading rabbinical interpretation as to the reasons the animal is put to death does not endow the animal with agency in the seduction and act, but rather seeks to eradicate the sin and its memory. For a discussion of the place of sexual prohibitions in the Torah, see Everett Fox's commentary, "On the Ritual Pollution of the Body," in *The Five Books of Moses: Genesis, Exodus, Leviticus, Numbers and Deuteronomy* (New York: Schocken Books, 1995), 556–57.

7. 1 Corinthians 6: 9, 7: 1, 29; Augustine, *The City of God*, trans. Marcus Dods, Christian Classics Ethereal Library, http://www.ccel.org/ccel/schaff/npnf102.iv.html (accessed July 10, 2013) chs. 13, 14; *The Confessions of Saint Augustine*, trans. Edward Bouverie Pusey, Sacred Texts, http://www.sacred-texts.com/chr/augconf/aug08.htm

(accessed July 10, 2013), book 3, ch. 8, 15; Alan Soble, "Correcting Some Misconceptions About St. Augustine's Sex," *Journal of the History of Sexuality* 11 (October 2002), 545; David M. Friedman, *A Mind of Its Own: A Cultural History of the Penis* (New York: Free Press, 2001), 37; Robert J. Darby, "William Acton's Antipodean Disciples: A Colonial Perspective on His Theories of Male Sexual (Dys)function," *Journal of the History of Sexuality* 13 (April 2004), 167.

8. John Boswell, *The Marriage of Likeness: Same-Sex Unions in Pre-Modern Europe* (New York: Vintage, 1995), 280; Pierre J. Payer, *Sex and the Penitentials: The Development of a Sexual Code, 550–1150* (Toronto: University of Toronto Press, 1984), 44–46; Erica Fudge, "Monstrous Acts: Bestiality in Early Modern England," *History Today* 50 (August 2000), 20–25.

9. Piers Beirne, *Confronting Animal Abuse: Law Criminology, and Human-Animal Relations* (Lanham, Md.: Rowman & Littlefield, 2009), 102; Joyce E. Salisbury, *The Beast Within: Animals in the Middle Ages* (New York: Routledge, 1994), 78–79, 90–91; Esther Cohen, "Law, Folklore and Animal Lore," *Past and Present* 110 (February 1986), 10–18; Beirne, "On the Sexual Assault of Animals: A Sociological View," in Angela N. H. Creager and William Chester Jordan, eds., *The Animal/Human Boundary: Historical Perspectives* (Rochester, N.Y.: University of Rochester Press, 2002), 222. Animal trials for sexual offenses were a subcategory of a larger body of trials that charged animals with a variety of offenses, from destroying agricultural crops to murder. In 1457, for example, a sow and her six piglets were imprisoned and tried for killing a five-year-old boy. The pigs received a court-appointed defense lawyer, and a parade of witnesses testified in the trial. Cohen, "Law, Folklore," 10. See also Paul Schiff Berman, "Rats, Pigs, and Statutes on Trial: The Creation of Cultural Narratives in the Prosecution of Animals and Inanimate Objects," *New York University Law Review* 69 (May 1994), 288–326.

10. Deuteronomy 23: 19. A medieval Jewish midrash argued that face-to-face intercourse is a mirror of a conversation with God whereas the other position is purely bestial. Jeffrey Richards, *Sex, Dissidence and Damnation: Minority Groups in the Middle Ages* (New York: Routledge, 1994), 30–31; Thomas Aquinas, *Summa Theologica*, Christian Classics Ethereal Library, http://www.ccel.org/ccel/aquinas/summa.pdf (accessed July 10, 2013) 1644, 4159. Pierre J. Payer, *Sex and the New Medieval Literature of Confession, 1150–1300* (Toronto: Pontifical Institute of Mediaeval Studies, 2009), 126–49; James A. Brundage, *Law, Sex and Christian Society in Medieval Europe* (Chicago: University of Chicago Press, 1987), 493; Arthur N. Gilbert, "Conceptions of Homosexuality and Sodomy in Western History," *Journal of Homosexuality* 6 (Fall–Winter 1980–81), 57–68; Salisbury, *The Beast Within*, 80–81, 94, 99.

11. This broad definition of sodomy lasted well into the eighteenth century. The term, according to Jeffery Merrick, "derived from the name of the Biblical city destroyed because of the sins of its inhabitants, could be applied to a considerable variety of nonprocreative sexual acts, ranging from masturbation to bestiality, including anal and oral intercourse within marriage." Merrick, "Sodomitical Inclinations in Early Eighteenth-Century Paris," *Eighteenth-Century Studies* 30 (Spring 1997), 290. Jonathan Goldberg

argues that the strong sanctions against alternate sexual practices aimed to accentuate the "'unnaturalness' of sodomy and thus its lack of relation to bonds between men." Goldberg, *Sodometries: Renaissance Texts, Modern Sexualities* (Stanford, Calif.: Stanford University Press, 1992), 239. Residues of the grouping of homosexuality and bestiality exist. Sweden, for example, decriminalized both as one in 1944. *Times Online*, November 12, 2008, http://www.timesonline.co.uk/tol/news/world/europe/article5140576.ece (accessed March 28, 2011). There is some statistical evidence suggesting that homosexual men are more likely to engage in bestiality than their heterosexual counterparts. Paul Cameron, Kirk Cameron, and Kay Proctor, "Effect of Homosexuality upon Public Health and Social Order," *Psychological Reports* 64 (June 1989), 1167–79; Mark E. Pietzyk, "Queer Science," *New Republic*, 211, October 3, 1994, 10–12. It is unclear if this proclivity, should it exist, is a result of psychological tendencies of homosexual men or of greater openness to sexual experimentation in the gay community. Both explanations could become powerful weapons in the hands of our homophobic culture. Ascribing this tendency to neuropsychological factors gives ammunition to those classifying homosexuality a mental deviant disorder. On the other hand, explaining the phenomenon in terms of cultural openness to experimentation could fuel attacks on the supposedly degenerate nature of gay culture.

12. As cited by Dekkers, *Dearest Pet*, 118; Eric Berkowitz, *Sex and Punishment: Four Thousand Years of Judging Desire* (Berkeley, Calif.: Counterpoint Press, 2012), 152; Jonas Liliequist, "Peasants Against Nature: Crossing the Boundaries Between Man and Animal in Seventeenth-and Eighteenth-Century Sweden," *Journal of the History of Sexuality* 1 (January 1991), 393–423; Torstein Jorgensen, "Illegal Sexual Behavior in Late Medieval Norway as Testified in Supplications to the Pope," *Journal of the History of Sexuality* 17 (September 2008), 344; Steven F. Kruger, "Conversion and Medieval Sexual, Religious and Racial Categories," in Karma Lochrie, Peggy McCracken, and James Schultz, eds., *Constructing Medieval Sexuality* (Minneapolis: University of Minnesota Press, 1997), 169; Katherine Crawford, *European Sexualities, 1400–1800* (New York: Cambridge University Press, 2007), 158; Fredric Garza Carvajal, *Butterflies Will Burn: Prosecuting Sodomites in Early Modern Spain and Mexico* (Austin: University of Texas Press, 2003), 166; John M. Efron, *Medicine and the German Jews: A History* (New Haven, Conn.: Yale University Press, 2001), 52; Barry S. Levy, *Quakers and the American Family: British Settlement in the Delaware Valley* (New York: Oxford University Press, 1992), 82.

13. Crawford, *European Sexualities*, 156–57; Alan Stewart, "Bribery, Buggery, and the Fall of Lord Chancellor Bacon," in Victoria Kahn and Lorna Hutson, eds., *Rhetoric and Law in Early Modern Europe* (New Haven, Conn.: Yale University Press, 2001), 125; F. E. Frenkel, "Sex-Crime and Its Socio-Historical Background," *Journal of the History of Ideas* 25 (July–September 1964), 333–52; A. D. Harvey, "Prosecutions for Sodomy in England at the Beginning of the Nineteenth Century," *Historical Journal* 21 (December 1978), 939–48, and "Bestiality in Late-Victorian England," *Journal of Legal History* 21 (September 2000), 85–88; Edward Coke, *The Third Part of the Institutes of the Laws of England*, 3 vols. (London, 1642), 3: 58; Keith Thomas, *Man and the Natural World:*

Changing Attitudes in England, 1500–1800 (New York: Pantheon Books, 1983), 38–39; Richard L. Greaves, *Society and Religion in Elizabethan England* (Minneapolis: University of Minnesota Press, 1981), 221.

14. "The Proceedings of Old Bailey, London's Central Criminal Court, 1674–1913," July 11, 1677, cases t16770711-1 and 2, in Old Bailey online, http://www.oldbaileyonline .org/ (accessed March 28, 2011).

15. Thomas, "'Not Having God Before His Eyes,'" 162–64; B. R. Burg, *Boys at Sea: Sodomy, Indecency, and Courts Martial in Nelson's Navy* (Houndmills: Palgrave Macmillan, 2007), 28–29.

16. *Boston Gazette* (Boston), November 11, 1734; *Boston Weekly Rehearsal* (Boston), November 18, 1734, p. 2; Lawrence Stone, *The Family, Sex and Marriage in England, 1500–1800* (London: Weidenfeld & Nicolson, 1977), 615–16; Arthur Cash, *John Wilkes: The Scandalous Father of Civil Liberty* (New Haven, Conn.: Yale University Press, 2006), 35; Harvey, "Prosecutions for Sodomy," 947; Arthur Gilbert, "Buggery and the British Navy, 1700–1861," *Journal of Social History* 10 (March 1976), 72–98; Thomas, *Man and the Natural World*, 118–19. According to Thomas, bestiality in seventeenth-century England was "a rural crime, most often involving cows and horses." B. J. Davey's study of rural crime in England between 1740 and 1780 noted that bastardy trials were the most common sexual prosecution, followed by proceedings against keeping brothels. Davey found "one or two cases of homosexuality" and a case of blackmail where one man threatened to accuse another of "buggery." Davey concludes that in the prosecution of sexual crimes, "the concern was economic, not moral." Davey, *Rural Crime in the Eighteenth Century: North Linconshire, 1740–1780* (Hull, UK: University of Hull Press, 1994), 39–44.

17. Michel Foucault, *The History of Sexuality: An Introduction*, trans. Robert Hurley, 3 vols. (New York: Vintage, 1976–84), 1: 59; Berkowitz, *Sex and Punishment*, 213–16. Julia Brown's comparative study of sexual regulations in different cultures found that bestiality was defined a punishable crime in 93 percent of the societies she surveyed. Brown, "A Comparative Study of Deviation from Sexual Mores," *American Sociological Review* 17 (April 1952), 135–46.

18. Virginia DeJohn Anderson, *Creatures of Empire: How Domestic Animals Transformed Early America* (New York: Oxford University Press, 2004), 205, notes that John Eliot, the Puritan missionary to the Indians, warned them against bestiality even though—not having domestic animals—such behavior was unlikely. Marie Hélène Huet, *Monstrous Imagination* (Cambridge, Mass.: Harvard University Press, 1993), 21–22; Thomas Laqueur, *Making Sex: Body and Gender from the Greeks to Freud* (Cambridge Mass.: Harvard University Press, 1990) 122, 151; Bernard W. Sheehan, *Savagism and Civility: Indians and Englishmen in Colonial Virginia* (New York: Cambridge University Press, 1980), 66–73; John H. Elliot, *Empires of the Atlantic World: Britain and Spain in America, 1492–1830* (New Haven, Conn.: Yale University Press 2006), 54; Quincy D. Newell, "'The Indians Generally Love Their Wives and Children': Native American Marriage and Sexual Practices in Missions San Francisco, Santa Clara, and San Jose," *Catholic Historical Review* 91 (January 2005), 68 n. 24; Anderson, *Creatures of Empire*, 204–5.

19. Anderson, *Creatures of Empire*, 169; William Bradford, *History of Plymouth Plantation, 1606–1646*, ed. William T. Davis (Boston: Scribner's, 1908 [orig. ca. 1650]), 238; Nathaniel Hawthorne, "The May-Pole of Merry Mount," in *Twice Told Tales* (Boston: Charles Bowen, 1836).

20. Samuel Danforth, *The Cry of Sodom Enquired Into; Upon Occasion of the Arraignment and Condemnation of Benjamin Goad, for his Prodigious Villany* (Cambridge, Mass., 1674), 6; John Canup, " 'The Cry of Sodom Enquired Into': Bestiality and the Wilderness of Human Nature in Seventeenth Century New England," *Proceedings of the American Antiquarian Society* 98 (1988), 113–19. On the relationship between the Torah and English sexual norms in the fifteenth and sixteenth centuries, see Naomi Tadmor, "Women and Wives: The Language of Marriage in Early Modern English Biblical Translations," *History Workshop Journal* 62 (Autumn 2006), 1–27.

21. John Cotton, *Abstract of the Laws of New England* (London, 1641), ch. 7, 20; Massachusetts Body of Liberties (1641) Hanover Historical Texts Project, http://history .hanover.edu/texts/masslib.html (accessed July 10, 2013) Capital Crimes, article 7. Plymouth similarly decreed that, "if any Person lyeth with a Beast or Bruit Creature, by Carnal Copulation, they shall surely be put to Death, and the Beast shall be slain and buried and not eaten." *The book of the general laws of the inhabitants of the jurisdiction of New-Plimouth* . . . (Cambridge, Mass., 1672). The willingness of Puritans to whip, torture, and execute sexual offenders contradicts the prevailing interpretation of Puritans' supposed treatment of sexual offenders "with patience and understanding" or the argument that that they created a legal order marked by restraint and compassion, which "shone forth as a model for others to emulate." Edmund S. Morgan, "The Puritans and Sex," *New England Quarterly* 15 (December 1942), 607; William E. Nelson, "The Utopian Legal Order of the Massachusetts Bay Colony, 1630–1686," *American Journal of Legal History* 47 (April 2005), 214, 230.

22. Anderson, *Creatures of Empire*, 169. Richard S. Dunn, ed., *The Journal of John Winthrop, 1639–1648* (Cambridge, Mass.: Harvard University Press, 1996), 197–98, 201–2; Danforth, *Cry of Sodom*, 11.

23. William Bradford, *Of Plymouth Plantation, 1620–1647*, with an introduction and notes by Samuel Eliot Morison (New York: Knopf, 1963), 320–21.

24. *The Public Records of the Colony of Connecticut 1636–1776*, ed. James H. Trumbull and Charles J. Hoadly, 15 vols. (Hartford: Press of the Case, Lockwood & Brainard Company, 1850–1890), 1: 157; The quote about Spencer is cited in John Murrin, " 'Things Fearful to Name': Bestiality in Early America," in Creager and Jordan, *The Animal/ Human Boundary*, 133; Seventeenth-century British America saw one execution for homosexual sodomy outside New England. In 1625 Virginia executed ship captain Richard Cornish for forcefully sodomizing his sailor. The circumstances, however, involve two capital crimes: rape and buggery. And while the Dutch colony of New Amsterdam did not prosecute bestiality, it executed or attempted to execute three men for homosexual sodomy. Richard Godbeer, *Sexual Revolution in Early America* (Baltimore: Johns Hopkins University Press, 2002), 110–11, 123–24; Murrin, " 'Things Fearful to Name,' " 123.

25. Anthropomorphizing animals was not unique to the New Haven Colony. William Byrd noted in 1710 in his diary that he put a bitch that killed a lamb "into a house with a ram that beat her violently to break her of her bad custom." Louis B. Wright and Marion Tinling, eds., *The Great American Gentleman: William Byrd of Westover in Virginia, His Secret Diary of the Years 1709–1712* (New York: Putnam's, 1963), 63.

26. Peter N. Moogk, "The Liturgy of Humiliation, Pain, and Death: The Execution of Criminals in New France," *Canadian Historical Review* 88 (March 2007), 107 n. 63; Eben Moglen, "Taking the Fifth: Reconsidering the Origins of the Constitutional Privilege Against Self-Incrimination," *Michigan Law Review* 92 (March 1994), 1086–1130; David D. Hall, *Worlds of Wonder, Days of Judgment: Popular Religious Belief in Early New England* (New York: Knopf, 1989), 172–76; Scott D. Seay, *Hanging Between Heaven and Earth: Capital Crime, Execution Preaching and Theology in Early New England* (DeKalb: Northern Illinois University Press, 2009).

27. In 1775 a thirteen-year-old Pueblo boy was convicted of having sex with a calf and was sentenced to eight days in prison and receiving twelve lashes each day, with the cause of his punishment being repeatedly told to him as he was being whipped. He was also forced to personally burn the calf alive and then exiled. Tracy Brown, "'Abominable Sin' in Colonial New Mexico: Spanish and Pueblo Perceptions of Same Sex Sexuality," in Thomas A. Foster, ed., *Long Before Stonewall: Histories of Same-Sex Sexuality in Early America* (New York: New York University Press, 2007), 70. On bestiality in colonial Louisiana, see Shannon Lee Dawdy, *Building the Devil's Empire: French Colonial New Orleans* (Chicago: University of Chicago Press, 2008), 172, 210. We thank Professor Dawdy for sharing her research with us.

28. John Murrin has similarly argued that in New England, "the active prosecution of witchcraft and bestiality rose and fell together," and that bestiality "discredited men in the way that witchcraft discredited women." According to Murrin, both crimes began as "unforgivable," but "were becoming forgivable by the end of the seventeenth century." Murrin, "'Things Fearful to Name,'" 137–43. See also Brundage, *Law, Sex and Christian Society*, 313.

29. Friedman, *A Mind of Its Own*, 4–5; Robert Muchembled, *A History of the Devil: From the Middle Ages to the Present*, trans. Jean Birrell (Cambridge, UK: Blackwell, 2003), 33–34; Retha M. Warnicke, "Sexual Heresy at the Court of Henry VIII," *Historical Journal* 30 (June 1987), 248–50; Janet Thompson, *Wives, Widows, Witches and Bitches: Women in Seventeenth-century Devon* (New York: Peter Lang, 1993), 124; Julia M. Garrett, "Dramatizing Deviance: Sociological Theory and *The Witch of Edmonton*," *Criticism* 49 (Summer 2007), 353; Hélène Cixous and Catherine Clément, *The Newly Born Woman*, trans. Betsy Wing (Minneapolis: University of Minnesota Press, 1986), 13.

30. John Denham, "A relation of a Quaker, that to the shame of his profession, attempted to bugger a mare near Colchester" (1659), in John Wardroper, *Lovers, Rakes and Rogues: A New Garner of Love-Songs and Merry Verses, 1580 to 1830* (London: Shelfmark Books, 1995), 216–18; Dunn, *The Journal of John Winthrop*, 254. See Barry Reay, "Popular Hostility Towards Quakers in Mid-Seventeenth-Century England," *Social History* 5 (October 1980), 387–407; Anne G. Myles, "Border Crossings: The Queer Erotics of

Quakerism in Seventeenth-Century New England," in Foster, *Long Before Stonewall*, 114–43.

31. *Litchfield Monitor*, January 4, 1797. Scotland, for instance, had no specific statute against bestiality. But the courts heard more cases against bestiality than witchcraft in the initial decades of the eighteenth century. Peter Maxwell-Stuart, "Witchcraft and Magic in Eighteenth-Century Scotland," in Owen Davies and Willem De Blecourt, eds., *Beyond the Witch Trials: Witchcraft and Magic in Enlightenment Europe* (Manchester, UK: Manchester University Press, 2004), 85–86.

32. A systematic search of digital Early American Newspapers turned up four cases: *New York Gazette* May 16, 1757, p. 3; *New York Gazette*, November 16, 1761, p. 2; *Connecticut Journal* (New Haven), December 2, 1774, p. 4; *Pennsylvania Evening Post, and Public Advertiser* (Philadelphia), June 4, 1783, p. 2. Also reported in *Freeman's Journal: or, North-American Intelligencer* (Philadelphia), June 4, 1783, p. 3. John M. Murrin and Clare A. Lyons uncovered two additional cases in 1748 and 1786. Murrin, " 'Things Fearful to Name,' " 142 nn. 36, 37; Lyons, "Mapping an Atlantic Sexual Culture: Homoeroticism in Eighteenth-Century Philadelphia," in Foster, *Long Before Stonewall*, 198 n. 44. The New Jersey and Pennsylvania executions testify to the persistence of the use of the death penalty against offenders outside New England in the eighteenth century. However, the cases, as far as we can tell, involved young men, not octogenarians.

33. William Blackstone, *Commentaries on the Laws of England*, 4 vols. (London, 1765–69), 4: ch. 15, sec. 4; Zephaniah Swift, *A System of the Laws of the State of Connecticut*, 2 vols. (Hartford, Conn., 1795), 2: 308–10.

34. [Laws, etc. (Session laws, 1700, October)] *An abstract or abridgment of the laws made and past by William Penn absolute proprietary, and governour in chief of the province of Pensilvania . . . , with the advice and consent of the . . . Generall-Assembly mett at New-Castle the fourteenth-day of October and continued . . . till the twenty-seventh of November in the year 1700* (Philadelphia: Reynier Jansen, 1701); [Laws, etc.] *The laws of the province of Pennsilvania collected into one volumn* [sic], *by order of the governour and Assembly of the said province* (Philadelphia: Andr. Bradford,, 1714); *The laws of the province of Pennsylvania, passed by the governour and General Assemblies of said province, held at Philadelphia in the years 1715, 1717 and 1718* (Philadelphia: Andrew Bradford, 1718). See also James D. Marietta and G. S. Rowe, *Crime and Justice in Pennsylvania, 1682–1800* (Philadelphia: University of Pennsylvania Press, 2006), 18–20. There is no record of bestiality prosecutions in the Dutch colony of New Amsterdam. The record does show, however, an execution for sodomy. In June 1660, Flemish soldier Jan Quisthout van der Linde was executed for forcing himself on Hendrick Harmeson, a white young boy. The soldier was first drummed out of the army, then tied inside a sack, and drowned. Daniel Allen Hearn, *Legal Executions in New York State: A Comprehensive Reference, 1639–1963* (Jefferson, N.C.: McFarland, 1997), 3.

35. [Laws, etc. (Session laws, 1697, October)] *Acts and laws, passed by the Great and General Court . . . of the Massachusetts-Bay* (Boston, 1697); *Acts and laws, passed by the General Court . . . of New-Hampshire* (Boston, 1718); *Acts and Laws of his Majesty's*

English colony of Connecticut (Hartford, Conn., 1702); Blackstone, *Commentaries*, 4:, ch. 15, sec. 4; Swift, *System of the Laws*, 2: 308.

36. "Summary of Newport Court Trial of Nathaniel Bowdish Jr., March 28, 1702," in Jane Fletcher Fiske, ed., *Rhode Island General Court of Trials, 1671–1704* (Boxford, Mass.: n.p., 1998), 208–9; General Sessions of the Peace at Salem, February 7, 1710, and November 27, 1705, Essex County Court of the General Sessions file papers, box 3; Bills of indictment against Benjamin Doroty and Edward Twist, November 29, 1705, General Sessions of the Peace at Salem, February 7, 1710, and November 27, 1705, Essex County Court of the General Sessions file papers, box 3; Dom Rex v. Andrew Davis, September 20, 1718, Connecticut State Archives, New London County Court records series, box 5, folder 5. We thank Elaine Forman Crane for bringing the Bowdish case to our attention.

37. Murrin, " 'Things Fearful to Name,' " 123–27; *New-York Mercury*, May 12, 1755; "Philopatris," *New-York Mercury*, April 26, 1756; *New York Gazette*, May 16, 1757; *New-York Gazette*, November 16, 1761; Marietta and Rowe, *Crime and Justice in Pennsylvania*, 40; Donna J. Spindel, *Crime and Society in North Carolina, 1663–1776* (Baton Rouge: Louisiana State University Press, 1989), 118–19.

38. Dror Wahrman, *The Making of the Modern Self: Identity and Culture in Eighteenth-Century England* (New Haven, Conn.: Yale University Press, 2004), 143–44; Aristotle [pseudonym], *The Works of Aristotle, the famous philosopher. In four parts . . .* (Philadelphia, 1799), 51–52. This quote is taken from the 1799 edition, but the theme appears in the other editions, some in an even more explicit form including illustrations of deformed birth brought about by bestiality. See for example the online version of the book, part 2, ch. 9, section 2, http://www.exclassics.com/arist/arist16.htm (accessed January 12, 2012); Elizabeth Reis, *Bodies in Doubt: An American History of Intersex* (Baltimore: Johns Hopkins University Press, 2009), 5; Mary E. Fissell, "Hairy Women and Naked Truths: Gender and the Politics of Knowledge in Aristotle's Masterpiece," *William and Mary Quarterly*, 3rd series, 60 (January 2003), 43–74. The age's repression of female sexuality was accompanied by suspicions of the insensitivity of some women to boundaries, particularly their willingness to have sex with different races. In fact, *Aristotle's Masterpiece* suggested that even if women were kept physically pure, some males, simply by virtue of their powerful mental imprint, could impregnate a woman. See also Huet, *Monstrous Imagination*; Dennis Todd, *Imagining Monsters: Miscreations of the Self in Eighteenth Century England* (Chicago: University of Chicago Press, 1995).

39. Isaac Backus, diary entry for Wednesday, January 23, 1771, *The Diary of Isaac Backus*, ed. William G. McLoughlin, 3 vols. (Providence, R.I.: Brown University Press, 1979), 2: 790. On the elevated status of Backus, see Jonathan D. Sassi, *A Republic of Righteousness: The Public Christianity of Post-Revolutionary New England Clergy* (New York: Oxford University Press, 2001), 70.

40. Adriana S. Benzaquén, *Encounters with Wild Children: Temptation and Disappointment in the Study of Human Nature* (Montreal: McGill-Queen's University Press, 2006), 43–45; John Wood Sweet, *Bodies Politic: Negotiating Race in the American North, 1730–1820* (Baltimore: Johns Hopkins University Press, 2003), 272–73, 290; Ritvo, *The*

Platypus and the Mermaid, 15–24; Julia Douthwaite, *"Homo ferus:* Between Monster and Model," *Eighteenth-Century Life* 21 (May 1997), 176–202; Karin Calvert, *Children in the House: The Material Culture of Early Childhood* (Boston: Northeastern University Press, 1992), 24–33.

41. Andrew Curran, "Monsters and the Self in the *Rêve de d'Alembert,*" *Eighteenth-Century Life,* 21 (May 1997), 62; François-Marie Arouet Voltaire, *Essai sur les mœurs et l'esprit des nations* (Paris: Chez Werdet et Lequien Fils, 1829 [orig. 1756]), 9; Ronald Schechter, *Obstinate Hebrews: Representations of Jews in France, 1715–1815* (Berkeley: University of California Press, 2003), 46–53. In this connection of humans and goats, Diderot and Voltaire may also have been thinking of classical satyrs, who were the offspring of such couplings. We thank David Bell for pointing us to the Voltaire passage and translating it from French.

42. Daniel Walker Howe, "Franklin, Edwards, and the Problem of Human Nature," in Barbara B. Oberg and Harry S. Stout, eds., *Benjamin Franklin, Jonathan Edwards, and the Representation of American Culture* (New York: Oxford University Press, 1993), 75; Christie Davies, "Sexual Taboos and Social Boundaries," *American Journal of Sociology* 87 (March 1982), 1033, 1060. The classical work on the subject remains Arthur O. Lovejoy, *The Great Chain of Being: A Study of the History of an Idea* (Cambridge, Mass.: Harvard University Press, 1936).

43. Qtd. by Ramon Gutierrez, *When Jesus Came, the Corn Mothers Went Away: Marriage, Sexuality, and Power in New Mexico, 1500–1846* (Stanford, Calif.: Stanford University Press, 1991), 18; Jacob Wallenberg in *"My son on the Galley"* (orig. 1781), qtd. by Sven-Erik Rose, "The Funny Business of the Swedish East India Company: Gender and Imperial Joke-Work in Jacob Wallenberg's Travel Writing," *Eighteenth-Century Studies* 33 (Winter 2000), 226; Marie E. McAllister, "Stories of the Origin of Syphilis in Eighteenth-Century England: Science, Myth, and Prejudice," *Eighteenth-Century Life* 24 (Winter 2000), 29; Wahrman, *Making of the Modern Self,* 127–40; Friedman, *A Mind of Its Own,* 112–13; Ritvo, *The Platypus and the Mermaid,* 129; Sweet, *Bodies Politic,* 273–74.

44. Thomas Jefferson, *Notes on the State of Virginia,* ed. Frank Shuffelton (New York: Penguin, 1999), 149–50; Sigmund Freud, *Totem and Taboo* [1913], in Strachey, *Standard Edition,* 13: 35. See also Robert A. Paul, "Did the Primal Crime Take Place?" *Ethos* 4 (Autumn 1976), 312. On the notion that sexual intercourse between white men and black slaves had bestial overtones, see Cynthia M. Kennedy, "'Nocturnal Adventures in Mulatto Alley': Sex in Charleston, South Carolina," in Thomas H. Appleton and Angela H. Boswell, eds., *Searching for Their Places: Women in the South Across Four Centuries* (Columbia: University of Missouri Press, 2003), 43; Linda Merians, "What They Are, Who We Are: Representations of the 'Hottentot' in Eighteenth-Century Britain," *Eighteenth-Century Life* 17 (November 1993), 29–30; Diane Miller Sommerville, *Rape and Race in the Nineteenth-Century South* (Chapel Hill: University of North Carolina Press, 2004), 228.

45. Walter Woodward shows that John Winthrop, Jr., succeeded in heading off Connecticut witchcraft prosecutions with similar tactics. Woodward, *Prospero's America:*

John Winthrop, Jr., Alchemy, and the Creation of New England Culture, 1606–1676 (Chapel Hill: University of North Carolina Press for the Omohundro Institute of Early American History and Culture, 2010).

46. Dom Rex v. Amos Green, Connecticut State Archives, New London County Superior Court series, September 1767, box 34, folder 12; *Connecticut Courant* (Hartford), October 5, 1767, p. 2; *Boston Post-Boy*, October 12, 1767, p. 3; Cornelia Hughes Dayton, *Women Before the Bar: Gender, Law, and Society in Connecticut, 1639–1789* (Chapel Hill: University of North Carolina Press for the Institute of Early American History and Culture, 1995), 164 n. 11.

47. Murrin, "'Things Fearful to Name,'" 140; *Connecticut Journal* (New Haven), September 21, 1770; *Boston Gazette*, September 2, 1771; *Massachusetts Spy* (Boston), May 14, 1772; *Providence Gazette* (Providence, RI), May 23, 1772; A Dialogue *between Elizabeth Smith, and John Sennet . . .* (Boston, 1773). The McKney case papers are in Suffolk Files, no. 148344, and the trial records are in the Supreme Judicial Court Record Book, 1778–1780, leaves 72 and 73, all in the Massachusetts Archives, Boston.

48. Peter Bowdish v. Isaac Baldwin, New London County Court Record Series, March 1770, Box 36, folder 9; Pardon Clark v. Asa Minor, June 1770, New London County Court record series, box 154, folder 2; Governor & Co v. Henry Burden, September 1782, New London County Court record series, box 34, folder 16; *Connecticut Courant* (Hartford), October 5, 1767, p. 2; *Boston Post-Boy*, October 12, 1767, p. 3.

49. John Adams, *Diary and Autobiography of John Adams*, ed. L. H. Butterfield, Leonard C. Faber, and Wendell D. Garrett, 4 vols. (Cambridge, Mass.: Harvard University Press, 1962), 1: 171–72. It is possible, of course, that vernacular stories like this circulated in seventeenth-century New England—but we have found no record of one, and vernacular jokes were seldom recorded. More broadly, we imagine that there was always a contest between the most rigorous Puritans and others who were more relaxed. Sometimes one side was dominant, sometimes the other. The periodic "awakenings" that swept through the region suggest this kind of tension.

50. Charles-Louis de Secondat, baron de La Brède et de Montesquieu, *L'Esprit des lois (The Spirit of Laws)* trans. Thomas Nugent (New York: Hafner Press, 1949), book 12, ch. 6, section 6, 189; Swift, *System of Laws*, 295, 308. On Montesquieu's popularity in the British Isles, see Michael Conforti, "An Inconvenient Forum: Power, Politics, and the Common Law in the Age of Mansfield" (Ph.D. diss., Fordham University, 2011), 85 n. 184. A search of the database of Early American Imprints, series 1: Evans, 1639–1800, yielded at least sixty-nine different citations of Montesquieu in eighteenth-century America. Beccaria was excerpted and quoted repeatedly in the American press after the Revolution. For example: *Pennsylvania Evening Herald and the American Monitor* (Philadelphia), February 2, 1786; *Loudon's New-York Packet*, December 1, 1786; *Pennsylvania Mercury* (Philadelphia), October 21, 1788. On Swift's indebtedness to Beccaria and Montesquieu, see Lawrence B. Goodheart, *The Solemn Sentence of Death: Capital Punishment in Connecticut* (Amherst: University of Massachusetts Press, 2011), 71.

51. Julian P. Boyd, ed., *The Papers of Thomas Jefferson*, 36 vols. to date (Princeton, N.J.: Princeton University Press, 1950–), 2: 325; *Freeman's Journal; or, The North-American Intelligencer* (Philadelphia) June 4, 1783, p. 3 and *Pennsylvania Evening Post, and Public Advertiser* (Philadelphia) June 4, 1783, p. 6; Negley K. Teeters, *"Hang by the Neck": The Legal Use of Scaffold and Noose, Gibbet, Stake, and Firing Squad from Colonial Times to the Present* (Springfield, Ill.: Charles C. Thomas, 1967), 111–12; George Painter, "The Sensibilities of Our Forefathers: The History of Sodomy Laws in the United States (1991–2005)," http://www.glapn.org/sodomylaws/sensibilities/introduction.htm (accessed February 2, 2011).

52. According to U.S. census data, in 1800 there were more than three times as many white men aged sixteen to forty-four years (37.4 percent of the whole male population) as there were white men over forty-five years (11.9 percent of the whole male population). In 1830, the first census to list white men aged eighty to eighty-nine years, they constituted less than three-tenths of 1 percent of white males (0.0029), whereas white men aged fifteen to twenty-nine years, the population most often associated with bestiality, constituted 29 percent of white males. These young men outnumbered octogenarians by almost exactly one hundred to one. In the 1790s the ratio would have been even more lopsided. See "Historical Statistics of the United States, Millenial Edition Online," http://hsus.cambridge.org/HSUSWeb/table/seriesfirst.do?id = Aa287–364 (accessed March 30, 2011). U.S. Department of Commerce, Bureau of the Census, "Population by Age, Sex, Race, and Nativity: 1790 to 1970," in *Historical Statistics of the United States: Colonial Times to 1970*, part 1 (Washington, D.C.: U.S. Census Bureau, 1975), 16.

53. Quotd in Carole Haber, *Beyond Sixty-Five: The Dilemma of Old Age in America's Past* (Cambridge: Cambridge University Press, 1983), 8; Robert V. Wells, *Population of the British Colonies in North America Before 1776* (Princeton, N.J.: Princeton University Press, 1975), 116–18 (cited in Haber, *Beyond Sixty-Five*, 8); Paula A. Scott, *Growing Old in the Early Republic: Spiritual, Social, and Economic Issues, 1790–1830* (New York: Garland, 1997), 9, 16; Haber, *Beyond Sixty-Five*, 8, 23; Scott, *Growing Old*, 33, 48.

54. Haber, *Beyond Sixty-Five*, 2–3.

55. Job 32:7; *The Old man's Calendar . . .* (Boston, 1781), 18. The quotation from Job 32:7 appears on the title page. This work went through five editions, including two Boston printings in 1781, one in London in 1783, another in Dover, N.H., in 1793, and finally one in the Berkshire town of Stockbridge, Mass., in 1794. Haber cites the quoted passage from the 1793 edition in *Beyond Sixty-Five*, 26, 43. W. Andrew Achenbaum, *Old Age in the New Land: The American Experience Since 1790* (Baltimore: Johns Hopkins University Press, 1978), 16–17.

56. Thomas, " 'Not Having God Before His Eyes,' " 160. Twenty-five men were prosecuted for attempting or committing bestiality between 1740 and 1850 in Somerset County, England. Only in three cases do the documents reveal the age of the defendants, and in all they were young—fourteen, twenty-two, and twenty-three years old. Polly Morris, "Sodomy and Male Honor: The Case of Somerset, 1740–1850," in Kent Gerard

and Gert Kekma, eds., *The Pursuit of Sodomy: Male Homosexuality in Renaissance and Enlightenment Europe* (New York: Harrington Park Press, 1989), 387.

57. According to Dayton, "by the end of the eighteen century, a consensus had been reached in Connecticut that only black men deserved to die on the gallows for sexual assault." *Women Before the Bar*, 282.

58. David Hackett Fischer, *Growing Old in America*, expanded ed. (New York: Oxford University Press, 1978), chs. 1 and 2, argued that age was exalted in early America (ca. 1607–1820), but that there was a transition toward the exaltation of youth in the decades from 1770 to 1820—a veritable revolution in age relations. If such motives were operating in the Farrell and Washburn cases, then one might expect the accusers and prosecutors of the two old men to be distinctly younger men. In fact it appears that the witnesses, prosecutors, and judges represented a cross-section of the adult male population, tilted somewhat toward age, which correlated with high office.

59. Laqueur similarly wrote that sex "is situational; it is explicable only within the context of battles over gender and power." *Making Sex*, 11.

Chapter 2. The Unlikely Prosecutions
of John Farrell and Gideon Washburn

1. Distance calculated from routes printed in *Fleets Pocket Almanack for the Year of Our Lord 1797* . . . . (Boston: T. & J. Fleet, 1796), 160, 161, 165 (as roads were later made more direct the distance fell to about eighty-nine miles. Judgments on Rev. Henry Williams based on comparative data in Richard D. Brown, *Knowledge Is Power: The Diffusion of Information in Early America, 1700–1865* (New York: Oxford University Press, 1989), appendix (on clergymen and clerical publications), 297–302. Harold Field Worthley reports that the records of the congregation prior to 1854 are lost. *Inventory of the Records of the Particular (Congregational Churches) of Massachusetts Gathered*, ed. Harold Field Worthley (Cambridge, Mass.: Harvard University Press, 1970), 324.

2. Compiled from Louis H. Everts, *History of the Connecticut Valley in Massachusetts*, 2 vols. (Philadelphia: Louis H. Everts, 1879), 2: 733–36; Richard D. Brown, "Shays's Rebellion and the Ratification of the Federal Constitution in Massachusetts," in Richard Beeman, Stephen Botein, and Edward C. Carter, II, eds., *Beyond Confederation: Origins of the Constitution and American National Identity* (Chapel Hill: Institute of Early American History and Culture and University of North Carolina Press, 1987), 123; Hampshire County's vote, including Hubbard's, is recorded in [Massachusetts Convention, 1788] *Debates, resolutions and other proceedings, of the Convention of the commonwealth of Massachusetts* . . . (Boston, 1788), 214. Perusal of the entire record reveals that most delegates did not speak or serve on committees. Though this record identifies "John Hubbard," his actual name was more likely Jonathan Atherton Hubbard, born in 1750, according to Ruth Ellen (Nickerson) Field, *A History of Leverett, Massachusetts, Together with a Genealogy of its Early Inhabitants* (Bountiful, Utah: Family History Publishers, 1996), 258.

3. [U.S. Bureau of the Census], *Heads of Families at the First Census of the United States Taken in the year 1790: Massachusetts* (Washington, D.C.: Government Printing Office, 1908), 9, 115; [U.S. Bureau of the Census], *Return of the Whole Number of Persons Within the Several Districts of the United States* [second census] (n.p.: n.d., [1801]), 11. The number of males over age sixteen (polls) is reported in Thomas and John Fleet, *A Pocket almanac for the year of our Lord 1794 . . . to which is annexed the Massachusetts register* (Boston, 1793), 55. Population for 1796 is an estimate based on the figures for 1790 and 1800 and assumes constant growth across the decade. This almanac puts the mileage from Montague to Sunderland (on the river) at ten miles, and like other Massachusetts almanacs omits Leverett entirely from its travel routes. Farrell's advertisement, "Cancers Cured," appears in the *Greenfield Gazette*, May 12, 1796, p. 4, and May 19, 1796, p. 3.

4. Peter Benes, "Itinerant Physicians, Healers, and Surgeon-Dentists in New England and New York, 1720–1825," in Peter Benes, ed., *Medicine and Healing: The Dublin Seminar for New England Folklife*, Annual Proceedings, July 14–15, 1990 (Boston: Boston University Press, 1990), 95–112. On particular surgical and chemical treatments see Elaine Forman Crane, ed., *The Diary of Elizabeth Drinker*, 3 vols. (Boston: Northeastern University Press, 1991), 3, 1741, 1741n (May 1, 1804), 1744 (May 17, 1804), 1993 (December 30, 1806), 2009 (February 12, 1807), which includes entries regarding an African American cancer doctor who treated members of Drinker's elite circle of acquaintances, in addition to a well-known allopathic physician and a Methodist preacher who also treated cancers.

5. *Connecticut Courant* (Hartford), October 31, 1785, p. 2; *Connecticut Gazette* (New London), November 23, 1791, p. 3; *Worcester Spy* (Worcester, Mass.), September 13, 1792, p. 4. Farrell does not appear in the Leverett census for either 1790 or 1800, nor does his name show up anywhere in Massachusetts, Connecticut, or Rhode Island in the 1790 list of heads of families. As a then seventy-nine-year old, it is not surprising, since many old men lived in the households of younger people, often a son or a daughter. That he was not living with a son seems likely inasmuch as no one by the name of Farrell headed a household anywhere in Massachusetts, though there was one each in Connecticut and Rhode Island.

6. From summons of September 20, 1796, signed by John Tucker, clerk of the court, Suffolk File no. 159835, Commonwealth v. Farrell, 1796, Massachusetts Archives; John Farrell case, September Term at Northampton, 1796, Supreme Judicial Court records, Massachusetts Archives.

7. Quotation from Farrell petition no. 1, n.d., Governor's Council Pardon File, Massachusetts Archives; Murrin, " 'Things Fearful to Name': Bestiality in Early America," in Angela N. H. Creager and William Chester Jordan, eds., *The Animal/Human Boundary: Historical Perspectives* (Rochester, N.Y.: University of Rochester Press, 2002), 132, 138, 142; Richard Godbeer, " 'The Cry of Sodom': Discourse, Intercourse, and Desire in Colonial New England," *William and Mary Quarterly* (*WMQ* hereafter), 3rd series, 52 (April 1995), 276; Godbeer, *Sexual Revolution in Early America* (Baltimore: Johns Hopkins University Press, 2002), 49–50.

8. John Adams, *Diary and Autobiography of John* Adams, 4 vols., ed. L. H. Butterfield et al. (Cambridge, Mass.: Harvard University Press, 1962), 1: 183 (December 18, 1760).

9. Simeon Strong, a resident of Amherst, just south of Leverett, heard the complaint against Farrell on June 25, 1796. This record and the indictment, Commonwealth v. Farrell, Northampton, September Term, 1796, are found in the Suffolk Files, no. 159835, Supreme Judicial Court records, Massachusetts Archives; *Hampshire Gazette* (Northampton), October 5, 1796; Murrin, "'Things Fearful to Name,'" 139–43. Without surveying every session of the Supreme Court of Judicature and the Supreme Judicial Court in every county for every year, one cannot state positively that no such indictment was brought in the intervening years.

10. *Federal Orrery* (Boston), May 5, 1796, p. 18, col. 2. Taken from *Hampshire Gazette* (Northampton), May 4, 1796; *State Gazette and Town and County Advertiser* (Providence), May 14, 1796, p. 152, dated at Northampton, April 29, 1796. We have found no printed copy of Dana's charge to the jury.

11. According to the census of 1800 the population had grown to 2,190 people, so if the rate of growth was relatively stable, the population would have approached 2,000 in 1796.

12. The trial report genre emerged after 1800, most notably for the trial of Jonathan Fairbanks for the murder of Elizabeth Fales in Dedham in 1801. Thereafter a relative handful of capital cases that aroused exceptional interest led printers, mostly in New England, New York, and Pennsylvania, to commission detailed reports that were retailed to the public and to lawyers and their student apprentices.

13. Quotation from Farrell petition no. 1, n.d., Governor's Council Pardon File, Massachusetts Archives. The assignment of Strong and Hooker is in Commonwealth v. Farrell, Northampton, September Term, 1796, Supreme Judicial Court records, Massachusetts Archives. As a matter of course, counsel was normally assigned one day before the trial, and sometimes on the same day.

14. *American Intelligencer* (West Springfield, Mass.), October 4, 1796, p. 3; *Hampshire Gazette* (Northampton), October 5, 1796, p. 3. The papers we found that reprinted the *American Intelligencer* report with the additional editorial comment were: *Columbian Centinel* (Boston), Oct. 8, 1796, p. 3; *New Hampshire and Vermont Journal: Or The Farmer's Weekly Museum* (Walpole, N.H.), Oct. 11, 1796, p. 3; *The Rising Sun* (Keene, N.H.), Oct. 11, 1796, p. 3; *Middlesex Gazette* (Middletown, Conn.), Oct. 14, 1796, p. 3; *Oracle of the Day* (Portsmouth, N.H.), Oct. 24, 1796, p. 3; *Rutland Herald* (Rutland, Vt.), Oct. 24, 1796, p. 2; *Otsego Herald; or, Western Advertiser* (Otsego, N.Y.), Oct. 27, 1796, p. 2.

15. William Potter, age sixty, was executed at New Haven in 1662, following the accusation of his son, who caught him engaged with a sow. His wife also testified to an incident with a dog in 1652, and on questioning, Potter admitted to numerous acts with animals, starting at the age of ten years. Murrin, "'Things Fearful to Name,'" 134–35. The pattern of behavior has been observed in the psychological literature on bestiality. Lawrence B. Goodheart, *Solemn Sentence of Death: Capital Punishment in Connecticut* (Amherst: University of Massachusetts Press, 2011), 22, 23, 26.

16. Nancy O. Phillips, ed., *Town Records of Derby Connecticut, 1655–1710* (New Haven, Conn.: Tuttle, Morehouse and Taylor, 1901), 270; Ada C. Haight, *The Richard Washburn Family Genealogy: A Family History of 200 Years with Some Connected Families* (Ossing, N.Y., Higginson Book, 1937), 1254; W. C. Sharpe, *The Washburn Family: Descendants of John of Plymouth Mass., and William of Stratford, Conn., and Hempstead, L.I.* (Seymour, Conn.: Record Print, 1892), 8; John Maltby, "Re: William Washburn, Derby CT, Abt 1700," *Washburn Family Genealogy Forum*, www.genealogy.com/genforum, accessed November 24, 1998; Samuel Orcutt, *The History of the Old Town of Derby, Connecticut, 1642–1880* (Springfield, Mass.: Springfield Printing, 1880), 109, 110, 129, 157; Phillips, *Town Records of Derby*, 180, 183, 186, 193, 224, 232, 279, 425. Note that the Washburn family also appeared in the records as Washborn, Washband, and Washbon.

17. The marriage was recorded in Derby's Record of Vital Statistics, Derby town hall, Derby, Conn. The other children of Gideon Washburn and Esther Alling were Asahel, born March 30, 1746; Anne, born January 30, 1748; Lucretia, born September 5, 1750; Mabel, born September 16, 1752; Eunice, born May 20, 1755; William, born May 1, 1757; and Sarah, born October 16, 1760. Mabel Thacher Rosemary Washburn, *Washburn Family Foundations in Normandy, England and America* (Greenfield, Ind.: Mitchell Printing, 1953), 149. Washburn's relationship with Ezra Stiles was rather remote. Four Stiles brothers immigrated to New England in the seventeenth century. Gideon Washburn's grandmother was daughter of Francis Stiles whereas Ezra Stiles descended from Francis's brother John. Henry Reed Stiles, *The Stiles Family in America* (Jersey City, N.J.: Doan & Pilson, printers, 1895), 471.

18. Derby Land Records, Derby town hall, Derby, Conn. 5: 106, 170, 226; Washburn, *Washburn Family Foundations*, 139–48.

19. Hollis A. Campbell, William C. Sharpe, and Frank G. Bassett, *Seymour, Past and Present* (Seymour, Conn.: W. C. Sharpe, 1902), 25–26, 95; Sharpe, *Seymour and Vicinity: Historical Collections* (Seymour, Conn.: Record Print, 1878), 40–41; "Records of Baptism, St. James Church, Derby," *New England Historical and Genealogical Register* 76 (1922), 135, 136, 138. By 1763 the small tribe was scattered and Chuse sold the land to Ebenezer Keeny, Joesph Hull, and Gideon's cousin John Wooster. The three were Seymour's first entrepreneurs who introduced manufacturing to the town.

20. In 1741 the Connecticut legislature decided that the best place for building a meetinghouse for the parish of Oxford was "on land belonging to Ephraim Washbourn." October 19, 1741, H. Trumbull and C. J. Hoadly, eds., *The Public Records of the Colony of Connecticut [1636–1776] . . . Transcribed and Published (in Accordance with a Resolution of the General assembly)*, 15 vols. (Hartford, Conn.: Brown and Parsons, 1850–90), 8: 427. Ephraim Washburn was also named collector and treasurer of the district of Oxford in Derby in the first meeting of the Oxford Parish. Ephraim Washburn signed one of the first claims of Connecticut to northeast Pennsylvania. In 1780 Ephraim Washburn built a paper mill in nearby Danbury, though the mill did not fare well and he quickly sold his share in it to another family. Norman Litchfield and Sabina Connolly Hoyt, *History of the Town of Oxford, Connecticut* (Oxford, Conn.: N. Litchfield, 1960), 9,

21, 23; William C. Sharpe, *History of Seymour Connecticut, with Biographies and Genealogies* (Seymour, Conn.: Record Print, 1879), 42, 44; Orcutt, *The History of the Old Town of Derby*, 147; Julian P. Boyd, ed., *The Susquehannah Company Papers*, 11 vols. (Ithaca, N.Y.: Cornell University Press, 1930–71), 1: 13; James Montgomery Bailey, *History of Danbury, Connecticut, 1684–1896* (New York: Burr Printing House, 1896), 258.

21. See also Historic House Committee, Bicentennial Commission, Oxford, Connecticut, *Early Houses of Oxford* (Derby, Conn.: [Historic House] Committee, 1976), 72. Other members of the family did not fare well even in the peripheral centers. When Gideon's cousin Samuel Washburn died in 1762, his debts were greater than the value of his estate and the probate court of New Haven ordered its sale to cover debts. Trumbull and Hoadly, *Public Records of the Colony*, 12: 30–31.

22. Roll of Company, 1746, *Collections of the Connecticut Historical Society*, 31 vols. (Hartford, Conn.: Connecticut Historical Society, 1860–1967), 15: 151; confession of Daniel Tucker, April 9, 1747, Connecticut State Archives, Crimes and Misdemeanors, 1st series, 4: 105a; Kenneth Scott, *Counterfeiting in Colonial America* (New York: Oxford University Press, 1957), 158, 161–67; William G. Domonell, *Newgate: From Copper Mine to State Prison* (Simsbury, Conn.: Simsbury Historical Society, 1998), 12; Trumbull and Hoadly, *Colonial Records of the Colony*, October 1751, 10: 66; Connecticut State Archives, Finance and Currency, series 2, 4: 66a; Washburn, *Washburn Family Foundations in Normandy, England and America*, 147; deposition of Samuel Wheler of Derby in regard to dissatisfaction of James Pritchard over his bargain with Thomas and Jerusha McDowland, July 4, 1760, Connecticut State Archives, Private Controversies, series 2, 31: 156i. Washburn enlisted in the second regiment of Connecticut under Col. Nathan Whiting of New Haven on April 3, 1758, was discharged on November 17, 1758, reenlisted in the same regiment on April 21, 1759 (this time he actually endorsed with his signature the list of soldiers in the company), and was discharged at a later date. He enlisted for the final time on April 9, 1761, and was discharged on December 4, 1761. *Collections of the Connecticut Historical Society*, 10: 30, 126, 127, 260. Fred Anderson, in *A People's Army: Massachusetts Soldiers and Society in the Seven Years' War* (Chapel Hill: University of North Carolina Press for the Institute of Early American History and Culture, 1984), 38–39, explains that farmers and laborers often enlisted so as to earn cash.

23. *New Milford Land Records*, New Milford town hall, New Milford, Conn., 10: 151, 256, 12: 50; 14: 165; 15: 79; 17: 422.

24. Christopher Collier, *All Politics Is Local: Family, Friends, and Provincial Interests in the Creation of the Constitution* (Hanover, N.H.: University Press of New England, 2003), 31. Reeve's first student in 1773 was his wife's cousin Aaron Burr, the future vice president of the United States. Thereafter Reeve took a number of students into his home before constructing a separate law school building in 1784. Alain Campbell White, *The History of the Town of Litchfield, Connecticut, 1720–1920* (Litchfield, Conn.: Enquirer Print, 1920), 98–109; Rachel Carley, *Litchfield: The Making of a New England Town* (Litchfield, Conn.: Litchfield Historical Society, 2011), 92–93; Litchfield Historical Society

(hereafter LHS), "History of the Litchfield Law School," http://www.litchfieldhistorical society.org/history/law_school.p hp, accessed March 7, 2011; John Langbein, "Blackstone, Litchfield, and Yale: The Founding of the Yale Law School," in Anthony T. Kronman, ed., *History of the Yale Law School* editor Anthony T. Kronman (New Haven, Conn.: Yale University Press, 2004), 23–32.

25. Catherine Keene Fields and Lisa C. Kightlinger, *To Ornament Their Minds: Sarah Pierce's Litchfield Female Academy, 1792–1833* (Litchfield, Conn.: Litchfield Historical Society, 1993); Lynne Templeton Brickley, "Sarah Pierce's Litchfield Female Academy, 1792–1833" (Ph.D. diss., Harvard University, 1985); Emily Noyes Vanderpoel, *Chronicles of a Pioneer School: The Litchfield Female Academy, Litchfield, Connecticut, 1792–1833* (Cambridge, Mass.: Harvard University Press, 1902); James Morris, *Memoirs of James Morris of South Farms in Litchfield, Written by Himself and Edited by His Grandson* (New Haven, Conn.: Yale University Press, 1933), 54.

26. Sanford v. Washburn et ux, Connecticut State Archives, Court Records, Supreme Court of Errors, RG 003, box 4, June 1795–June 1798; *Litchfield Land Records*, Litchfield town hall, Litchfield, Conn., 14: 390; 15: 131; 17: 436–38; Carley, *Litchfield*, 72.

27. James Morris, "Litchfield County Report" (1815) in Christopher P. Bickford et al., eds., *Voices of the New Republic: Connecticut Towns 1800–1832*, 2 vols. (New Haven, Conn.: Memoirs of the Connecticut Academy of Arts and Sciences, 2003), vol. 1, *What They Said*, 136; Samuel Hart, *Old Connecticut: Historical Papers on People, Places, Traditions, and Early Anglicanism* (Hartford, Conn.: Transcendental Books, 1976), 221; Bruce Steiner, "New England Anglicanism: A Genteel Faith?" *WMQ*, 3rd series, 27 (1970), 122–35, and "Anglican Office-Holding in Pre-Revolutionary Connecticut: The Parameters of New England Community," *WMQ*, 3rd series, 31 (1974), 247–81. See also Bruce Steiner, *Connecticut Anglicans in the Revolutionary Era: A Study in Communal Tensions* (Hartford, Conn.: American Revolutionary Bicentennial Commission of Connecticut, 1978).

28. White, *History of the Town of Litchfield*, 186; committee report, Sanford v. Washburn, Connecticut State Archives; receipt for reimbursement for William Washburn, August 26, 1796 and November 14, 1796, Northfield Congregational Church Papers, LHS.

29. *Litchfield Town Records*, Litchfield Town Hall, Litchfield, Conn., 1: 191; *Litchfield Land Records*, March 6, 1797, 17: 437–38; Litchfield Tax Records for 1797, Litchfield Town Hall, Litchfield, Conn. In comparison, William Washburn's taxable income would rank him in the top 27 percent of members of the First Congregational Church in Litchfield itself, and at the top 25 percent of the South Farm region of Litchfield. Washburn's herd was small in comparison to most farmers in the state. On average, Connecticut farms had seventeen domestic animals per person. Bruce C. Daniels, "Economic Development in Colonial and Revolutionary Connecticut: An Overview," *WMQ*, 3rd series, 37 (July 1980), 432–33.

30. Connecticut State Archives, Litchfield County Superior Court, Papers by Subject: Misc. Material 1752–1920, box 335; James Morris Justice of the Peace Books Litchfield County SS, Litchfield, March 19, 1792, entry 22, LHS; Jesse Root, *Reports of Cases*

Adjudged in the Superior Court and in the Supreme Court of Errors in the State of Connect-icut, 2 vols. (Hartford, Conn.: Hudson and Goodwin, 1802), 2: 499–503; Sanford v. Washburn, Connecticut State Archives. We thank Linda Hocking for bringing the entry from James Morris's Justice of the Peace book to our attention.

31. Morris, Justice of the Peace Books, entry 22; Root, *Reports of Cases*, 2: 499–503, 505–7; Sanford v. Washburn.

32. Litchfield County Superior Court, August Term 1799, bill of indictment against Gideon Washburn, Connecticut State Archives, Crimes and Misdemeanors, 2nd series, 2: 87a. Goodheart, *The Solemn Sentence of Death*, 97, provides a sketch of the Washburn case as a mysterious curiosity.

33. Dwight C. Kilburne, *The Bench and Bar of Litchfield County, Connecticut, 1709 – 1909: Biographical Sketches of Members, History and Catalogue of the Litchfield Law School* (Litchfield, Conn.: D. C. Kilbourn, 1909).

34. Uriah Tracy, *Reflections on Monroe's View, of the conduct of the Executive, as published in the United States, under the signature of Scipio* (Philadelphia, 1798), 84–85; Dorothy Deming to Julius Deming, June 20, 1799, Quincy Collection, LHS. The coalition that coalesced around Jefferson and Madison to challenge the Washington and Adams administrations had many labels including, most commonly, Republicans, Democratic-Republicans, the French party, and Jeffersonians.

35. John Allen, speech in Congress, July 5, 1798, *Annals of Congress*, 5th Congress, 2nd sess., 2098; John Allen to Julius Deming, May 24, 1798, Alice Wolcott Collection, LHS.

36. On Allen's reputation as an alcoholic, see for example Julius Deming to Lynde McCurdy, April 1, 1801, Quincy Collection, LHS. George Woodruff, *A Genealogical Register of the Inhabitants of the Town of Litchfield, Connecticut* (Hartford, Conn.: Case Lockwood & Brainard Company, 1900), 8. The announcement of Allen's decision not to seek reelection to Congress in the *Litchfield Monitor* on August 28, 1799, read: "We announce with much Regret the Resignation of the Hon. John Allen Esq of his Seat in Congress of the United States. The Reasons assigned for this Gentleman's decline, are not within our Knowledge; we however presume that no pecuniary Motives, nor the most virulent disorganizing Abuse, in any Crisis or imminent and sudden danger, are Objects of sufficient impression to withdraw him from the Post. The vile Slander of exclusive Patriots, which so far imposes on the Credulity, or Forbearance of the Public as to pass off with Indifference and Impunity, is under any circumstances of Resignation an Evil of no less common Concern."

37. Unknown writer to Pierpont Edwards, December 28, 1799, Pierpont Edwards Papers, Yale University, box 8, folder 1.

38. David Waldstreicher and Stephen R. Grossbart, "Abraham Bishop's Vocation; or, the Mediation of Jeffersonian Politics," *Journal of the Early Republic* 18 (Winter 1998), 635; Sidney Hayden, *Washington and His Masonic Compeers* (Whitefish, Mont.: Kessinger Publishing, 2003 [Orig. 1866]), 318; Mary-Jo Kline, ed., *Political Correspondence and Public Papers of Aaron Burr*, 2 vols. (Princeton, N.J.: Princeton University Press,

1983), 1: lix; Cathy N. Davidson, introduction to Hannah W. Foster, *The Coquette*, Early American Women Writers (New York: Oxford University Press, 1986), xi; Kristie Hamilton, "An Assault on the Will: Republican Virtue and the City in Hannah Webster Foster's 'The Coquette,'" *Early American Literature* 24 (Fall 1989), 135–51; Nancy Isenberg, "The 'Little Emperor': Aaron Burr, Dandyism, and the Sexual Politics of Treason," in Jeffrey L. Pasley, Andrew W. Robertson, and David Waldstreicher, eds., *Beyond the Founders: New Approaches to the Political History of the Early American Republic* (Chapel Hill: University of North Carolina Press, 2004), 129–58.

    39. *Connecticut Courant*, September 9, 1799.

    40. *Litchfield Monitor*, September 4, 1799.

    41. *Litchfield Monitor*, September 4, 1799; "Preliminary Remarks of Chief Justice Jesse Root at the Sentencing of Gideon Washburn," *Litchfield Monitor*, October 2, 1799; Jesse Root to Lynde Lord, October 25, 1799, LHS; Litchfield Co. Superior Court Executions on Judgment Cases, box 1, 1798–1816, Litchfield Superior Court Executions 1798–1802 Inclusive, LHS.

Chapter 3. Sexual Crisis in the Age of Revolution

    1. Richard D. Brown, "'Tried, Convicted, and Condemned, in Almost Every Barroom and Barber's Shop': Anti-Irish Prejudice in the Trial of Dominic Daley and James Halligan, Northampton, Massachusetts, 1806," *New England Quarterly* 84 (June 2011), 205–33.

    2. Bestiality among elderly men, while very rarely recorded, is not unknown. As noted in Chapter 1, William Potter, one of the original founders of the New Haven Colony, was sixty years old in 1662 when his son caught him having sex with a sow. Confronted, Potter confessed to a lifelong fondness for bestiality. In fact, in addition to the incident with the sow cited in Chapter 1, his wife had caught him red-handed a few years earlier having sex with a bitch and forgave him only after he promised to stop; and the family hanged the animal that "seduced" him. In 1662, however, Mrs. Potter was no longer in a forgiving mood and her husband was tried and sentenced to die. Before he went to the gallows Potter went through his farm and identified his sexual partners—a sow, two heifers, three sheep, and two pigs. The man and his animals were then executed together. John Murrin, "'Things Fearful to Name': Bestiality in Early America," in Angela N. H. Creager and William Chester Jordan, eds., *The Animal/Human Boundary: Historical Perspectives* (Rochester, N.Y.: University of Rochester Press, 2002), 134–35. Potter's history, however rare, is confirmed by the professional literature. Nearly three centuries later, two young Missouri women, aged nineteen and twenty-one, testified in 1926 that they saw through a barn's window seventy-two-year-old H. Wilson mounting a mare from behind. They entered the barn and startled the old man, who ran out naked. Wilson countered that an injury suffered fourteen years earlier made it impossible for him to engage in intercourse and a physician corroborated his statement. The jury, however, believed the women, and Wilson was sentenced to two years in prison. A. F.

Niemoeller, *Bestiality and the Law: A Resume of the Law and Punishment for Bestiality with Typical Cases from Fifteenth Century to the Present* (Girard, Kan.: Halderman-Julius, 1946), 28–29. In some cases senile dementia or Alzheimer's dementia may lead to the collapse of inhibitions and result in abnormal sexual behavior. And there are some, albeit very rare, documented modern cases of elderly men engaging in such behavior. For example, in August 2002, eighty-one-year-old S. A. Balderson, of Richmond County, Virginia, was convicted of having sex with cows in a Westmoreland County pasture. A police detective filmed Balderson going from cow to cow while wearing only a t-shirt, shoes, and sunglasses. The court ordered two years of counseling for Balderson. August 26, 2002, http://www.fredericksburg.com/News/FLS/2002/082002/08262002/sentenced (accessed April 14, 2011).

3. We do not suggest that sex with dogs, cows, and horses is impossible. Men have succeeded in getting their way even with aggressive canine breeds. On October 20, 2006, Pierce County, Washington, charged twenty-six-year-old Michael Patrick McPhail for penetrating his female pit bull terrier. McPhail's wife, who captured the incident on her cell phone camera, felt pity for the squealing and crying dog and called the police. See http://seattletimes.nwsource.com/html/localnews/2003314312_webbestiality20.html, accesed April 14, 2011.

4. Mic Hunter, "Uncovering the Relationship Between a Client's Adult Compulsive Sexual Behavior and Childhood Sexual Abuse," in Mic Hunter et al., eds., *Adult Survivors of Sexual Abuse: Treatment Innovations* (Thousand Oaks, Calif.: Sage Publications, 1995), 56–79; Gary Duffield, Angela Hassiotis, and Eileen Vizard, "Zoophilia in Young Sexual Abusers," *Journal of Forensic Psychiatry* 9 (September 1998), 294–304; William A. Alvarez and Jack P. Freinhar, "A Prevalence Study of Bestiality (Zoophilia) in Psychiatric In-patients, Medical In-patients, and Psychiatric Staff," *International Journal of Psychosomatics* 38(1991), 45–47; Walter Bacmeister, "Murder Committed by a Man Aged Sixty-three Years as Result of Constantly Troubled Conscience over Bestiality Performed at Seventeen Years of Age," *Journal of Criminal Psychopathology* 5 (July 1943), 169. A study of seventeenth-century sex in Middlesex, Mass., points out that members of the same families were accused of sexual crimes and that family members of John Lawrence, who was accused of bestiality in 1679, for example, were tried for a variety of sexual crimes. We did not find similar histories in the Washburn and Farrell families. Roger Thompson, *Sex in Middlesex: Popular Mores in a Massachusetts County, 1649–1699* (Amherst: University of Massachusetts Press, 1986), 100.

5. Wayne Brekhus, "Social Marking and the Mental Coloring of Identity: Sexual Identity Construction and Maintenance in the United States," *Sociological Forum* 11 (September 1996), 507–8.

6. Mark E. Kann, "Sexual Desire, Crime, and Punishment in the Early Republic," in Thomas A. Foster, ed., *Long Before Stonewall: Histories of Same-Sex Sexuality in Early America* (New York: New York University Press, 2007), 281.

7. Diary of John Adams, December 18, 1760, John Adams Diary, vol. 6, December 2, 1760, March 3, 1761, in *Adams Family Papers: An Electronic Archive*, Massachusetts

Historical Society, http://www.masshist.org/digitaladams/aea/cfm/doc.cfm?id=D6 &numrecs=25&archive=all&hi=on&mode=&query=Savile&queryid=&rec=6& start=1&tag=text#firstmatch (accessed April 14, 2011). See also Thomas A. Foster, *Sex and the Eighteenth-Century Man: Massachusetts and the History of Sexuality in America* (Boston: Beacon Press, 2006), 160–61.

8. Entry for September 20, 1860, Charles F. Winslow Diary, Charles Frederick Winslow Papers, Massachusetts Historical Society, Boston. We thank Professor Nancy Shoemaker for bringing this entry to our attention.

9. Moses C. Welch, *The Gospel to Be Preached to All Men, Illustrated in a Sermon Delivered in Windham, at the Execution of Samuel Freeman* (Windham, Conn.: Byrne, 1805), 30. Such outbursts, from colonial witch hunts to modern hysterias about sexual abuse in day-care centers, generally feature a measure of inexplicable randomness; in 1692, bizarre accusations by young girls led to a murderous hysteria in Salem, but the same type of accusations were dismissed in Stamford, Conn.; in the 1980s, some communities believed that toddlers' sexual talk bespoke abuse whereas others treated it as age-appropriate psychosexual inquiry. Richard Godbeer, *Escaping Salem: The Other Witch Hunt of 1692* (New York, 2005); John Demos, *The Enemy Within: 2000 Years of Witch-Hunting in the Western World* (New York: Viking, 2008).

10. Richard Godbeer, *Sexual Revolution in Early America* (Baltimore: Johns Hopkins University Press, 2002), chs. 7–9; Faramerz Dabhoiwala, *The Origins of Sex: A History of the First Sexual Revolution* (New York: Oxford University Press, 2012), ch. 2. We wish to clarify the very limited parameters of our psychohistorical inquiry. Unlike Paul Boyer and Stephen Nissenbaum, who traced the actions of individual accusers to specific neuroses or Oedipal conflicts, our study merely tries to make sense of the atmosphere that gave rise to these accusations. Boyer and Nissenbaum, *Salem Possessed: The Social Origins of Witchcraft* (Cambridge, Mass.: Harvard University Press, 1974). Why individuals decide to act in a specific way at a specific moment is beyond most historical inquiries. Our study neither assigns specific psychoanalytically theorized motivation to the actions and words of specific individuals nor applies a particular psychoanalytic model or theory.

11. Benjamin Rush, *Medical Inquiries and Observations upon the Diseases of the Mind* (Philadelphia: Kimber & Richardson, 1812), 347–48.

12. Rush, *Medical Inquiries*, 347; Thomas W. Laqueur, *Solitary Sex: A Cultural History of Masturbation* (New York: Zone Books, 2003), 47.

13. Pat Moloney, "Savages in the Scottish Enlightenment's History of Desire," *Journal of the History of Sexuality* 14 (July 2005), 236–44; Robin Ganev, "Milkmaids, Ploughmen, and Sex in Eighteenth-Century Britain," *Journal of the History of Sexuality* 16 (January 2007), 42.

14. Michel Foucault, *The History of Sexuality: An Introduction*, 3 vols., trans Robert Hurley (New York: Vintage, 1976–84), 1: 116, 35; Bernd W. Krysmanski, *Hogarth's Hidden Parts: Satiric Allusion, Erotic Wit, Blasphemous Bawdiness and Dark Humor in Eighteenth-Century English Art* (New York: Georg Olms, 2010); Dror Wahrman, *The Making of the*

Modern Self (New Haven, Conn.: Yale University Press, 2004), 21. See also Charles Taylor, *Sources of the Self: The Making of Modern Identity* (Cambridge, Mass.: Harvard University Press, 1989); David M. Halperin, "Forgetting Foucault: Acts, Identities, and the History of Sexuality," *Representations* 63 (Summer 1998), 93–120.

15. Thomas W. Laqueur, *Making Sex: Body and Gender from the Greeks to Freud* (Cambridge, Mass: Harvard University Press, 1990), ch. 5; Karen Harvey, "The Century of Sex? Gender, Bodies and Sexuality in the Long Eighteenth Century," *Historical Journal* 45 (December 2002), 899–916.

16. A classic work on sentimental novels remains Cathy N. Davidson, *Revolution and the Word: The Rise of the Novel in America* (New York: Oxford University Press, 1986). See also Ruth H. Bloch, "Changing Conceptions of Sexuality and Romance in Eighteenth-Century America," *William and Mary Quarterly* (*WMQ* hereafter), 3rd series, 60 (January 2003), 13–42: Bruce Burgett, *Sentimental Bodies: Sex, Gender, and Citizenship in the Early Republic* (Princeton, N.J.: Princeton University Press, 1998), chapter 4; Laqueur, *Solitary Sex*, 302–58; Martha Tomhave Blauvelt, *The Works of the Heart: Young Women and Emotion, 1780–1830* (Charlottesville: University of Virginia Press, 2007), 32–48; Moloney, "Savages in the Scottish Enlightenment's History of Desire," 236–41; Michael Ignatieff, "John Millar and Individualism," in Istvan Hont and Ignatieff, eds., *Wealth and Virtue: The Shaping of Political Economy in the Scottish Enlightenment* (Cambridge: Cambridge University Press, 1983), 337–38; Dabhoiwala, *Origins of Sex*, 169–79.

17. *Saturday Night's Post*, London, April 13, 1780, in Rictor Norton (ed.), "Burke Proposes Abolition of the Pillory, 1780," *Homosexuality in Eighteenth-Century England: A Sourcebook*, 23 February 2007, updated 3 April 2007, http://rictornorton.co.uk/eigh teen/1780burk.htm, accessed on August 14, 2013.

18. House of Commons, April 11, 1780, in Norton (ed.), "Burke Proposes Abolition of the Pillory, 1780."

19. Thomas Potter and John Wilkes, *An Essay on Woman* (London, 1763), 2, 3–4; Jeremy Bentham, "Offences Against One's Self: Paederasty" (1785), http://www.columbia .edu/cu/lweb/eresources/exhibitions/sw25/bentham/index.html (accessed April 14, 2011). The essay was first published in the *Journal of Homosexuality* 3 (Summer 1978), 389–405, and 4 (Fall 1978), 91–107. B. R. Burg, *Sodomy and the Perception of Evil: English Sea Rovers in the Seventeenth-Century Caribbean* (New York: New York University Press, 1983), 37–38; Richard Godbeer, "'The Cry of Sodom': Discourse, Intercourse, and Desire in Colonial New England," *WMQ*, 3rd series, 52 (1995): 276–77; Arthur N. Gilbert, "Buggery and the British Navy, 1700–1861," *Journal of Social History* 10 (Autumn 1976), 72; James Raven, *Judging New Wealth: Popular Publishing and Responses to Commerce in England, 1750–1800* (Oxford: Oxford University Press, 1992), 150; Elizabeth Campbell Denliner, "The Garment and the Man: Masculine Desire in Harris's List of Covent-Garden Ladies, 1764–1793," *Journal of the History of Sexuality* 11 (July 2002), 389; Randolph Trumbach, "Sex, Gender, and Sexual Identity in Modern Culture: Male Sodomy and Female Prostitution in Enlightenment London," *Journal of the History of Sexuality*

2 (October 1991), 186–203; Anna Clark, "The Chevalier d'Eon and Wilkes: Masculinity and Politics in the Eighteenth Century," *Eighteenth-Century Studies* 32 (Fall 1998), 19–48; Dennis Rubini, "Sexuality in Augustan England: Sodomy, Politics, Elite Circles and Society," in Kent Gerard, ed., *The Pursuit of Sodomy: Male Homosexuality in Renaissance and Enlightenment Europe* (New York: Routledge, 1989), 349–82; Pamela Cheek, *Sexual Antipodes: Enlightenment Globalization and the Placing of Sex* (Stanford, Calif.: Stanford University Press, 2003), 95–98.

20. Randoph Trumbach, "London's Sodomites: Homosexual Behavior and Western Culture in the 18th Century," *Journal of Social History* 11 (Autumn 1977), 9; Trumbach, "Sex, Gender, and Sexual Identity in Modern Culture," 190; David F. Greenberg, *The Construction of Homosexuality* (Chicago: University of Chicago Press, 1988), 338–39; A. D. Harvey, "Prosecution for Sodomy in England at the Beginning of the Nineteenth Century," *Historical Journal* 21 (December 1978), 939–48; H. G. Cocks, *Nameless Offences: Homosexual Desire in the Nineteenth Century* (Cambridge: Cambridge University Press, 2003), 20–24; Robert B. Shoemaker, "The Old Bailey Proceedings and the Representation of Crime and Criminal Justice in Eighteenth-Century London," *Journal of British Studies* 47 (July 2008), 559–80.

21. Isabel V. Hull, *Sexuality, State, and Civil Society in Germany, 1700–1815* (Ithaca, N.Y.: Cornell University Press, 1996), 340, 344–50; William Benemann, *Male-Male Intimacy in Early America: Beyond Romantic Friendships* (New York: Routledge, 2006), 39; Gilbert, "Buggery and the British Navy," 81; B. R. Burg, *Boys at Sea: Sodomy, Indecency, and Courts Martial in Nelson's Navy* (Houndmills: Palgrave Macmillan, 2007); Robert J. Corber, "Representing the 'Unspeakable': William Godwin and the Politics of Homophobia," *Journal of the History of Sexuality* 1 (July 1990), 85–101.

22. Katherine Crawford, *European Sexualities, 1400–1800* (New York: Cambridge University Press, 1997), 205; Matthew J. Kinservik, *Sex, Scandal, and Celebrity in Late Eighteenth-Century England* (London: Palgrave Macmillan, 2007). Similarly, anxieties over masculinity erupted in force in Germany following Napoleon's routing of the Prussian military at Jena and Auerstaedt in 1806. Peter Uwe Hohendahl, "The New Man: Theories of Masculinity Around 1800," *Goethe Yearbook* 15 (2008), 187–215.

23. Arthur N. Gilbert, "Sexual Deviance and Disaster During the Napoleonic Wars," in *Albion: A Quarterly Journal Concerned with British Studies* 9 (Spring 1977), 102, 113; Gilbert, "Buggery and the British Navy," 73; H. G. Cocks, "Safeguarding Civility: Sodomy, Class and Moral Reform in Early Nineteenth-Century England," *Past and Present* 190 (February 2006), 121–46; Katherine Binhammer, "The Sex Panic of the 1790s," *Journal of the History of Sexuality* 6 (January 1996) 409–34; Corber, "Representing the 'Unspeakable'"; Netta Murray Goldsmith, *The Worst of Crimes: Homosexuality and the Law in Eighteenth-Century London* (Brookfield, Vt.: Ashgate, 1998). A. D. Harvey proposes that the "*major* source of this hostility towards sexual deviancy was itself sexual neurosis; and the coincidence in time of the most vicious persecutions of homosexuals with the development of the sexual ethic subsequently misnamed *Victorian* is altogether too remarkable to be ignored." Harvey, "Prosecutions for Sodomy in England," 947.

Brian Henry, *Dublin Hanged: Crime, Law Enforcement and Punishment in Late Eighteenth-Century Ireland* (Dublin: Irish Academic Press, 1994), reports 242 hangings in Dublin from 1780 to 1795, none of which were for sodomy.

24. Gilbert, "Buggery and the British Navy," 81–87; Gilbert, "Sexual Deviance and Disaster," 111.

25. Commonwealth of Massachusetts v. Joshua Clark, September 25, 1787, Supreme Judicial Court Record Book, September 1788–April 1789, p. 185, Suffolk Files, v, 1177: case # 15920. The preceding notation follows the system of identifying records in the Massachusetts Archives, Boston, where the records of nearly all capital judicial proceedings are located, Essex County excepted. The *Otsego Herald* used the following text on September 19, 1799: "Sodomy. Gideon Washburn, an old Man of 86 years, was lately found guilty on an indictment for Beastiality, at the Superior Court, at Litchfield in Connecticut, and received sentence of DEATH; to be executed on the 15th of November next." The conflation appeared in religious tracts such as *The Constitution and standards of the Associated-Reformed Church in North America* (New York, 1799), 323–24. Jonathan Goldberg suggested that men convicted of bestiality were brutally punished to accentuate the " 'unnaturalness' of sodomy and thus its lack of relation to bonds between men." Goldberg, *Sodometries: Renaissance Texts, Modern Sexualities* (Stanford, Calif.: Stanford University Press, 1992), 239.

26. Clare A. Lyons, *Sex Among the Rabble: An Intimate History of Gender and Power in the Age of Revolution, Philadelphia, 1730–1830* (Chapel Hill: University of North Carolina Press and Omohundro Institute of Early American History and Culture, 2006), 181. On the urban sexual scene at the end of the eighteenth century, see also Godbeer, *Sexual Revolution in Early America*, ch. 8; Christine Stansell, *City of Women: Sex and Class in New York, 1789–1860* (New York: Knopf, 1982), ch. 2. On the connection between the Enlightenment and sexual autonomy, see also Jay Fliegleman, *Prodigals and Pilgrims: The American Revolution Against Patriarchal Authority* (New York: Cambridge University Press, 1982), ch. 5.

27. Foster, *Sex and the Eighteenth-Century Man*, 173–74; Clare A. Lyons, "Mapping an Atlantic Sexual Culture: Homoeroticism in Eighteenth-Century Philadelphia," *WMQ*, 3rd series, 60 (January 2003), 121–43; *Cuckold's Chronicle: Being Select Trials for Adultery, Imbecility, Incest, Ravishment, &c.*, vol. 1 (Boston: n.p., 1798), a reprint of H. Lemoin's London edition of 1793.

28. Leslie C. Patrick-Stamp, "The Prison Sentence Docket for 1795: Inmates at the First State Penitentiary," *Pennsylvania History* 60 (1993), 366; *Morning Chronicle* (New York), March 21, 1803; Benemann, *Male-Male Intimacy in Early America*, 71–92. Penal reformers in the early nineteenth century argued that excessive passion led to sodomy and recommended secluding incarcerated offenders to check desire.

29. William Bradford, *An Enquiry How Far the Punishment of Death is Necessary in Pennsylvania. With Notes and Illustrations* (Philadelphia, 1793), 20–21. On the time line of legal revisions of antisodomy laws in the United States, see George Painter, *The Sensibilities of Our Forefathers: The History of Sodomy Laws in the United States*, http://www .glapn.org/sodomylaws/sensibilities/introduction.htm (accessed February 14, 2011). For

the Massachusetts revision, which matched the Pennsylvania penalty, see Irene Q. Brown and Richard D. Brown, *The Hanging of Ephraim Wheeler: A Story of Rape, Incest, and Justice in Early America* (Cambridge, Mass.: Harvard University Press, 2003), 198. Connecticut did not distinguish in the prosecution of bestiality between minors and adults. In 1821 Connecticut revised its punishment for bestiality from death to life imprisonment, but while offenders under fifteen were deemed too young to stand prosecution for sodomy, no minimum age was required for bestiality charges. Nancy Hathaway Steenburg, *Children and the Criminal Law in Connecticut, 1635–1855: Changing Perceptions of Childhood* (New York: Routledge, 2005), 124–25.

30. T. A. Milford, "Boston's Theater Controversy and Liberal Notions of Advantage," *New England Quarterly* 72 (1999), 81–82. In 1792 a divided state legislature voted to allow local option on theaters, ending the blanket prohibition that had been enacted in 1750. See also Jacqueline Barbara Carr, *After the Siege: A Social History of Boston, 1775–1800* (Boston: Northeastern University Press, 2005), and Heather S. Nathans, *Early American Theatre from the Revolution to Thomas Jefferson: Into the Hands of the People* (New York: Cambridge University Press, 2003).

31. S. F. Leander, "On Modern Novels, and their Effects," *Massachusetts Magazine; or, Monthly Museum . . .* , November 1791, 3, 662: Foster, *The Coquette*, 112–13; *The Public Records of the Colony of Connecticut, 1636–1776*, James H. Trumbull and Charles J. Hoadly, eds., 15 vols. (Hartford: Press of the Case, Lockwood & Brainard Company, 1850–1890), 10: 25; Richard Gaskins, "Changes in the Criminal Law in Eighteenth-Century Connecticut," *American Journal of Legal History* 25 (October 1981), 309–42.

32. Nathaniel Emmons, *A Discourse, Delivered November 3, 1790, at the Particular Request of a Number of Respectable Men in Franklin, who were Forming a Society, for the Reformation of Morals* (Providence, [1790]), 4, 26, 27. Franklin is located in the southwest corner of Norfolk County, close to the boundaries of Worcester County and Rhode Island.

33. Lyman Beecher, *The Practicability of Suppressing Vice, by Means of Societies Instituted for That Purpose: A Sermon, Delivered Before the Moral Society in East-Hampton (Long-Island.) September 21, 1803* (New London, Conn.: Samuel Green, 1804), 10–11, 12.

34. Emmons, *A Discourse*, 28, 29; Beecher, *The Practicability of Suppressing Vice*, 22.

35. Emmons, *A Discourse*, 16; Beecher, *The Practicability of Suppressing Vice*, 18; Emmons, *A Discourse*, 15. He quoted Richard Price, *Observations on the Importance of the American Revolution, and the means of making it a benefit to the world* (London, 1784). This work was reprinted in Boston and Philadelphia, among other places. Emmons may have used the 1785 New Haven edition. In 1781 Yale had honored George Washington and Richard Price with honorary degrees.

36. Joan Hoff Wilson, "The Illusion of Change: Women and the American Revolution," in Alfred F. Young, ed., *The American Revolution: Explorations in the History of American Radicalism* (DeKalb: Northern Illinois University Press, 1976), 405; Daniel Scott Smith, "The Dating of the American Sexual Revolution: Evidence and Interpretation," in Michael Gordon, ed., *The American Family in Social-Historical Perspective*, 2nd

ed. (New York: St. Martin's Press, 1978), 427; Daniel Scott Smith, "Parental Power and Marriage Patterns: An Analysis of Historical Trends in Hingham, Massachusetts," *Journal of Marriage and Family* 35 (August 1973), 419–28; Gloria Main, "Rocking the Cradle: Downsizing the New England Family," *Journal of Interdisciplinary History* 37 (Summer 2006) 43–46; Carl Degler, *At Odds: Women and Family in America from the Revolution to the Present* (New York: Oxford University Press, 1980), 11–12; Gary B. Nash, *The Urban Crucible: Social Change, Political Consciousness, and the Origins of the American Revolution* (Cambridge, Mass.: Harvard University Press, 1979), 313; Laurel Thatcher Ulrich, *A Midwife's Tale: The Life of Martha Ballard, Based on Her Diary, 1785–1812* (New York: Vintage, 1990), 147–49.

37. William Nelson, *Americanization of the Common Law: The Impact of Legal Change in Massachusetts Society, 1760–1830* (Cambridge, Mass.: Harvard University Press, 1975), 36–37; Cornelia Hughes Dayton, *Women Before the Bar: Gender, Law, and Society in Connecticut, 1639–1789* (Chapel Hill: University of North Carolina Press for the Institute of Early American History and Culture, 1995), 287 n.12. The proceeding against Priscilla Warfield is recorded in Edward W. Hanson's notes on "Supreme Judicial Court Criminal Cases, 1776–1800," 41, compiled in support of the multivolume *Robert Treat Paine Papers*, which Hanson is editing and generously shared with us, March 2011. William E. Nelson, "Emerging Notions of Criminal Law in the Revolutionary Era: A Historical Perspective," *New York University Law Review* 42 (1967), 450–82. A study of English courts similarly shows a dramatic reduction in infanticide cases in Chester Court of Great Sessions, 1650–1800, from sixty-three cases in 1650–99 to thirty-one cases in 1700–49, to eighteen cases in 1750–1800, with a reduction of women hanged from twenty to four, to three. Mark Jackson, *New-Born Child Murder: Women, Illegitimacy and the Courts in Eighteenth-Century England* (Manchester, UK: Manchester University Press, 1996), 38. On the cessation of executions, see Daniel Allen Hearn, *Legal Executions in New York State: A Comprehensive Reference, 1639–1963* (Jefferson, N.C.: McFarland, 1997), *Legal Executions in New England: A Comprehensive Reference, 1623–1960* (Jefferson, N.C.: McFarland, 1999), and *Legal Executions in New Jersey: A Comprehensive Registry, 1691–1963* (Jefferson, N.C.: McFarland, 2005).

38. Data compiled from Hanson's notes on "Supreme Judicial Court Criminal Cases." Incest was seldom prosecuted as incest: instead, lewd and lascivious behavior was the more common charge. Brown and Brown, *Hanging of Ephraim Wheeler*, 60–61, 95, 271–72. The 1759 prosecution of twenty-nine-year-old Huldah Dudley for committing incest with Judah Clark, her seventy-six-year-old stepfather, is treated in Donald L. Hafner, "'To Be Set upon the Gallows for the Space of One Hour': A Tale of Crime and Punishment in Colonial Lincoln, Massachusetts," in *Center Affiliated Faculty Publications*, Boston College Center for Human Rights and International Justice (July 2006), 1–26.

39. Jonathan Edwards to Sally Burr, January 29, 1770, Reeve Family Papers, Yale University Manuscript and Archives Collection. See also Godbeer, *Sexual Revolution in Early America*, 290.

40. Benjamin Rush to David Ramsay (March or April 1788), in *The Letters of Benjamin Rush*, ed. L. H. Butterfield, 2 vols. (Princeton, N.J.: Princeton University Press, 1951), 1: 454; Kann, "Sexual Desire, 279; Foster, *Sex and the Eighteenth-Century Man*, xv, 65; Charles Burr Todd, *In Olde Connecticut, Being a Record of the Quaint, Curious and Romantic Happenings There in Colonial Times and Later* (New York: Grafton Press, 1906), 189; Mariah Wolcott to Frederick Wolcott, n.d. (probably 1786), and to Elizabeth Stoughton Wolcott, November 15, 1789; Mariann Goodrich to Fredrick Wolcott, November 15, 1789, Wolcott Collection, Litchfield Historical Society (LHS hereafter).

41. Todd, *In Olde Connecticut*, 190; Charles Beecher, ed., *Autobiography, Correspondence, Etc., of Lyman Beecher, D.D.*, 2 vols. (New York: Harper, 1864), 1: 26; Mariah Wolcott to Frederick Wolcott, n.d. (1798?), Wolcott Collection, LHS; Richard J. Purcell, *Connecticut in Transition: 1775–1818* (Middletown, Conn.: Wesleyan University Press, 1963 [orig. 1918]), 27.

42. James Morris, *Memoirs of James Morris of South Farm in Litchfield, Written by Himself and Edited by His Grandson* (New Haven, Conn.: Yale University Press, 1933), 54; William Kenrick, *The Whole Duty of Woman: A New Edition with Considerable Improvements* (Litchfield, 1798 [orig. 1753]),18 (a play on Richard Allestree's pious classic *The Whole Duty of Man* [London, 1658]); Laura Hadley Moseley, ed., *The Diaries of Julia Cowles* (New Haven, Conn.: Yale University Press, 1931), 36–37; *Connecticut Courant* (Hartford), supplement, July 29, 1799, p. 3.

43. James Morris, "A Statistical Account of Several Towns in the County of Litchfield, Litchfield County Report" (1815), in Christopher P. Bickford, Carolyn C. Cooper, and Sandra L. Rux, eds., *Voices of the New Republic: Connecticut Towns, 1800–1832*, 2 vols. (New Haven, Conn.: Memoirs of the Connecticut Academy of Arts and Sciences, 2003), vol. 1, *What They Said*, 133; Goodwin v. Harrison, Connecticut State Archives record group no. 003, Litchfield County Court Files, 1751–1855.

44. Moseley, *The Diaries of Julia Cowles*, 37; Dorothy Deming to Julius Deming, June 20, 1799, Quincy Collection, LHS.

45. Mary Douglas, *Purity and Danger: An Analysis of Concepts of Pollution and Taboo* (New York: Routledge Classics, 2002 [orig. 1966]), xi.

Chapter 4. Fearful Rulers in Anxious Times

1. Compiled from Governor's Council Pardon Files, 1780–89, Massachusetts Archives. Those pardoned included: Michael Scott, burglary, 1785; Potter Allen, burglary, 1787; and Daniel Foster, manslaughter, 1789. The death sentence of Edward Johnson, also a burglar, was commuted in 1789 to life imprisonment. This discussion of Massachusetts pardons draws on Irene Quenzler Brown and Richard D. Brown, "Pardons Won and Pardons Lost" (paper, annual meeting, American Historical Association, Boston, January 5, 2001).

2. "Caleb Strong," in Clifford K. Shipton, *Sibley's Harvard Graduates: Biographical Sketches of Those Who Attended Harvard College*, vol. 16, *1764–1767* (Boston: Massachusetts Historical Society, 1972), 94–110.

3. Edward Coke, *The Third Part of the Institutes of the Laws of England*, 3 vols. (London, 1642), 3: 58; Samuel Danforth, *The Cry of Sodom Enquired Into; Upon Occasion of the Arraignment and Condemnation of Benjamin Goad, for his Prodigious Villany* (Cambridge, Mass., 1674), 24.

4. Farrell petition no.1, n.d., Governor's Council Pardon File, Massachusetts Archives.

5. Examination of the Suffolk Files from 1750 to 1800, Massachusetts Archives, revealed no such cases. According to Edward Hanson's compilation of the prosecutions made by the Massachusetts attorneys general Robert Treat Paine and James Sullivan from 1776 to 1800, in addition to Farrell's case there were only two other sodomy-related trials, both in western Massachusetts. In Worcester County Isaac Coburn was found guilty in 1788 and sentenced to one hour on the gallows plus thirty stripes for assault with intent to commit sodomy; and in 1789 in Hampshire County Joshua Clark was found not guilty of sodomy.

6. Death Penalty Information Center, "Execution Database by State," http://www .deathpenaltyinfo.org/executions-us-1608–2002-espy-file (accessed January 3, 2013); Stuart Banner, *The Death Penalty: An American History* (Cambridge, Mass.: Harvard University Press, 2002), 54; Richard Gaskins, "Changes in the Criminal Law in Eighteenth Century Connecticut," *American Journal of Legal History* 25 (October 1981), 309–42.

7. *The Public Records of the Colony of Connecticut 1636–1776*, ed. James H. Trumbull and Charles J. Hoadly, 15 vols. (Hartford: Press of the Case, Lockwood & Brainard Company, 1850–1890), 8: 419, 469; 9: 49–50, 52; *The Weekly Oracle* (New London, Conn.), June 17, 1797; *Litchfield Monitor*, June 28, 1797.

8. Isaac Frasier (or Frazier), executed September 7, 1768. Lawrence Goodheart, *The Solemn Sentence of Death: Capital Punishment in Connecticut* (Amherst: University of Massachusetts Press, 2011), 66–68.

9. Hoadly et al., *Public Records of the State of Connecticut*, 8: 469; Washburn Petition, October 14, 1799, Connecticut State Archives, Crimes and Misdemeanors, 2nd series, 2: 87b.

10. Zephaniah Swift, *A System of the Laws of the State of Connecticut*, 2 vols. (Hartford, Conn., 1795), 2: 310; Washburn's Petition. In bestiality cases involving blacks, the courts also did not uphold the common law requirement of having two witnesses per incident. William M. Wiecek, "The Statutory Law of Slavery and Race in the Thirteen Mainland Colonies of North America," *William and Mary Quarterly* (*WMQ* hereafter), 3rd series, 34 (April 1977), 274.

11. Connecticut State Archives, House Journal, October 22, 23, 24, 25, 28, 29, 1799; Hoadly et al., *Public Records of the State of Connecticut*, 9: 437–38; Connecticut State Archives, Crimes and Misdemeanors, 2nd series, 2: 87c; *Litchfield Monitor*, November 6, 1799.

12. Mary Douglas, *Purity and Danger: An Analysis of Concepts of Pollution and Taboo* (New York: Routledge Classics, 2002 [orig. 1966]), 200. The *Age of Reason* went through

seven American printings in 1794, including in Boston and Worcester, Mass., as well as in New York and Philadelphia. In the following year there were three more printings in New York and Philadelphia.

13. Richard D. Brown, *Knowledge Is Power: The Diffusion of Information in Early-America, 1700–1865* (New York: Oxford University Press, 1989), 169–71.

14. The literature on these developments is vast, and the citations below are but a sample of the scholarship that informs our thinking. Christopher Grasso, *A Speaking Aristocracy: Transforming Public Discourse in Eighteenth-Century Connecticut* (Chapel Hill: University of North Carolina Press, 1999); Nathan O. Hatch, *The Democratization of American Christianity* (New Haven, Conn.: Yale University Press, 1989); Dee E. Andrews, *The Methodists and Revolutionary America, 1760–1800: The Shaping of an Evangelical Culture* (Princeton, N.J.: Princeton University Press, 2000); Thomas S. Kidd, *The Protestant Interest: New England After Puritanism* (New Haven, Conn.: Yale University Press, 2004); James M. Banner, Jr., *To the Hartford Convention: The Federalists and the Origins of Party Politics in Massachusetts, 1789–1815* (New York: Knopf, 1969); Ronald P. Formisano, *The Transformation of Political Culture: Massachusetts Parties, 1790s-1840s* (New York: Oxford University Press, 1983); David W. Kling, *A Field of Divine Wonders: The New Divinity and Village Revivals in Northwestern Connecticut* (University Park: Pennsylvania State University Press, 1993); Jonathan D. Sassi, *A Republic of Righteousness: The Public Christianity of the Post-Revolutionary New England Clergy* (New York: Oxford University Press, 2001); John L. Brooke, *The Heart of the Commonwealth: Society and Political Culture in Worcester County, Massachusetts, 1713–1861* (New York: Cambridge University Press, 1989); Winifred Barr Rothenberg, *From Market-Places to a Market Economy: The Transformation of Rural Massachusetts, 1750–1850* (Chicago: University of Chicago Press, 1992); Christopher Clark, *The Roots of Rural Capitalism: Western Massachusetts 1780–1860* (Ithaca, N.Y.: Cornell University Press, 1990); Brown, *Knowledge Is Power*. On the interior's view of immigrants, see Richard D. Brown, " 'Tried, Convicted, and Condemned, in Almost Every Bar-room and Barber's Shop': Anti-Irish Prejudice in the Trial of Dominic Daley and James Halligan, Northampton, Massachusetts, 1806," *New England Quarterly* 84 (June 2011), 205–33.

15. *Philadelphia Aurora*, July 6, 1795; Jonathan Maxcy, *An Oration delivered in the Baptist Meeting-House in Providence, July 4, a.d. 1795, at the celebration of the nineteenth anniversary of American Independence* (Providence, 1795), 18, 19; for capacity of the meetinghouse, see Henry Jackson, *An Account of the Churches in Rhode-Island* (Providence, R.I.: G. H. Whitney, 1853), 86; Joanne B. Freeman, *Affairs of Honor: National Politics in the Early Republic* (New Haven, Conn.: Yale University Press, 2001), xiii; Stanley Elkins and Eric McKitrick, *The Age of Federalism: The Early American Republic, 1788–1800* (New York: Oxford University Press, 1993), 416–22.

16. The Champion quote is cited by Charles Roy Keller, *The Second Great Awakening in Connecticut* (New Haven, Conn.: Yale University Press, 1942), 26. On New England and the Quasi-War with France see James Roger Sharp, *American Politics in the Early Republic: The New Nation in Crisis* (New Haven, Conn.: Yale University Press, 1993),

146–54; Elkins and McKitrick, *The Age of Federalism*, 524–28; Nathan Perl-Rosenthal, "Private Letters and Public Diplomacy: The Adams Network and the Quasi-War, 1797–1798," *Journal of the Early Republic* 31 (Summer 2011), 283–311; William Stinchcombe, *The XYZ Affair* (Westport, Conn.: Greenwood Press, 1980), 22–28; Alexander DeConde, *The Quasi-War: The Politics and Diplomacy of the Undeclared War with France, 1797–1801* (New York: Scribner's, 1966), 25–29.

17. Uriah Tracy, *Reflections on Monroe's View, of the conduct of the Executive, as published in the United States, under the signature of Scipio* (Philadelphia, 1798) p. 18; Keith Arbour, "Benjamin Franklin as Weird Sister: William Cobbett and the Federalist Philadelphia's Fears of Democracy," in Doron Ben-Atar and Barbara B. Oberg, eds., *Federalists Reconsidered* (Charlottesville: University of Virginia Press, 1998), 187–98; Elkins and McKitrick, *Age of Federalism*, 420–21.

18. Hannah Webster Foster, *The Coquette; or, The History of Eliza Wharton* (Boston, 1797), ed. Cathy N. Davidson (New York: Oxford University Press, 1986), xi, 63; Bruce Burgett, *Sentimental Bodies: Sex, Gender, and Citizenship in the Early Republic* (Princeton, N.J.: Princeton University Press, 1998), 88–95; Rachel Hope Cleves, "'Jacobins in this Country': The United States, Great Britain, and Trans-Atlantic Anti-Jacobinism," *Early American Studies* 8 (Spring 2010), 418–28; Gillian Brown, "Consent, Coquetry, and Consequences," *American Literary History* 9 (Winter 1997), 244; Kristie Hamilton, "An Assault on the Will: Republican Virtue and the City in Hannah Webster Foster's 'The Coquette,'" *Early American Literature* 24 (Fall 1989), 135–51; Sharon M. Harris, "Hannah Webster Foster's *The Coquette*: Critiquing Franklin's America," in Harris, ed., *"Redefining the Political Novel": American Women Writers, 1797–1901* (Knoxville: University of Tennessee Press, 1995), 1–22.

19. Quoted in Philip H. Jordan, Jr., "Connecticut Politics During the Revolution and Confederation, 1776–1789" (Ph.D. diss., Yale University, 1962), 297; David P. Szatmary, *Shays' Rebellion: The Making of an Agrarian Insurrection* (Amherst: University of Massachusetts Press, 1980), 116–17; Christopher Collier, *All Politics Is Local: Family, Friends, and Provincial Interests in the Creation of the Constitution* (Hanover, N.H.: University Press of New England, 2003), 98.

20. Richard Bushman, *The Refinement of America: Persons, Houses, Cities* (New York: Knopf, 1992), ch. 3, "Bodies and Minds," 61–83. One who continued to soil his clothes butchering livestock even after he was a distinguished member of Congress and guest at President Washington's table was James Abraham Hillhouse of New Haven. See Karen Sue Kauffman, "In the Society of Our Friends: Two Generations of the Hillhouse Family, 1770–1840" (Ph.D. diss., University of Connecticut, 1996).

21. Alan V. Briceland, "The Philadelphia Aurora, the New England Illuminati, and the Election of 1800," *Pennsylvania Magazine of History and Biography* 100 (January 1976), 3; Banner, *To the Hartford Convention*, 15–22; David Waldstreicher and Stephen R. Grossbart, "Abraham Bishop's Vocation; or, the Mediation of Jeffersonian Politics," *Journal of the Early Republic* 18 (Winter 1998), 617–57; Grasso, *A Speaking Aristocracy*, 414–31; Henry Adams, *History of the United States of America During the Administrations*

of Thomas Jefferson, 2 vols. (New York: Library of America, 1986 [orig. 1889–91]), 57. Though they were mostly short-lived, papers bearing the Republican appellation appeared in Danbury, Fairfield, Hartford, New London, Norwalk, and Norwich, among others. See Jeffrey L. Pasley, *The Tyranny of Printers: Newspaper Politics in the Early American Republic* (Charlottesville: University of Virginia Press, 2001), 153–75; Clarence Brigham, *History and Bibliography of American Newspapers* 2 vols. (Worcester, Mass.: American Antiquarian Society, 1947), 1: 16–62.

22. *The United States Elevated to Glory and Honor. A Sermon Preached before His Excellency Jonathan Trumbull . . . and the Honorable the General Assembly of the State of Connecticut, convened at Hartford, at the Anniversary Election, May 8th, 1783* (New Haven, Conn., 1783).

23. Jon Butler, *Awash in a Sea of Faith: Christianizing the American People* (Cambridge, Mass.: Harvard University Press, 1990), 267; Richard D. Shiels, "The Feminization of American Congregationalism, 1730–1835," *American Quarterly* 33 (Spring 1981), 46–62; Mary Kupiec Cayton, "The Expanding World of Jacob Norton: Reading, Revivalism, and the Construction of a 'Second Great Awakening' in New England, 1787–1804," *Journal of the Early Republic* 26 (Summer 2006), 231; Susan Juster and Ellen Hartigan-O'Connor, "The 'Angel Delusion' of 1806–1811: Frustration and Fantasy in Northern New England," *Journal of the Early Republic* 22 (Fall 2002), 375–404.

24. Johann N. Neem, "Creating Social Capital in the Early American Republic: The View from Connecticut," *Journal of Interdisciplinary History* 39 (Spring 2009), 479; Thomas Kidd, "Passing as a Pastor: Clerical Imposture in the Colonial Atlantic World," *Religion and American Culture* 14 (Summer 2004), 174; James R. Rohrer, *Keepers of the Covenant: Frontier Missions and the Decline of Congregationalism, 1774–1818* (New York: Oxford University Press, 1995), 4.

25. Timothy Dwight, *A Discourse on Some Events of the Last Century* (New Haven, Conn.: Ezra Read, 1801), 25; Gary Nash, "The American Clergy and the French Revolution," *WMQ*, 3rd series, 22 (July 1965), 392–412; Butler, *Awash in a Sea of Faith*, 218–19; Ruth Bloch, *Visionary Republic: Millennial Themes in American Thought, 1756–1800* (New York: Cambridge University Press, 1985), 154–59; Grasso, *A Speaking Aristocracy*, 350–51; Banner, *To the Hartford Convention*, 19, 156–64.

26. Otis as cited by Banner, *To the Hartford Convention*, 94; 108; John Allen speech, May 3, 1798, *Annals of Congress* (Washington: Gales & Seaton, 1851), 1578; James Gould, *An Oration, pronounced at Litchfield; on the Anniversary of the Independence of the United States of America* (Litchfield, Conn., 1798), 10, 12; Uriah Tracy to Oliver Wolcott, August 7, 1800, in George Gibbs, *Memoirs of the Administrations of Washington and John Adams Edited from the Papers of Oliver Wolcott Secretary of the Treasury*, 2 vols. (New York: William van Norden, 1846), 2: 400; Erasmus, "Thomas Paine," *Balance and Columbian Repository* (Hudson, NY) December 28, 1802; Faramerz Dabhoiwala, *The Origins of Sex: A History of the First Sexual Revolution* (New York: Oxford University Press, 2012), 80; Michael Durey, *Transatlantic Radicals and the Early American Republic* (Lawrence: University Press of Kansas, 1997); Rogers M. Smith, "Constructing American National

Identity: Strategies of the Federalists," in Ben-Atar and Oberg, *Federalists Reconsidered*, 19–40. Italics added to characterization of Thomas Paine.

27. Grasso, *A Speaking Aristocracy*, 367; Sassi, *A Republic of Righteousness*, 52–53; Kling, *Field of Divine Wonders*, 62; Azel Backus, *Absalom's Conspiracy: A Sermon Preached at the General Election*. . . . (Hartford, Conn., 1798), 41. Ironically, the illuminati charge was first leveled by the Jesuit Augustin de Barruel, *Memoirs Illustrating the History of Jacobinism*. This work, originally published in French in 1797, was immediately translated into English and published in London the same year. The following year its translator, the Hon. Robert Clifford, published *Application of Barruel's Memoirs of Jacobinism to the Secret Societies of Ireland and Great Britain. By the translator of that work* (London, 1798). In 1799 the Hartford printers Hudson and Goodwin printed Barruel's *Memoirs* for a New York City publisher. The close connections between Federalists and English anti-Jacobins facilitated dissemination and adoption of the conspiracy idea.

28. Mark R. Valeri, *Joseph Bellamy's New England: The Origins of New Divinity in Revolutionary America* (New York: Oxford University Press, 1994), 58; Stephen Foster, "A Connecticut Separate Church: Strict Congregationalism in Cornwall, 1780–1809," *New England Quarterly* 39 (September 1966), 309–33.

29. Cited by Richard D. Birdsall, "The Second Great Awakening and the New England Social Order," *Church History* 39 (September 1970), 347. The historical controversy over the extent of Dwight's power and influence notwithstanding, critics charged he turned Connecticut into "almost totally an ecclesiastical state, ruled by the President of the College, as a Monarch." John Ogden, *A View of the Calvinistic Clubs in the United States* (Litchfield, Conn., 1797), 14.

30. Calvin Chapin, *A Sermon Delivered, 14th January, 1817 at the Funeral of the Rev. Timothy Dwight* (New Haven, Conn.: Maltby, Goldsmith & Company, 1817), 22, 24; John R. Fitzmier, *New England's Moral Legislator: Timothy Dwight, 1752—1817* (Bloomington: Indiana University Press, 1998), 5; Colin Wells, *The Devil and Doctor Dwight: Satire and Theology in the Early American Republic* (Chapel Hill: University of North Carolina Press, 2002), 3, 37; Robert J. Imholt, "Timothy Dwight: Federalist Pope of Connecticut," *New England Quarterly* 73 (September 2000), 386–411; Kling, *Field of Divine Wonders*, 6–7, 80, 95–103, 167–94; Sassi, *A Republic of Righteousness*, 56–83; Grasso, *A Speaking Aristocracy*, 329; William R. Sutton, "Benevolent Calvinism and the Moral Judgment of God: The Influence of Nathaniel Taylor in Revivalism in the Second Great Awakening," *Religion and American Culture: A Journal of Interpretation* 2 (Winter 1992), 24–26.

31. Dwight, *A Discourse*, 19, 35; Timothy Dwight, *The Nature and Danger of Infidel Philosophy* (New Haven, Conn., 1798), 95.

32. Edward Griffin to William Sprague, September 1832, cited by Kling, *Field of Divine Wonders*, 3; James Russell, "American Revivals," in *The Weekly Christian Teacher*, 3 vols. (Glasgow: A Fulerton, 1837–40), II: 292; Kling, *Field of Divine Wonders*, 38–41, 151–52; Keller, *The Second Great Awakening in Connecticut*, 36–37; Bloch, *Visionary Republic*, 121–22; Birdsall, "The Second Great Awakening and the New England Social Order," 352; Sassi, *A Republic of Righteousness*, 14; Mary Kupiec Cayton, "The Expanding

World of Jacob Norton: Reading, Revivalism, and the Construction of a 'Second Great Awakening' in New England, 1787–1804," *Journal of the Early Republic* 26 (Summer 2006), 244–45. The evidence from the Farrell and Washburn trials and their surrounding contexts support the view of Richard Hofstadter, Henry May, and Steven Novak, who saw the events of the late 1790s as a Calvinist-Federalist counterrevolution. Hoftstadter, "The Paranoid Style in American Politics," *Harper's Magazine* (November 1964), 77–86, and in his *The Paranoid Style in American Politics, and other Essays* (New York: Knopf, 1965); May, *The Enlightenment in America* (New York: Oxford University Press, 1976), 275; Novak, "The College in the Dartmouth College Case: A Reinterpretation," *New England Quarterly* 47 (December 1974), 553. For an opposing view, see Neil Brody Miller, "'Proper Subjects for Public Inquiry': The First Unitarian Controversy and the Transformation of Federalist Print Culture," *Early American Literature* 43 (2008), 106.

33. Henry Williams's one published sermon is evangelical: *A Sermon Preached at Shutesbury, in September 1809* (Greenfield, Mass.: John Denio, 1810), quotations from 1, 19. For the Hampshire Missionary Society, see *Report of the Trustees to the Hampshire Missionary Society at Their Annual Meeting at Northampton, on the Last Thursday in August*, A.D. 1802 (Northampton, Mass.: William Butler, 1802), 7. Anna Clark has argued that in dramatic moments of social upheaval, societies tend to prosecute sexual outsiders and transgressors. Clark, "Twilight Moments," *Journal of the History of Sexuality* 14 (January–April 2005), 142.

34. James Morris, "A Statistical Account of Several Towns in the County of Litchfield, Litchfield County Report" (1815), in Christopher B. Bickford, Carolyn C. Cooper, and Sandra L. Rux, eds., *Voices of the New Republic: Connecticut Towns 1800–1832*, 2 vols. (New Haven, Conn.: Memoirs of the Connecticut Academy of Arts and Sciences, 2003), vol. 1, *What They Said*, 132; Franklin Bowditch Dexter, ed., *The Literary Diary of Ezra Stiles*, 3 vols. (New York: Scribbner's, 1901), 3: 419; *Litchfield Monitor*, August 10, 1796; Dexter, *The Literary Diary of Ezra Stiles*, 3: 417; Frederick Wolcott to Oliver Wolcott, Sr., June 29, 1795, Wolcott Collection, Litchfield Historical Society (LHS hereafter).

35. James Dana, *The Folly of Practical Atheism: a Discourse Delivered in the Chapel of Yale-College, on Lord's Day, November 23, 1794* (New Haven, Conn., 1794); *Christianity, the Wisdom of God: a Sermon Preached October 17, 1798 at the Ordination of the Rev. Dan Huntington to the Pastoral Care of the First Church and Society in Litchfield, Connecticut* (Litchfield, Conn., 1799), 6, 8, 22, 25.

36. Dan Huntington, *Memories, Counsels, and Reflections* (Cambridge, Mass.: Metcalf and Company, 1857), 52; Dan Huntington, letter to ed., *Connecticut Evangelical Magazine*, July 8, 1808, 313; Edward F. Hayward, *Lyman Beecher* (Boston: Pilgrim Press, 1904), 27; Benjamin Tallmadge to Tapping Reeve, December 7, 1807, in Reeve Family Papers, Fairfield Historical Society, Fairfield, Conn.

37. Elihu Hubbard Smith noted in his diary in 1798 that he heard Huntington deliver "a handsome & moral discourse; with which I was more pleased than expected." James E. Cronin, ed., *The Diary of Elihu Hubbard Smith* (Philadelphia: American Philosophical Society, 1973); Huntington, *Memories, Counsels, and Reflections*, 55; Stanley

Griswold to Dan Huntington, November 25, 1801, in Stanley Griswold, *Church and State a Political Union, Formed by the Enemies of Both Illustrated in Correspondence Between the Rev. Stanley Griswold and the Rev. Dan Huntington, and Between Col. Ephraim Kirby and the Rev. Joseph Lyman* (n.p., 1802), 20–21.

38. Frederick Wolcott to Oliver Wolcott, Sr., May 1791, Wolcott Collection, LHS; *American Mercury* (Hartford) August 11, 1794, and April 6, 1795; Ephraim Kirby to Ruth Kirby, May 7, 1796, and E. Kirby to Jacob Van Fleck, January 23, 1797, Ephraim Kirby Papers, Duke University. See also James R. Beasley, "Emerging Republicanism and the Standing Order: The Appropriation Act Controversy in Connecticut, 1793–1795," *WMQ*, 3rd series, 29 (October 1972), 596; Andrew Siegel, "'Steady Habits' Under Siege: The Defense of Federalism in Jeffersonian Connecticut," in Ben-Atar and Oberg, *Federalists Reconsidered*, 202; E. Kirby to R. Kirby, May 7, 1796, and E. Kirby to Van Fleck, January 23, 1797.

39. Ephraim Kirby to Stephen Twining, February 10, 1800, Miscellaneous Papers, LHS; E. Kirby to Joseph Lyman, September 15, 1801, in Griswold, *Church and State*, 33; Uriah Tracy to John Adams, April 8, 1799, in Gibbs, *Memoirs of the Administrations*, 2: 232; E. Kirby to Lyman, October 10, 1801, in Griswold, *Church and State*, 48, 49. Kirby exchanged the accusations with Joseph Lyman of Hatfield, Mass., who was a close associate of Huntington. When Huntington moved to head the Congregational church of Middletown in 1809, Lyman delivered his installation sermon. Joseph Lyman, *A Sermon at the Installation of Rev. Dan Huntington* (Middletown, Conn.: T. Dunning, 1809).

40. Dan Huntington to Stanley Griswold, September 29, 1801, in Griswold, *Church and State*, 14.

41. Stanley Griswold, *Truth Its Own Test and God Its Only Judge; or, An Inquiry—How Far Men May Claim Authority Over Each Other's Religious Opinions? A Discourse Delivered at New-Milford, October 12th, 1800* (Bridgeport, Conn.: Lazarus Beach, 1800), 30; Griswold to Dan Huntington, September 29, 1801, October 23, 1801, and November 25, 1801, in Griswold, *Church and State*, 9, 11–12, 17, 20–21, 27–28; Sassi, *A Republic of Righteousness*, 257 n. 83.

42. *The Bee* (New London), October 9, 1799; Pasley, *Tyranny of Printers*, 140–42; Richard D. Brown, "The Emergence of Urban Society in Rural Massachusetts, 1760–1820," *Journal of American History* 61 (June 1974), 41; Brown, *Knowledge Is Power*, 65–81.

43. Brown, "Emergence of Urban Society," 41; Steven C. Bullock, *Revolutionary Brotherhood: Freemasonry and the Transformation of the American Social Order, 1730–1840* (Chapel Hill: University of North Carolina Press and Institute of Early American History and Culture, 1996).

44. Jedidiah Morse, *A Sermon, Delivered at the New North Church in Boston, in the Morning and in the Afternoon at Charlestown, May 9th, 1798, Being the Day Recommended by John Adams, President of the United States of America, for Solemn Humiliation, Fasting, and Prayer* (Boston, 1798), 10; *The Bee* (New London) November 20, 1799; Vernon Stauffer, "New England and the Bavarian Illuminati," *Studies in History, Economics and Public Law*, 82 (1918), 229–36; Bullock, *Revolutionary Brotherhood*, 173–75; Charles C. Bradshaw,

"The New England Illuminati: Conspiracy and Causality in Charles Brockden Brown's Wieland," *New England Quarterly* 76 (September 2003), 361; Sassi, *A Republic of Righteousness*, 79; Bryan Waterman, "The Bavarian Illuminati, the Early American Novel, and the Histories of the Public Sphere," *WMQ*, 3rd series, 62 (January 2005), 19; Butler, *Awash in a Sea of Faith*, 219–20; John L. Brooke, "Ancient Lodges and Self-Created Societies: Voluntary Association and the Public Sphere in the Early Republic," in Ronald Hoffman and Peter J. Albert, eds., *"Launching the Extended Republic": The Federalist Era* (Charlottesville: University Press of Virginia, 1996), 320.

45. Increase N. Tarbox, ed., *Diary of Thomas Robbins, D.D., 1796–1854*, 2 vols. (Boston: Beacon Press, 1886–87), 1: 76, 87; General Association of Connecticut, *Contributions to the Ecclesiastical History of Connecticut; Prepared Under the Direction of the General Association to Commemorate the Completion of One Hundred and Fifty Years* (New Haven, Conn.: W.L. Kingsley, 1861), 313–14; John Brooke, "Ancient Lodges and Self-Created Societies: Voluntary Association and the Public Sphere in the Early Republic," in *Launching the "Extended Republic": The Federalist Era*, ed. Ronald Hoffman and Peter J. Albert (Charlottesville: University Press of Virginia, 1996), 277–83, 296–309, 316–22, 325, 353, 355. See also Dorothy Ann Lipson, *Freemasonry in Federalist Connecticut* (Princeton, N.J.: Princeton University Press, 1977).

46. *American Mercury* (Hartford), March 9, 1795; Journal of the St. Paul Masonic Lodge, Litchfield, Conn. We thank the Lodge of St. Paul for allowing us to examine its records. In July 1799, while Washburn was awaiting trial in jail, Kirby and Allen engaged in a public conflict in the pages of the local newspaper in which Allen, who by then had joined the Society of Cincinnati, accused his former fellow Freemason of "malevolent designs" to vilify him in secret and "insult him in public," in a highly partisan manner during the town's Fourth of July celebrations. Kirby replied that the personal attacks on him had "necessarily driven [him] into this warfare" against the "*Radicals* who have crept" into political office. *Litchfield Monitor* (Litchfield), July 24, 1799.

47. Richard Godbeer, *The Overflowing of Friendship: Love Between Men and the Creation of the American Republic* (Baltimore: Johns Hopkins University Press, 2009), 184; Margaret C. Jacob, *Living the Enlightenment: Freemasonry and Politics in Eighteenth-Century Europe* (New York: Oxford University Press, 1991), 5–6; Thomas A. Foster, "Antimasonic Satire, Sodomy, and Eighteenth-Century Masculinity in *The Boston Evening Post*," *WMQ*, 3rd series, 60 (2003): 171–84; Clare A. Lyons, "Mapping an Atlantic Sexual Culture: Homoeroticism in Eighteenth-Century Philadelphia," *WMQ* , 3rd series, 60 (2003), 137–38, 152.

48. A decade later Connecticut revised the 1699 statute under which Phoebe Thomson was tried, so that when an illegitimate infant was found dead the presumption of murder was lifted. Indeed the last time a woman was executed in Connecticut for this crime was 1753, and in Massachusetts it was 1788. In 1808 when this crime came before the Superior Court at Norwich, Justice Zephaniah Swift's charge to the grand jury called for more understanding treatment of defendants in such cases. His whole charge was printed at the request of the grand jurors in *The Courier* (Norwich, Conn.), February 3,

1808, p. 2, col. 103. The issue is discussed in Goodheart, *The Solemn Sentence of Death*, 76, 77.

49. Connecticut State Archives, Litchfield County Superior Court, 1798, 1797, box 195, Jesse Clark for Bigamy; *Connecticut Courant* (Hartford), September 9, 1799.

50. Swift, *A System of Laws*, 2: 310–11. Swift remarked that the fact that the poet Virgil condoned "the passion of a shepherd for beautiful boy . . . [was] striking evidence of the depravity, corruption, and debauchery of the Romans at that period."

Chapter 5. Puritan Twilight in the New England Republics

1. Farrell petition no. 2, Nov. 30, 1796, Governor's Council Pardon File, Massachusetts Archives.

2. Farrell petition no. 3, n.d., Governor's Council Pardon File, Massachusetts Archives. Italics added.

3. Farrell's advertisement in *The Phenix, or Windham Herald* (Windham, Conn.), Oct. 29, 1791, p. 3, explained "if he effects not the cure he expects no reward."

4. Farrell petition c.3, from Worcester County, twenty-one signatures. Governor's Council Pardon File, Massachusetts Archives. A small number of signatures came from Hampshire County, though the petition identified signers as Worcester County residents. One Hampshire signer was Seth Field of Leverett, the older brother of Jonathan Field, a farmer who testified in Farrell's trial. Ruth E. N. Field, *A History of Leverett, Massachusetts: Together with a Genealogy of Its Early Inhabitants* (Bountiful, Utah: Family History Publishers, 1996), 199–200). Information on Boylston signatories is in William O. Dupuis, *History of Boylston, 1742–1786* (Boylston, Mass.: Boylston Historical Commission, 1976), 21–22, 26–30, 46; Matthew Davenport, *A Brief Historical Sketch of the Town of Boylston* (Lancaster, Mass.: Carter Andrews and Company, 1831), 14; Boylston, Massachusetts, *Centennial Celebration of the Incorporation of the Town of Boylston, Massachusetts* (Worcester, Mass.: Press of Sanford and Davis, 1887), 93–98, 103. In his page 3 advertisement of May 12, 1796 in the *Greenfield Gazette*, Farrell had reported, "He has resided in Boylston, near Worcester, several years, and has had great success in curing many of the long standing and of the rose kind."

5. On Pelham and its residents, see Gregory H. Nobles, "Shays's Neighbors: The Context of Rebellion in Pelham, Massachusetts," in Robert A. Gross, ed., *In Debt to Shays: The Bicentennial of an Agrarian Rebellion* (Charlottesville: University of Virginia Press, 1993), 185–203 and 367–72, and Charles O. Parmenter, *History of Pelham, Mass. from 1738 to 1898* (Amherst, Mass.: Press of Carpenter and Morehouse, 1898), 386–87, 389–90, 394, 425, 504. See also Gregory H. Nobles, "The Politics of Patriarchy in Shay's Rebellion: The Case of Henry McCulloch," in Peter Benes, ed., *Families and Children: Dublin Seminar Series for New England Folklife Annual Proceedings, 1985* (Boston: Boston University Press, 1987).

6. Petition of David Thomas et al., Farrell Case, Governor's Council Pardon File, Massachusetts Archives.

7. V. A. C. Gatrell, *The Hanging Tree: Execution and the English People, 1770–1868* (Oxford: Oxford University Press, 1994), 618, records fifty executions in the years 1805 to 1832. A 1762 case of Catholic prosecution of a Protestant in Toulouse, France, suggests the same general atavistic phenomenon; see David D. Bien, *The Calas Affair: Persecution, Toleration, and Heresy in Eighteenth-Century Toulouse* (Princeton, N.J.: Princeton University Press, 1960).

8. K. G. Davis, ed., *Documents of the American Revolution, 1770–1783* , 21 vols., Colonial Office Series (Shannon, Ireland: Irish University Press, 1972–81), 15: 241. Franklin, the last royal governor of New Jersey, was sent to Litchfield after he violated the relaxed conditions of his confinement in Connecticut and made contact with British military commanders. On April 22, 1776, the Continental Congress requested Governor John Trumbull of Connecticut to place Franklin in "close confinement, prohibiting to him the use of pen, ink, and paper, or the access of any person or persons, but such as are properly licensed for that purpose by Governor Trumbull." Litchfield's jail measured up to these requirements and it is likely that conditions only worsened in the twenty-two years that passed between the incarceration of Franklin and that of Washburn. Larry R. Gerlach, *William Franklin: New Jersey's Last Royal Governor* (Trenton, N.J.: New Jersey Historical Commission, 1975), 32–35.

9. Litchfield's jailer, Reuben Webster, submitted the following expense report to the state on September 2, 1799: "To boarding Gideon Washburn from the 6th of Inst august Untill the 30th of the same 3 Weeks & 1 Day _ $4„71; To 1 turnkey on said Washburn _[$0]„33; For attending gideon Washburn to Court [$]1." "Bill of Gideon Washburn Expenses in Gaole 1800, Order drawn & delivd D. W. Lewis Esq.," February 10, 1800, Tapping Reeve Collection, Litchfield Historical Society (LHS hereafter). The invoice from the Litchfield jail demonstrates that Washburn was at the local jail. However, Washburn's name appears on the roster of prisoners who spent some time in New Gate Prison in Simsbury, Conn., in 1799. Washburn probably spent at least a few days in that state institution, where living conditions were notoriously inhumane. In 1773 the colony of Connecticut turned the old copper mines in Simsbury into the state's prison. The committee that selected New Gate was impressed by the natural makings of the mine that seemed to create a sealed structure. The state did not even bother to put a fence around the property, figuring that prisoners would not be able to climb out unassisted. The inmates, however, quickly found ways to escape. Many did and others revolted against the terrible conditions in the damp dark mines. In 1782 the state built two stone buildings above the mine's shafts. When it reopened in 1790, New Gate had a very different look. To get out of their lodging tunnels prisoners had to climb up a twenty-five-foot ladder, and come through the shaft's opening into a passage room. From there they climbed up another short ladder and came out through a trap door in the floor of the guardroom built above their lodgings. William G. Domonell, *New Gate: From Copper Mine to State Prison* (Simsbury Conn.: Simsbury Historical Society, 2001), 12–32; Richard Phelps, *New Gate Connecticut: Its Origin and Early History* (Rockport, Maine, 1996 [orig. 1876]), 89.

10. *Litchfield Monitor*, January 15, 1800; the state of Connecticut reimbursed Lynde Lord in the amount of eighteen shillings for the cost of erecting the gallows. Invoice for compensated expenses for Lynde Lord by the State of Connecticut, February 12, 1800, Superior Court Executions on Judgment Cases box 1, 1798–1816, Litchfield Co. Superior Court Executions 1798–1802 Inclusive, Miscellaneous Court Records, LHS. The fact that Lord actually built the gallows does not rule out the possibility of a last-minute commuting of the sentence. In 1776, for example, Lord reported that "I caused the within named John Thomas to be taken from the common Gaol in Litchfield to the place of Execution and there Set upon a Gallows with a Rope Round his Neck for the full term of one hour. & Then tied to the Tail of a Cart and Transported to four of the most public places in the Town of Litchfield and there whiped on his naked body thirty nine [times?] in the Whole." Lynde Lord, February 21, 1776, Miscellaneous Papers, LHS.

11. "Test Lynde Lord Sheriff Resolve of Assembly &c Gideon Washburn," Litchfield Co. Superior Court Executions on Judgment Cases, box 1, 1798–1816, LHS; *Litchfield Monitor*, January. 15, 1800.

12. Leviticus 20:15; Samuel Danforth, *The Cry of Sodom Enquired Into; Upon Occasion of the Arraignment and Condemnation of Benjamin Goad, for His Prodigious Villany* (Cambridge, Mass., 1674), 31; Cotton Mather, *Magnalia Christi Americana; or, The Ecclesiastical History of New England*, 2 vols. (London, 1702), 2: 401, 405–7; Zephaniah Swift, *A System of the Laws of the State of Connecticut*, 2 vols. (Hartford, Conn., 1795), 2: 310; Jeremy Bentham, "Offences Against One's Self," online ed., *Stonewall and Beyond: Lesbian and Gay Culture*, http://www.columbia.edu/cu/lweb/eresources/exhibitions/sw25/bentham/index.html (accessed March 8, 2010).

13. Litchfield Deed Records, Litchfield town hall, Litchfield, Conn., 14: 131–32, 15: 436–37, 17: 107, 131–32, 158; Mabel Thacher Rosemary Washburn, *Washburn Family Foundations in Normandy, England and America* (Greenfield, Ind.: Mitchell Printing, 1953), 149–51. For the reversal of William Washburn's legal fortunes, see "Supreme Court of Errors. Washburn v. Merrills (1803)," in Thomas Day, ed., *Report of Cases Argued and Determined in the Supreme Court of Errors of the State of Connecticut, in the Years 1802–1813*, 5 vols. (Hartford, Conn.: Banks Law Publishing Company, 1806–23), 1: 139–41. Like Farrell, Gideon Washburn does not appear by name in the census records. The census of 1790 reported that in the Litchfield household of William Washburn lived three males and three females who were over the age of sixteen. By 1800, following the death of Gideon, the census reported that the William Washburn house included, in addition to the head of the household and his wife, one woman older than forty-five years old and four children under the age of ten—his sons William and Joseph and his daughters Martha and Sarah. William Washburn and his family appear as residents of Middlebury in Addison County in the 1810 Vermont census. Ron and Sally Selleck and Linda Williams, "West Cemetery Index," Middlebury, Vt., 2002, http://midddigital.middlebury.edu/cemeteryindexes/MiddleburyWest.html (accessed January 14, 2013).

14. Daniel A. Cohen, *Pillars of Salt, Monuments of Grace: New England Crime Literature and the Origins of American Popular Culture, 1674–1860* (New York: Oxford University Press, 1993); Scott D. Seay, *Hanging Between Heaven and Earth: Capital Crime,*

Execution Preaching, and Theology in Early New England (DeKalb: Northern Illinois University Press, 2009); Irene Q. Brown and Richard D. Brown, *The Hanging of Ephraim Wheeler: A Story of Rape, Incest, and Justice in Early* America (Cambridge, Mass.: Harvard University Press, 2003), 63; Stuart Banner, *The Death Penalty: An American History* (Cambridge, Mass.: Harvard University Press, 2003), chs. 1 and 2.

15. James Morris, "A Statistical Account of Several Towns in the County of Litchfield, Litchfield County Report," in Christopher B. Bickford, Carolyn C. Cooper, and Sandra L. Rux, eds., *Voices of the New Republic: Connecticut Towns 1800–1832*, 2 vols. (New Haven, Conn.: Memoirs of the Connecticut Academy of Arts and Sciences, 2003), vol. 1, *What They Said*, 133. The custom in Connecticut was to bury people who commit suicide at an intersection of four roads. Samuel G. Goodrich, *Recollections of A Lifetime on Men and Things I Have Seen: In a Series of Familiar Letters to a Friend*, 2 vols. (New York: Miller, Orton and Mulligan, 1856), I, 30. Washburn's final resting place is unknown.

16. *Litchfield Monitor*, October 2, 1799, p. 1.

17. Bill of indictment against Gideon Washburn, Connecticut State Archives; *Litchfield Monitor*, September 4, 1799; Frederick Wolcott to Elizabeth Wolcott, September 27, 1802, Wollcott Papers, LHS. Even though both Tracy and Allen were Litchfield residents and the town was a Federalist stronghold, the state's Republicans targeted the town in their campaign to bring Jeffersonian republicanism to Connecticut.

18. There is no mention of the Farrell trial in James R. Trumbull, *History of Northampton, Massachusetts, from Its Settlement in 1654* (Northampton, Mass.: Press of Gazette Printing, 1898–1902), nor in Field, *A History of Leverett*. The same is true for county histories. Though the history of Litchfield is well chronicled, Washburn's crime and punishment have not been remembered.

19. Goodheart, *Solemn Sentence of Death*, 71–72; Swift, *A System of the Laws*, 5: 295.

20. Swift, *A System of the Laws*, 2: 328, 331.

21. John Brooke, *The Heart of the Commonwealth: Society and Political Culture in Worcester County, Massachusetts, 1713–1861* (New York: Cambridge University Press, 1989), develops a parallel argument in which the tension operates between a Harringtonian communitarian outlook and a Lockean individualist worldview. The tensions between agriculture and commercial and industrial development are treated in Christopher Clark, *The Roots of Rural Capitalism: Western Massachusetts, 1780–1860* (Ithaca, N.Y.: Cornell University Press, 1990).

22. Stella H. Sutherland, *Population Distribution in Colonial America* (New York: Columbia University Press, 1936), Robert V. Wells, *The Population of the British Colonies in America Before 1776: A Survey of Census Data* (Princeton: Princeton University Press, 1975), United States. Census Office, *Return of the Whole Number of Persons Within the Several Districts of the United States*, also titled *First Census of the United States, 1790* (Philadelphia: Childs and Swaine, 1791).

23. Advertisements in *Hampshire Gazette* (Northampton), February 10, 1796, p. 4. This issue was selected at random from the year 1796.

24. John Adams, "A Dissertation on the Canon and Feudal Law," no. 4, *Boston Gazette*, October 21, 1765, in *Papers of John Adams*, vol. 1, September 1755– October 1773, ed. Robert J. Taylor et al. (Cambridge, Mass.: Harvard University Press, 1977), 127.

25. Samuel Miller, *A Brief Retrospect of the Eighteenth Century: Part the First: In Three Volumes: Containing a Sketch of the Revolutions and Improvements in Science, Arts, and Literature, During That Period* (London: J. Johnson, 1805), 3: 296, 298, 304, 305, 321. Miller (1769–1850) was a Delaware native who, after a twenty-year career in New York City, took a professorship at Princeton Theological Seminary in 1813, where he remained until 1849.

26. John Adams, Quincy, November 13, 1815, *Works of John Adams, Second President of the United States*, 3 vols., ed. Charles Francis Adams (Boston: Little, Brown, and Company, 1856), 10: 174.

27. Thomas Jefferson, Monticello, January 11, 1816, *The Writings of Thomas Jefferson*, 20 vols., ed. Albert Ellery Bergh (Washington, D.C.: Thomas Jefferson Memorial Association, 1903–4), 14: 393.

28. Brown and Brown, *The Hanging of Ephraim Wheeler*, 201–3, 212–15. In 1805, while Strong was serving as governor of Massachusetts, in connection with the completion of its new state prison the state undertook a general review of its penal code, a review that led in 1808 to the abolition of branding, whipping, and other corporal punishments in Massachusetts, excepting only the death penalty. See Samuel Sewall and Nathan Dane, *Communication from the Hon. Samuel Sewall, Esq. and the Hon. Nathan Dane, Esq. Accompanied with Several Bills for the Regulation of the State Prison and the Alteration of the Criminal Laws of the Commonwealth* (Boston: Young & Minns, 1805).

INDEX

Page numbers in italics refer to illustrations.

ACKNOWLEDGMENTS

Many generous colleagues and friends helped our research in spite of the subject. Historians properly begin by thanking the custodians of primary sources: archivists. Linda Hocking of the Litchfield Historical Society has helped this research since Doron first showed up at the society's offices a decade ago. Linda found documents, solved transcription puzzles, and was our first reader. We wish to thank the professional staff of state employees at the Connecticut and Massachusetts State Archives. In particular, Connecticut archivist Bruce Stark provided New London County documents that were extremely useful. We also thank Michael Comeau of the Secretary of State's office at the Massachusetts Archives as well as Elizabeth Bouvier, who oversees the records of that state's Supreme Judicial Court. Elise Bernier-Feeley, local history specialist at the Forbes Library, Northampton, provided assistance, as did Marie Lamoureux, a genealogy specialist at the American Antiquarian Society. We also thank the town clerk of Leverett, Massachusetts, and the public employees of the Hampshire County Registry of Probate and the Land Records Office, both in Northampton.

Research for this study was assisted in part by a fellowship awarded to Doron Ben-Atar by the Dorothy and Lewis B. Cullman Center for Scholars and Writers as well as research support granted to Ben-Atar by Fordham University. We benefited from thoughtful discussions of our project at the Boston Early American History Seminar at the Massachusetts Historical Society, the Philadelphia Early American History Seminar (aka the Zuckerman salon), the Muriel Gardiner Program in Psychoanalysis and the Humanities of the Western New England Institute for Psychoanalysis, the University of Connecticut History Department graduate student luncheon series, and the Program in Renaissance and Early Modern Studies at Brown University.

Authors ask friends and colleagues to read drafts, and we were fortunate to have their suggestions. David Bell of Princeton, Daniel Richter of the University of Pennsylvania, and John Demos of Yale provided invaluable suggestions that helped us structure the book and sharpen its argument. Debbie Pollak, Doron's partner in playwriting, read the entire manuscript and supplied helpful feedback. Peter Gay inspired Doron to combine psychoanalysis and history and has been a friend and confidant for over two decades. Robert King of the Yale Child Study Center advised us on the psychiatric and psychoanalytic elements of this study. Richard Gyug of Fordham and Kenneth Gouwens of the University of Connecticut checked our discussion of medieval and early modern Europe. David Bell did the same for eighteenth-century Europe.

Catherine Fields, director of the Litchfield Historical Society, supported the project in many ways. Lynn Templeton Brickley shared her research and encyclopedic knowledge of the history of Litchfield. The Rev. Edward W. Hanson, editor of the Robert Treat Paine papers, generously offered his invaluable compilation of criminal cases in the Massachusetts Superior Court of Judicature and its successor, the Supreme Judicial Court, 1776–1800, all taken from the minute books of those courts and now housed in the Massachusetts Archives, Boston. We are also deeply grateful to the Museum Director of the Old New-Gate Prison, Karin Peterson, of the Connecticut State Historic Preservation Office in the Department of Economic and Community Development. She compiled the table on inmates housed at Connecticut's prison. Other scholars whose critical views improved this book include Mary Sarah Bilder, Irene Quenzler Brown, Patricia Cline Cohen, Elaine Forman Crane, Shannon Lee Dawdy, Cornelia Hughes Dayton, Steve Deyle, Ann Fabian, Timothy Gilfoyle, Richard Godbeer, Jane Kamensky, Bruce Mann, John Murrin, and Nancy Shoemaker. We are grateful to Robert Lockhart, senior editor of the University of Pennsylvania Press, for his advice and support and we thank Rachel Taube for guiding us through the production process.

We thank the following institutions for allowing us to use their images: Abby Aldrich Rockefeller Folk Art Museum of the Colonial Williamsburg Foundation, American Antiquarian Society, Boston Public Library, Forbes Library of Northampton, Metropolitan Museum of Art in New York, Museum of Fine Arts in Boston, National Gallery in London, and New York Public Library. Special thanks to Litchfield Historical Society and to Yale University's Art Gallery for waiving the usual fees for using images. Jackie Penny of the American Antiquarian Society, Ellen Miles and Linda Thrift of the National Portrait Gallery, and Rebecca Grunberger of the Metropolitan Museum of Art helped us locate paintings and their owners. The curators of the Litchfield Historical Society, first Jeannie Ingram and then Julie Frey Leone, helped this project for over a decade. We thank Mr. Frederick Strong Moseley, who graciously invited us to take our own digital image of the Gilbert Stuart portrait of his ancestor Caleb Strong.

Finally, we thank our families. Though our children, Assaf, Heddy, and Daniel Ben-Atar and Josiah and Nicholas Brown (and their spouses) may have found it strange that we were writing a book treating bestiality, we did not hear complaints. Finally, we especially appreciate the good nature of our wives, Jo Ben-Atar and Irene Quenzler Brown, who, we suspect, heard more accounts of unseemly behavior than they would have preferred.